The Way We Civilise

Born in 1944, Rosalind Kidd is a graduate of Griffith University. Her PhD thesis, based on an unprecedented investigation into the files of Queensland's Aboriginal department, provided the groundwork for this book. At Griffith University, she served as student representative on the Humanities Course Review Committee, and has been a member of the steering committee of the university's Queensland Studies Centre for several years.

Kidd has worked as senior researcher for an international study on criminology, and also submitted a report to the 1996 Stolen Children Inquiry. From this background of intensive research into official records, she writes fulltime on a variety of projects. In April 1996 Kidd served as expert witness for the Aboriginal complainants at the Human Rights and Equal Opportunities Commission Inquiry into underpaid wages on Palm Island.

Presently she works as a freelance researcher, unaffiliated with academic or political bodies, investigating official records and providing reports for various claimants in native title cases. She lives with her artist husband and two dogs on the outskirts of Brisbane; and has three children and two grandchildren.

The Way We Civilise

Aboriginal Affairs
— the untold story

Rosalind Kidd

University of Queensland Press

First published 1997 by University of Queensland Press
Box 42, St Lucia, Queensland 4067 Australia
Reprinted 1997

Typeset by University of Queensland Press
Printed in Australia by McPherson's Printing Group

Cataloguing in Publication Data
National Library of Australia

Kidd, Ros. (Rosalind) 1944–   .
  The way we civilise : Aboriginal affairs — the untold
  story.

  1. Aborigines, Australian — Queensland — Government
  relations. 2. Aborigines, Australian — Legal status, laws,
  etc. — Queensland. 3. Aborigines, Australian — Queensland
  — Cultural assimilation. 4. Aborigines, Australian —
  Queensland — Treatment — History. I. Title.

  Includes index.

305.89915

ISBN 0 7022 2961 X

Cover photograph: 1907 Beaudesert, "Two families —
William Smith and another." Courtesy John Oxley Library.

Contents

Foreword

I am a descendant through my mother's father, the late Fred Waddy, of the Jiman people of the Upper Dawson River region in Central Queensland. My view of Australian history is fundamentally shaped by this fact of my genealogy and my investigations of the fate of my grandfather's nation.

The Jiman people were routed following an incident at the Hornet Bank homestead on the banks of the Dawson River in 1857. Vigilante groups rode throughout the area for months afterward indiscriminately slaughtering my ancestors. By 1917, the few surviving Jiman people and their associates remaining in the area were incarcerated at the Bundalla reserve, also on the banks of the Dawson River, under the charge of a superintendent.

In 1925, they were marched by force with their belongings on bullock-drawn drays to the present site at Woorabinda Aboriginal community some 400 kilometres to the north in Central Queensland. The last of the old Jiman people who established Woorabinda was a man who continued to reside there until he died in 1996. His funeral was attended by police who arrested a number of the mourners. There are other Jiman elders who continue to reside throughout Queensland and elsewhere in Australia.

In December 1996 some of us reunited at the Taroom

Town Hall overlooking the upper reaches of the Dawson River to discuss a proposal for a major dam construction in our country. We visited the trench graves at old Bundalla, now a grazing homestead, and contemplated those who are buried there, and who may be inundated by the dam waters. They were the victims of epidemics, thought to be the "Spanish flu" and possibily other influenzas.

Few Australians know the history of their nation as it is told by the colonial files and memoranda. They have had instead a diet of mythology and jingoistic revisionism. I was confronted in 1990, while serving in the Senior Executive Service of the Queensland Public Service, with the possibility of doing a simple thing to disrupt the Australian silence and amnesia about the fate of Aboriginal nations such as my own. Ros Kidd contacted me and asked if she might have access to Departmental files to carry out research on the administration of Aboriginal affairs in that State. I arranged for her access to the files within the limits of Government policy and looked forward to the results. She was the first scholar to approach me with such a request.

Her timing was fortunate. After her thesis was examined, it became apparent that she had unearthed the evidence of systematic abuse of Aboriginal rights, and this evidence came to be used in a wage justice case brought by a group of Aboriginal people of Palm Island in the far north of the State. Because of her careful research, their case before the Human Rights and Equal Opportunity Commission was successful. However, the Queensland Government rejected the recommendations of the Commission and the Palm Islanders will now seek wage justice before the federal court. Dr Kidd suffered assertions from the Queensland government that her work misrepesented matters, while she made her thesis available to Aboriginal people and in particular to assist the Palm Islanders. Scholars of Aboriginal affairs in Queensland rallied to support her, many understanding from their own experiences just how difficult it is in Queensland to comply with the requirements of scholarship and integrity.

In a thorough and compelling way, Dr Kidd's work corrects the ahistoricism which plagues the vision of Australia as the land of the "fair go".

It is therefore gratifying to me to commend, to what will be I trust a wide readership, this account of the administration of Aboriginal affairs in Queensland from 1840 to 1988. Because of her work, more people will doubt the school textbook version of Australian history which positioned Aboriginal people as the dark historical backdrop to the grand adventures of "explorers". This account does not tell a history of "savages" and unnamed "natives", but it restitutes Aboriginal people as human beings with a knowable and known past. Her examination of the colonial memoirs and memoranda tells of lives carefully documented in the files of the various Aboriginal Protectors and their successors.

Dr Kidd's detailed analysis of documents throughout the twentieth century opens up new perspectives for our understanding of race relations. This knowledge is essential if we are to counter the regular eruption of ill-informed "race debates". Her critical revelations of government operations of recent years should give pause for thought to Aboriginal and non-Aboriginal Queenslanders alike.

More Aboriginal people will be able to go to the sources of Dr Kidd's thesis with a new understanding obtained from reading this book. Good history, such as Dr Kidd

writes, can have the effect of assisting in the pursuit of
justice. I thank her for her courage, persistence and scholarship.

Marcia Langton
Director, Centre for Indigenous Natural and
Cultural Resource Management
Northern Territory University
March 1997

Preface

Government bureaucracies are notoriously reticent about exposing their operations to outsiders. The department of Aboriginal and Islander Affairs has rated, along with the departments of Health and Police, as one of the most reluctant, perhaps even secretive, about access to documents under its control. For most of this century the department has exercised almost monopoly control over all aspects of Aboriginal life in Queensland.

Its store of historical information is therefore invaluable, whether to contextualise personal and family experiences of Aboriginal people, to provide an understanding of social and administrative practices, or to act as a data resource for revisionist accounts mounted to challenge "official" commentaries on activities of past and present governments.

As the first academic researcher to gain virtually unlimited access to the department's storehouse of material, I spent fifteen months perusing thousands of files, many previously closed to scrutiny. Many months were also spent reading material held by the Anglican and Presbyterian churches in Queensland and Queensland State Archives. The accumulated body of information formed the basis for my doctoral thesis entitled "Regulating Bodies: administrations and Aborigines in Queensland 1840–1988", completed in 1994.

There are two major differences between this book and the thesis. First, a thesis is required to reveal the progression of arguments by reference to statements verifiable from either primary sources or from accredited writers in the field, or by building on its own framework as this is explicitly established. It is also expected to corroborate or challenge a wide range of texts in order to stake out a distinctive theoretical territory of its own. Second, it was my intention that the finished thesis would do justice to the enormous range of issues and variety of individuals whose activities and ideologies comprised Aboriginal affairs in Queensland over the last 150 years. I sought to provide multiple points of reference and a dense tapestry of contemporary accounts which could activate areas of Aboriginal experience previously neglected in historical writings.

The finished thesis ran to over 700 pages and over 2,000 footnotes. Such a comprehensive document will assist future academic researchers. More importantly, the exhaustive referencing supplies previously inaccessible archival documentation as support for contemporary Aboriginal projects seeking to discover the administrative past, and operates as a comprehensive resource repertoire for Aboriginal activism. Readers seeking detailed documentation should refer to the thesis.[1]

In contrast, this book is both shorter in length and more direct in style. In presenting much of the material and historical analysis of the thesis in a form accessible to wide public readership the intention remains to challenge the conventional parameters of race relations debates and to stimulate new perspectives on the governing of Queensland's Aboriginal population.

The way we civilise

This, in plain language, is how we deal with the aborigines: On occupying new territory the aboriginal inhabitants are treated exactly in the same way as the wild beasts or birds the settlers may find there. Their lives and their property, the nets, canoes, and weapons which represent as much labor to them as the stock and buildings of the white settler, are held by the Europeans as being at their absolute disposal. Their goods are taken, their children forcibly stolen, their women carried away, entirely at the caprice of the white men. The least show of resistance is answered by a rifle bullet; in fact, the first introduction between blacks and whites is often marked by the unprovoked murder of some of the former — in order to make a commencement of the work of "civilising" them. Little difference is made between the treatment of blacks at first disposed to be friendly and those who from the very outset assume a hostile attitude. As a rule the blacks have been friendly at first, and the longer they have endured provocation without retaliating the worse they have fared, for the more ferocious savages have inspired some fear, and have therefore been comparatively unmolested …

Many, perhaps the majority [of settlers] have stood aside in silent disgust whilst these things were being done, actuated by the same motives that keep humane men from shooting or molesting animals which neither annoy nor are of service to them … But the protests of the minority have been disregarded by the people of the settled districts; the majority of outsiders who take no part in the outrages

*have been either apathetic or inclined to shield their companions,
and the white brutes who fancied the amusement have murdered,
ravished, and robbed the blacks without let or hindrance. Not only
have they been unchecked, but the Government of the colony has
been always at hand to save them from the consequences of their
crime.*

*When the blacks, stung to retaliation by outrages committed on
their tribe, or hearing the fate of their neighbors, have taken the
initiative and shed white blood, or speared white men's stock, the
native police have been sent to "disperse" them. What disperse
means is well enough known. The word has been adopted into bush
slang as a convenient euphemism for wholesale massacre. Of this
force we have already said that it is impossible to write about it with
patience. It is enough to say of it that this body, organised and paid
by us, is sent to do work which its officers are forbidden to report in
detail, and that a true record of its proceedings would shame us
before our fellow-countrymen in every part of the British Empire ...*

*Murder and counter murder, outrage repaid by violence, theft by
robbery, so the dreary tale continues, till at last the blacks, starved,
cowed, and broken-hearted, their numbers thinned, their courage
overcome, submit to their fate, and disease and liquor finish the
work which we pay our native police to begin.*

*This is the ordinary course of events, but occasionally a vari-
ation occurs, and the process of quieting the blacks is unusually
prolonged. This is particularly the case in the North, where the
blacks are more determined, better armed, and have more mountain
and scrub retreats than in other parts of the colony. In the Cape
York Peninsula the race conflict has hardly diminished in intensity
since the whites began it by robbing and shooting the blacks on the
occasion of the first rush to the Palmer ... No doubt [Aboriginal]
numbers have been greatly thinned, but they have not been cowed.
Consequently there is no part of Queensland in which more Euro-*

pean lives have been lost, or where the bush is so thoroughly unsafe for the single traveller ...

Evidently settlement must be delayed until the work of extermination is complete — a consummation of which there is no present prospect — or until some more rational and humane method of dealing with the blacks is adopted. It is surely advisable, even at this the eleventh hour, to try the more creditable alternative, and to see whether we cannot efface some portion at least of the stain which attaches to us.

The Queenslander
Editorial
1 May 1880

Introduction

After one hundred years of intensive government controls the chronic destitution of a great many Aboriginal Queenslanders remains a national scandal. In 1897 the first law was passed in Queensland authorising the state to act as guardian of Aboriginal interests and setting up a network of "protectors" to regulate all aspects of Aboriginal lives including freedom of movement, place of residence, employment, finances and family life. How are we to understand this abject failure of government when so little information is available?

Notions of "benign settlement" and "doomed race" which filled histories until the early 1970s have since been discredited by researchers who revealed the extent of "frontier" conflict. The activities of government during this century have, however, remained hidden from similar public scrutiny. Until now our limited knowledge of the recent history of Aboriginal affairs in Queensland has been gleaned largely from official pronouncements in departmental reports, in parliament and in the media. Endemic poverty, trashed housing, unemployment and alcohol-related violence and despair are portrayed as aspects of an "Aboriginal problem" which seemingly defies resolution.

This book changes the focus of our inquiry. If, as is the case, the state government has had almost total control over

Aboriginal lives for a century, then it is the operations of state government which should be investigated to reveal the reasons for the disastrous conditions which persist for so many of those who were for so long their unwilling wards.

In studying the administration of Aboriginal people over the 150-year period to 1988 this book ranges beyond the conventional repression/liberation frameworks which have dominated Aboriginal studies during the last 20 years. Attention to official documents at any particular time shows clearly that administration is not reducible to race relations. Police protectors, government ministers, missionaries, departmental officers, health advisers and state and federal bureaucrats operate from a variety of interest bases, pursue conflicting ideologies and demonstrate varying commitments to "Aboriginal affairs". Such a broad spectrum of investigation needs an approach which is focused enough to produce a strong narrative but flexible enough to respect the fullest sweep of voices and experiences.

I have turned to the work of French philosopher Michel Foucault for the conceptual tools which might do justice to this project. In particular I am interested in his concept of *governmentality* which he described as denoting the field of reformative intentions and bungled operations of governments. The constant devising and implementing of supposedly more effective strategies exemplified what he dubbed the "eternal optimism" of governments. But at the same time, Foucault argued, such optimism is constantly sabotaged by the conflicts and complexities arising from the sheer quantity and extent of official interventions. Governmentality therefore, he said, is also inherently blighted by "congenital failure".[1]

This, then, is a study of the eternal optimism and the

congenital failure of successive Queensland governments as their activities impacted on Aboriginal lives. It identifies and investigates the contexts which gave rise to changing policies and practices in a domain even today misperceived, if not mislabelled, the "Aboriginal problem". In focusing on the workings of government this book provides a different and more comprehensive account than those grounded in racial conflict: it provides evidence which should make us all — Aboriginal and non-Aboriginal alike — question the propriety of those who wield power over our lives.

Abbreviations

AAC	Aboriginal Advisory Council
AAL	Aboriginal Advancement League
ABM	Australian Board of Missions
ACTU	Australian Council of Trade Unions
ADC	Aboriginal Development Commission
AEU	Amalgamated Engineering Union
AHT	Aboriginal Health Team
AIC	Aboriginal and Islanders' Commission
AITM	Australian Institute of Tropical Medicine
ALFC	Aboriginal Land Fund Commission
ALS	Aboriginal Legal Service
ATSIAL	Aboriginal and Torres Strait Islander Advancement League
ATSIC	Aboriginal and Torres Strait Islander Commission
ATSILS	Aboriginal and Torres Strait Islander Legal Service
AWU	Australian Workers' Union
BOEMAR	Board of Ecumenical Missions and Relations
BWIU	Building Workers' Industrial Union
CAA	Council for Aboriginal Affairs
CDEP	Community Development and Employment Program
CES	Commonwealth Employment Services
CIB	Criminal Investigation Branch
CSHA	Commonwealth-State Housing Agreement
DAA	Department of Aboriginal Affairs
DAIA	Department of Aboriginal and Islander Affairs
DCS	Department of Community Services
DNA	Department of Native Affairs
DOGIT	Deed of Grant in Trust
FAIRA	Foundation for Aboriginal and Islander Research Action
FCAA	Federal Council for the Advancement of Aborigines

FCAATSI	Federal Council for the Advancement of Aborigines and Torres Strait Islanders
FEDFA	Federated Engine Drivers' and Firemen's Association
MCW	Maternal and Child Welfare
NAC	National Aboriginal Council
NHMRC	National Health and Medical Research Council
NTC	National Tribal Council
OAA	Office of Aboriginal Affairs
OPAL	One People of Australia League
QIMR	Queensland Institute of Medical Research
QNU	Queensland Nurses Union
QPD	Queensland Police Department
QPM	Queensland Police Museum
QSA	Queensland State Archives
SAHT	State Aboriginal Housing Trust
SFS	Supplementary Feeding Scheme
TLC	Trades and Labour Council
UGA	United Graziers' Association

Acknowledgments

Although the creation of this book was a relatively solitary task, many people gave me valuable support and assistance during the five-year genesis of the PhD thesis on which it is based. At an academic level, my Griffith University supervisors, Professor Mark Finnane and Dr Dugald Williamson, were always generous with their time and enthusiasm, and encouraged my pursuit of the unexpected.

The friendship and interest of a range of people lightened the task of research for the thesis. Particularly fond memories persist of the months spent on the fourth floor at Charlotte Chambers; willing assistance was also much appreciated from archival staff at the Anglican and Presbyterian churches, the Queensland Police Museum and Queensland State Archives. Dr David Cilento kindly endorsed the use of diaries and letterbooks of his father, Sir Raphael Cilento.

I am particularly indebted to Professor Marcia Langton who, as Assistant Divisional Head of Rights and Culture in Queensland's Aboriginal department in 1991, authorised my all-but unlimited access to records under departmental control. I thank the department for generously extending to me workspace, delivery of thousands of files, and photocopying facilities during my fifteen-month perusal of government correspondence.

This gratitude survives attacks by the Borbidge government on my professional integrity in its attempts to exclude information of past government practices from judicial scrutiny. The actions of crown law in the Human Rights and Equal Opportunities Commission inquiry into underpaid Aboriginal workers on Palm Island, and the cavalier dismissal by the government of findings which so resoundingly went against it, gave dramatic significance to the rewriting of the final chapter in this book. I greatly value the friendship and advocacy of Bob Haebich, solicitor for the complainants, during, and after, this Inquiry.

Special mention goes to Kathy Frankland and Margaret Reid for their work in upgrading file numbers of material which has been relocated at Queensland State Archives since my research at the department. They have also been foremost in a band of determined supporters who strengthened my resolve that governments should not succeed in intimidating those who seek to put historical information in the public forum.

The enthusiasm of my editors at University of Queensland Press, Sue Abbey and Felicity Shea, has heightened my enjoyment in the reworking of the thesis. Their accessibility and easy approach made the project less daunting.

Unquestionably, my greatest debt is to my husband Barry, without whose care and conviction over more than thirty years I would never have found freedom.

Map of Queensland including Aboriginal settlements and missions.

1
Problems of law

Extending the processes of European law into the vast "northern sector", as Queensland was termed in the mid-1800s, was always going to be difficult. Distance from Sydney, shortages of trustworthy personnel and tight finances were just a few of the obstacles. Add to these a mobile and determined indigenous population, a scattering of ambitious squatters, and floating bands of disorderly shearers, doggers, fencers, miners and entrepreneurs, and issues of policing and justice take on almost insoluble prospects. In this context, management of race relations during the nineteenth century was inevitably complex and capricious.

A new settlement

Alert to the degradation of "tame natives" reduced to begging in the streets of Sydney town, clergymen recommended that a mission for displaced Aborigines should be included in plans for the new convict colony of Moreton Bay. But the colonial government faced huge costs to build and maintain the penal outpost which operated from 1825, and the mission was unfunded.

From the early days commandants of the convict settlement utilised Aboriginal expertise, offering rewards for those who tracked and returned absconding prisoners. In fact this policy inflamed hostilities. Escapes from the cruelty of prison discipline were frequent and local tribes were exposed to arbitrary vengeance from serving and ticket-of-leave men. Although there are several well-chronicled instances of escapees living with, and as, Aborigines over long periods of time, the official line was that escapees faced almost certain death from the "ferocious race of people who would murder a European for any part of his clothing or possessions".[1] Distrust of Europeans soon intensified to such an extent that the Moreton Bay authorities requested, unsuccessfully, that funding should be made available to win confidence through gifts of tomahawks, blankets and fish-hooks.

The processing of racial clashes in colonial courts of law had always been problematic. As early as 1805 advocates had proclaimed the impossibility of justice for Aboriginal litigants. Languages and concepts could not be reconciled, prompting the suggestion that a separate category of "just punishment" should apply. It was argued that without any conception of a Christian god Aboriginal people could not swear evidence and were therefore "incapable of being brought before a Criminal Court, either as Criminals or as Evidence".[2]

The frequent procedural exclusion of Aborigines from early courts of law is seen as indicative of the dominant squatter hierarchy's wilful flouting of British law and their repudiation of the humanity of the indigenous race. In such terms, it is argued, settlers pursued with impunity private dispensation of "justice".[3] In fact legal argument in 1827 made just the opposite point: "Why were so many [Aboriginal people], who have of late been apprehended for the murder of British subjects, turned loose from the gaols? They were rightfully turned out, because they could not legally be tried ... "[4]

Documentary evidence suggests that the failures of law masked neither racial indifference nor doctrinal paralysis. Rather, legal processes were continually debated and adjusted. Perhaps, it was proposed in the benchmark 1836 case of *R. versus Jack Congo Murrell*, Aborigines were not even subject to colonial laws. This would pertain if, as was argued, colonial occupation was a result of conquest rather than settlement. On a majority decision, however, this contention was rejected. According to international jurisprudence, Australia's "peaceful settlement" conveyed with it British subjectivity for the indigenous population, extending to them the full rights and responsibilities of British laws.[5]

Difficulties in the fair application of such laws were also addressed. The New South Wales parliament enacted legislation in 1839 to allow Aboriginal evidence on affirmation rather than on oath, following the damning House of Commons Select Committee inquiry in Britain into the treatment of the "Native Inhabitants of British Settlement". This law was subsequently disallowed on the grounds that to allow "heathens" to give evidence would be "contrary to the principles of British Jurisprudence".[6]

While theorists debated Aboriginal status in rarefied legal circles, church personnel continued their efforts on a more practical level. Each year brought greater abuse and degradation of dispossessed Aboriginal families, and in the early 1830s Rev John Dunmore Lang of the Presbyterian church canvassed Europe for men willing to establish missions in the new colonies. As a result, twenty Moravian

(Lutheran) missionaries arrived in Moreton Bay in 1838 and commenced work on 640 acres near Eagle Farm assigned to them by Commandant Cotton. The government matched the £310 raised by private subscription, adding three cows for good measure.

The "German mission" at Nundah was never a success. In time a few local Aborigines were enticed to cultivate crops and on occasion left their children at the school. But the major attraction, it appears, was from snatching produce in night-time raids. Despite government outlays of £1,298 between 1837 and 1840, self-sufficiency remained elusive. No doubt constrained by a severe economic depression in New South Wales, it was said that Governor Gipps viewed the site "with the eye rather of a rapacious landlord"[7] on his inspection in 1842. Future grants were tied to the mission's relocation out of Brisbane. Attempts to find an alternative position proved abortive, and within two years the mission ceased.

Reports of early mission experiences reveal that local tribes exploited the missions rather than the reverse. In general missionaries were dismayed that attendance at school or work had to be bought with gifts of food. And several reminiscences describe the laughter and mimicry which erupted as soon as missionaries' backs were turned.[8] Religious fervour was sorely tested. A second Lutheran mission at Keppel Bay was started in 1840 and survived eighteen years of near starvation before closing. On Stradbroke Island the Catholics set up a mission in 1843 to save Aboriginal souls from "unhealthy intercourse" between the women and the white pilots stationed at Amity Point. It folded after three years of Aboriginal rejection and missionary despair.

With the opening of Moreton Bay as a free settlement in 1842 Aboriginal activities came under the umbrella of administrative documentation. Processes of policing and law were initially delegated to an elderly police magistrate stationed on the Clarence River in northern New South Wales. He was soon replaced by Dr Stephen Simpson, commissioner of crown lands at Moreton Bay. This latter position required Dr Simpson to "communicate" with local Aborigines as well as to "repress the predatory attacks of the natives, and to keep order among all classes". In one of his earliest reports of Aboriginal activities, sent annually to the colonial secretary in Sydney, he noted two hundred Aboriginal people near the settlement. Quite a few men and women worked at odd jobs around the settlement, he wrote, but "upon the whole with little advantage to their moral condition".[9]

Frequent raids on crops and stores and the spearing of cattle severely disrupted the Moreton Bay settlement during the 1840s. Figures are given of sixteen European deaths and nine woundings between 1841 and 1844 alone, prompting ruthless massacres of local Aboriginal groups. But it was the activities of Aborigines in outlying areas which caused most concern. During these years triennial tribal gatherings of several thousand Aborigines were not uncommon in south-east Queensland, usually coinciding with the maturation of the bunya pine nuts. Bilingual Moravian missionaries later wrote of a decision taken at one of these assemblies to mount a campaign against the white intruders and their introduced animals,[10] a campaign which lasted twenty years and took an estimated 250 white lives.[11]

Dr Simpson's reports corroborate the notion of orchestrated hostilities. The 3,000 Aborigines living between the

Tweed River and Wide Bay and the 1,500 from the dividing ranges, he wrote, "rarely or never visit the Stations in the vicinity without pillage and often bloodshed". In vain he proposed that official Aboriginal reserves be allocated at Ipswich, Rosewood, and at Mt Zion (Nundah) where the "most numerous and troublesome" coastal tribes spent time. Meanwhile, with only four constables and one chief constable under the control of police magistrate Captain John Wickham, effective law enforcement was negligible.

The rapid "opening up" of the new colony also exposed deficiencies in the legal system itself. Frequent miscarriage and obstruction of justice occurred because of prohibitive costs in transporting all litigants and witnesses to trial in Sydney. Despite there being nearly 3,000 people in the northern colony, courts of petty sessions were not set up until 1848 in Moreton Bay, Ipswich, Cressbrook and Darling Downs. But they handled only summary convictions or civil cases involving fines or debts under £50. Adjudicating on breaches of employment contracts under the *Masters and Servants Acts* and drunkenness, these courts were concerned mainly with the "moral condition" of the colony. A contemporary historian described them as "most convenient institutions for the station owners ... whether the public did receive any real benefit is an open question".[12]

It was said that violent crime was not only largely unpunished, but positively thrived in the absence of higher court facilities. "Many offences that merited exemplary punishment", observed a visiting Supreme Court judge, "have been committed from the prospect of impunity on which those who committed them calculated".[13] There were howls of outrage when the military contingent withdrew in 1848, and public protests that settlers were left exposed to attack from escaped convicts and displaced Aborigines.

It would be a further two years before Circuit Courts were set up in Brisbane to deal with crimes of violence. And one of the first cases resulted in a three-year gaol sentence for a soldier found guilty of wounding an Aboriginal man. In 1857 the Supreme Court of Queensland was established, presided over by a single judge who held sessions in Brisbane, Ipswich, Toowoomba and Maryborough.

Policing the colony

Aggressive immigration campaigns accelerated the encroachment of white settlement over Aboriginal lands. Indeed when Queensland achieved independent colonial status in December 1858 only 7,000 of the 25,000 settlers lived in Brisbane. They were grossly outnumbered by the Aboriginal population, estimated as upwards of 100,000 people.[14] Mindful of inevitable "clashes", the new government appointed doctors at Wide Bay and in the Burnett district, each on a £20 annual retainer, as "Surgeons to the Aborigines".

Finances were critical. In 1860 the expected colonial income was listed as £160,000. Against this was expenditure of £149,319 including provision of £50 for defence expenses of Aborigines brought before the Supreme Court and a further £20 for interpreters. Treasury holdings in June 1860 fell to 7d. Police manpower stood at only ninety-one with responsibility for an estimated occupied area of 195,500 square miles. Officers carried additional unpaid duties as clerks of petty sessions, rangers of crown lands, inspectors of slaughter houses, registrars of births, deaths, and marriages, bailiffs of Courts of Requests, and servers of summons.

Policing at the rapidly expanding frontiers was necessarily precarious. As squatters sought to "clear" their holdings by leading punitive expeditions against local Aboriginal tribes, a state of almost open warfare existed. Evidence from newspapers of the time gives Aboriginal casualties in the Port Curtis area alone in the mid-nineteenth century of around 1,000, against 28 white deaths in the same area.[15] With critical shortages of manpower and finances, the colonial government turned to the policing agency which had for several decades operated cheaply and "efficiently" in the southern colonies — the native police force.

Inaugurated in Victoria in 1842 and consolidated in New South Wales in 1848 under Captain Frederick Walker, the native police force operated in groups of ten or twelve non-local Aborigines under a white commander. Officially the recruitment term for troopers was five years, but frequently they were "taken up" into service when drunk or otherwise entrapped. Many were ex-prisoners offered the chance to serve their time outside prison confines. As the primary policing arm of governments in remote areas, this force quickly gained notoriety for arbitrary ambush and wilful murder in all colonies.

Called to Moreton Bay to combat Aboriginal offensives, two units had operated from Brisbane's Sandgate since 1853. They were led by Lieutenant Frederick Wheeler, known as a ruthless and sadistic killer of Aborigines.[16] By 1860 there were 128 troopers in four outlying police districts. Instructions from the native trooper commandant at Rockhampton reveal the aggressive intent: "It is the duty of the Officers at all times and opportunities to disperse any large assembly of Blacks. Such meetings of natives invariably lead to depredations and murder".[17] Not surprisingly, an official inquiry following a massacre at Hornet Bank in 1858 found that native police presence frequently aggravated relations between Aborigines and whites.

But the training and deployment of Aborigines as agents of force was risky. It was a common concern that deserting and disbanded troopers often rejoined their tribes to turn their new martial skills against encroaching settlers. And contemporary evidence suggests recent assertions that troopers were given *carte blanche* in assaults on rural Aboriginal women, so long as they refrained from interfering with women in the towns,[18] may be over-simplistic. One critic of the force alleged at the time that "gins consorting with the troopers kept hostile tribes informed of the detachment's whereabouts", thereby facilitating retaliatory ambushes.[19]

Certainly paranoia made existence perilous for all Aborigines. Native police officer William Hill wrote that life was never safe and "the only wise thing to do on seeing a black was to shoot, and shoot straight".[20] Colonial historian George Rusden described the force as "a mere machine for murder".[21] But the troopers themselves were also victim to arbitrary violence from their commanders who had almost total discretion over conduct and discipline. One such officer described the troopers as as easy to manage as children, and blithely advised firmness in dispatching "a bob, a nip of whisky, or a flogging".[22] Several troopers were flogged to death by their officers.

A campaign in Brisbane's *Queenslander* newspaper exposed the scandalous activities of the native police force, but the resultant parliamentary committee inquiry in 1861

exonerated the system and laid blame at the feet of a few
negligent officers. Hardly surprising considering that every
member of the committee was a squatter, and fellow landholders with public commissions refused to give evidence.
It transpired that former native police commandant Captain Walker had been recruited and paid by local squatters
in the Dawson area to run a private squad of troopers for
their benefit. The general attitude was that the native police
force was available to perform the killings which were
otherwise illegal. Editorial comment in the *Queensland
Guardian* went further, announcing: "... no white man who
shot an Aborigine, in self-defence or in sport, should be
exposed to trial or sentence".[23]

Documents show that pastoralists besieged the colonial
secretary with demands for native police, even offering to
cover the costs for several years. Without such "protection",
wrote one Darling Downs manager, "we can't get men at
any price" to work the properties.[24] A resolution passed at
a public meeting at Rockhampton proposed that any station owner or manager should be able to mount a "dispersal" assault against Aborigines with total legal immunity for
any consequences providing they had consent of one magistrate.[25]

In 1866 premier Robert Herbert proclaimed: "... the
only way to deter [Aborigines] from attacks upon life and
property is to convince them of the superior power of the
white man by the frequent and unexpected presence of an
organized patrol in every part of the thinly populated
districts, and by the prompt punishment of crime".[26] The
"punishment of crime" in country areas was the province
of local justices and magistrates, a semi-legal body of men

with links to both police and law. But did they resolve irregularities in law enforcement, or compound them?

Local justices

Local judiciaries signified position rather than profession. Magistracies in nineteenth-century New South Wales are shown to have operated as "a form of colonial honours system", carrying the imprimatur of gentility but requiring no qualifications of rank, property or expertise. Magistrate's positions were temporary and tenure of office was reliant on annual votes through colonial parliaments. Appointments were often dispensed as rewards for political supporters, although unpopular magistrates could be abruptly transferred to obscure areas.

Rural justices of the peace, on the other hand, were usually prominent landowners nominated by local squatters. As settlement pushed outwards, men of "position" were co-opted into acting as legal and administrative deputies. But any legal training or even knowledge of law was purely coincidental for either the paid magistrates or the unpaid justices. Wide discretionary powers and isolation from official surveillance enabled this tier of legal operatives to act as "both tyrants and flunkeys".[27]

Many landowners refused to take on these additional, and often unpopular, duties. Even so, contemporary historian William Coote noted that by 1860 "a cloud of magistrates hovered over the land, for there were even then one hundred and fifty-three gentlemen on the commission of the peace".[28] Their multiple status — as arbiters of justice, supporters of policing, and often landholders themselves in need of native police "expertise" — compounded the probability of partiality.

So disreputable were their performances that it was necessary in 1861 for the attorney-general to issue a directive insisting that magistrates act to protect Aborigines as much as Europeans. In support, one correspondent declared that even where magistrates found accused Aborigines innocent, irate landowners routinely resorted to murder. He continued: "There are many other cases where Magistrates through ignorance or 'want of moral courage' have not extended to Aborigines the protection of law to which they are entitled … I only know one case where the Magistrate resisted the slaughter of unoffending blacks and even he was pressured and his brother threatened the native police officer with his gun and saved the station from further bloodshed … a strong feeling prevails that the government connived at these practices".[29] In fact it was common practice for native police officers to be promoted through the ranks of the provincial magistracy, and many police regarded magistrates' courts as merely mechanisms to process offenders.

An incident at Ipswich at this time demonstrates the incestuous linkages between positions of law enforcement and legal adjudication. After holding an inquiry into the deaths of three Aborigines on the Fassifern property of local JP John Hardie, the coroner Dr Challinor reported to the attorney-general that Hardie had sworn a false statement alleging the deaths resulted from a tribal fight. Challinor argued that evidence established "the shooting of the blacks is unequivocally traced to Sgt Wheeler and the detachment of native police under his command" which Hardie had demanded the local police magistrate send to his property. With both the police magistrate and the JP implicated in the deaths, Challinor pleaded for a rehearing of evidence before a disinterested justice. The attorney-general refused. Within one month a petition was circulated and lodged with parliament opposing Challinor's reappointment as district magistrate. Challinor subsequently leaked to the press full details of the magisterial hearings and the attorney-general's letter refusing to lay blame.

Calls for action

Challinor was widely known as "the champion of the Aborigines". As the member of parliament for Ipswich, he was perhaps the most prominent of a range of men calling for government action to resolve the Aboriginal plight as settlement terminated nomadic subsistence. At the 1861 native police inquiry, at which the general condition of Aborigines in the colony was also raised, Challinor called for the appointment of official protectors to defend the rights of Aborigines, a measure not officially implemented until 1897.

To provide employment for adult Aborigines while their children received basic schooling, Challinor recommended a government-supported venture to produce cotton on a commercial basis. The notion of a Missionary Cotton Company, rather than a farm of edible crops, was also advocated by several missionaries including Mr Zillman of the aborted mission at Nundah.

Government files of around this time contain a wealth of suggestions for the accommodation and normalisation of Aboriginal presence in the "occupied" areas. One correspondent writing in 1864 maintained that missions failed because educated children had little option but to return to families already struggling with destitution and disease on marginal pockets of land. He argued that the annexation of hunting grounds, deprival of food, and restriction of liberty of the Aboriginal inhabitants "does not comply with the ideas of British justice nor with religious precepts".[30]

Rev William Ridley, who had travelled among rural Aboriginal groups since 1850, was more emphatic. Aboriginal aggression was the direct result of actions by convicts and their descendants in evicting people from fertile land, necessitating the spearing of cattle to prevent starvation. Since the government granted the land to the squatters, he lectured the colonial secretary, the government had a duty to supply food to Aboriginal families as compensation. Neither the public nor the authorities backed Rev Ridley's proposal for regular ration issues, although a few blankets were distributed annually to destitute families.

The Herbert government did reserve some pockets of land for missions in the south of the colony in 1864 but not necessarily in places of greatest need. Rev William Larkin's application for a grant of land at Roma where he had been ministering for three years was knocked back, even though the venture was fully funded from private donations. In protest Rev Larkin applied to Governor Bowen, arguing that he had the support of several members of parliament, including Dr Challinor. Bowen informed Larkin that only the government could act to improve the conditions of Aborigines.[31]

Religious organisations pursued their "philanthropic" goals. A mission and sugar plantation venture did get off the ground at Beenleigh in 1866 but ran only a few years. Attempts at this time by Rev Fuller on Fraser Island (where he taught Aborigines in their own dialect and compiled a register of 1000 words) and subsequently on Hinchinbrook

Island also failed, the latter because native troopers had shot all the men prior to his arrival.[32] Nevertheless, Aboriginal Protection Societies or Aboriginal Friends' committees were running by the early 1870s at Ipswich, Brisbane, Warwick and Toowoomba.

But in the "unsettled" areas, meanwhile, the situation was disturbingly familiar. Discoveries of gold on the Mary River and at Gympie intensified demands for "protection" at a time when northern districts were also broached. "In order to push out the native police to these more unsettled districts", reported the police commissioner in 1866, "I have been compelled to break up or reduce the inside stations".

The weaker white police presence both emboldened Aboriginal aggression and intensified white attrition. At Rockhampton, where ambushes of up to two hundred armed Aborigines forced the partial abandonment of the new town,[33] rampaging troopers attacked Aboriginal groups at random, often hunting down those peacefully working in station paddocks. And at Maryborough, an area notorious for its vigilante raids by local whites and executions by native troopers, a nineteenth-century historian recorded campaigns by nearly two thousand Aborigines in devastating attacks on local timber-fellers.[34]

Despite its increasing notoriety, police commissioner Seymour insisted the force of 150 native troopers was essential to "check the outrages of the aborigines", then thought to number 50,000. In 1872 a training depot was established to ensure greater "efficiency". Seymour also acknowledged that white officers of suitable character were difficult to find; many had no previous experience in handling men nor did they receive any training before active duty. An officer with the native police later wrote revealingly, "it will be obvious to any Queenslander of those days that some episodes connected with the doings of the force cannot be published ... the 'boys' got beyond control in certain circumstances".[35]

The opening up of the northern sectors exposed police deficiencies. At Gilberton the gold diggings themselves were subject to frequent raids. The audacious ease of the ambushes was accentuated by the impotence of police: "The Officer in Command goes out with white constables and a black tracker and they return with horses knocked up and men tired and they never see a black".[36] Seymour criticised the casual approach of the newcomers. On the Palmer and Hodgkinson goldfields, he lamented, travellers straggled along in leisurely groups, failed to keep watch at night camps, and often left huts unattended for weeks at a time. Then the increasingly frustrated targets of black offensives took the law into their own hands. A later statement by a mining warden at the diggings reveals the general attitude: "Where there are no Acts of Parliament, and where there is no mantle of police protection", he wrote, the killers of Aborigines "were no more murderers than you or I".[37]

*   *   *

It is undeniable that deplorable atrocities were committed upon Aboriginal people during the nineteenth century. Examination of the difficulties and inconsistencies in extending and controlling agents of police and law in a remote colony suggests that failure of legal protection for Aborigines was inextricably rooted in logistical problems. The legal fraternity, parliamentarians, police, religious bodies, new settlers, landholders and miners, pursued a range of interests which are not reducible to a singular vector of repressive racism.

By the late 1860s the new colony was faced with two separate aspects of a single imponderable: what to do with the Aborigines? As white occupation spread to the "unsettled" north and west, the rogue native police force remained the easiest solution for a government lacking both the funds and the men, and perhaps even the will, to ensure the normal conventions of law. In the "settled" corner, the possibility of regularising the position of displaced Aboriginal families in white society was seemingly repudiated by the consistent failure of missionary ventures.

2
Learning to labour

By the latter half of the nineteenth century it was evident some form of official action was necessary to deal with the growing numbers of destitute adults and children in closely settled areas, as well as to arrest the rapid degeneration of the race in the remote regions of Queensland. But what procedures could be implemented to manage this range of problems?

In fact, a ready strategy of reform was already operating in the colonies at this time to regulate "problem" sectors of the population, namely the industrial schools and reformatories movement. A brief sketch of the emergence and rationale of this movement will allow a comparison to be made with the terminology of debate and the remedial programs proposed to redress the "Aboriginal problem".

"Problem" populations

Philanthropists and social commentators in late eighteenth-century Britain were alarmed to discover in their proudest cities large and rapidly multiplying populations of what they described as unwashed, immoral, uneducated, unchristian, unemployed and lawless slum-dwellers. It was the counting and categorising of social groups by the emerging "science" of social statistics that gave substance and potency to these concerns. Surveys to detect and register petty theft, criminal assault, matrimonial status, legitimacy of children, occupation, religion and schooling were converted into maps of criminal and moral conduct. Such information was said to represent a political barometer of the moral health of the country.[1]

One outcome of such specification and correlation of data was the linking of moral "degradation" with criminal behaviour. This motivated demands for official intervention to rescue children from incipient corruption, especially those whose poverty excluded them from national schools. From the 1840s a few "ragged schools" operated as "preventive agencies for the suppression of crime". Set up by philanthropic bodies in the slum areas, ragged schools fostered order and obedience and "the awakening of moral and religious principle".[2] This latter was not so much a matter of spirituality but of indoctrination in behavioural norms of punctuality, diligence, cleanliness and submissiveness *through* religious practices of self-criticism and prayerful obedience.

Government-backed reform schools, on the other hand, removed children from degenerate circumstances for retraining. In general, parental consent was sought for such "removals". However, "paupers, mendicants, vagabonds, foundlings, and deserted children" as well as those deemed to be "vicious or in moral danger"[3] could be classified as delinquent *because of* their problematic status and sent to reformatories.

Parental consent to child removals was effectively abolished in 1854, when a law was passed widening the state's powers of compulsory committal.[4] Further refinements in

1857 enabled any child between seven and fourteen years to be sent to a certified industrial school if parents could not guarantee good behaviour.[5] By the turn of the century 30,000, or one in every 230 juveniles between five and fifteen years in Britain, were under the jurisdiction of reformatory and industrial schools.[6]

The preventive dimension was the key focus of reformatories. It was argued that charity only entrenched "pauperism" by encouraging dependency and demoralisation. Industrial training, on the other hand, would fit youngsters with the moral and practical skills crucial for independence. To this end, inmates from reformatories were apprenticed out for menial work from the age of ten. The state controlled both employment and wages until the age of twenty-one.

In Australia the reformatory conviction is evident from earliest colonial days. Only two years after it became a free settlement Moreton Bay was host to a Benevolent Society set up to promote "the physical and moral well-being of the destitute labouring classes".[7] White children deemed to be "at risk" from a corrupting environment in New South Wales could be removed without parental consent after 1852 and placed in service to responsible families. In Hobart from the 1860s young females could be forcibly removed from the streets, given basic training, and apprenticed out as domestics.[8]

In Queensland, the 1865 *Industrial and Reformatories Schools Act* authorised the removal of any destitute child under seventeen found wandering or begging in the streets, any child dwelling with a reputed thief, prostitute or drunkard, and *any child born of an Aboriginal or half-caste mother*. Under the 1879 *Orphanages Act* children deemed to be deserted or neglected could be confined and later hired out in domestic or farm service. The police commissioner himself called for a girls' reformatory: "There are in Brisbane alone over fifty girls, under 14 years of age, who are being "dragged up" in the lowest haunts of vice, and who, unless rescued in time, have no other life than one of infamy and crime".[9] The mentality of rescue and reform is reflected in the predominance of committals for "neglect" rather than for legal violations in the latter half of the century, especially with regard to females.[10]

It is apparent that the practice of identification and legalised removal of "problem" individuals was common in nineteenth-century Britain and in colonial Australia. Unschooled young children, females, the poor, itinerants, the destitute, the homeless, or those whose associates were judged as unreliable or unsuitable, fell increasingly under the gaze of officialdom. How do these concerns over problematic sectors of the European population relate to nineteenth-century proposals to alleviate distress and destitution among Aborigines?

Remedial programs

The farming or industrial basis of the early missions has already been noted. There were several reasons why the harnessing of Aboriginal labour was essential for all missionary ventures. First, government support was sporadic, if at all, and church bodies were unable to provision either the pastors or their "flocks" beyond the first few months. Second, the rationale for these remedial enclaves was one of self-contained communities detached from the vices and degradation of the colonial towns. It was proposed, as we have seen, that Aboriginal children be taught regularity, diligence and basic skills, while their parents learned that persistence and industry would bring its own rewards of reliable food, shelter and security.

Correspondence from the 1860s confirms the reformatory perspective of the missionary ventures. The master of the Gladstone National School argued that because of the "nomadic propensities" of the adults it would be necessary for young Aborigines to be strictly supervised if farm training was to counter the "baneful influence" of corrupting Europeans and "disruptive" families.[11] Nundah Lutheran missionary, Mr Zillman, argued that a cotton farm would provide employment for adults while schooling for children would "raise them to a better condition".[12] From Roma, Rev Larkin proposed to "concentrate on youth" since the adults were too set in their ways. His scheme has a familiar ring. Young Aborigines would be housed, clothed and trained for hiring out as tradesmen and domestic servants.[13]

The low level of educational goals — domestic training for girls, farm labour for boys — also derives from the European rationale which decreed that slum children were to be given only a start in life, not an unearned educational privilege.[14] This attitude was neatly encapsulated by a leading British philanthropist who based his training ethos on "the Bible and the Spade for the boy, the Bible, broom, and needle, for the girl".[15]

The key factor for the collapse of missions was the indifference and the mobility of local Aboriginal groups, characteristics which were read as indices of Aboriginal indolence. But official exasperation with "idleness" and "wandering" was not simply an expression of racial repudiation. Rather it derived from a longstanding European presumption that nomadism and vagabondage were allied to criminal propensity.

In mid-nineteenth-century England it was estimated that 50,000 of the criminal population of 150,000 were vagrants, perceived as occupying an anomalous position between criminal and pauper, pursuing idle and disorderly modes of life which affronted the prevalent work ethos. "The nomad", wrote social commentator Henry Mayhew with regard to "Non-Workers, or in other words, the Dangerous Classes of the Metropolis",[16] "is distinguished from the civilised man by his repugnance to regular and continuous labour — by his want of providence in laying up a store for the future ... by the looseness of his notions as to property".[17] Thus constancy and the will to work were regarded as essential constituents of self-determination and social responsibility.

Aboriginal labour was essential for the cost-effectiveness of the missions, and was central to remedial ideology. A third reason for harnessing Aboriginal potential derived from the labour needs of the rapidly expanding colony which had become acute after the withdrawal of the convicts. It was conventional wisdom that Europeans were genetically unfit to labour in tropical climates, and as northern areas opened up to sugar and sheep farming displaced Aboriginal families were seen as a ready labour pool.

The goldrushes of the 1860s and 1870s compounded chronic labour shortages and many pastoral properties were totally dependent on their Aboriginal workers, as correspondence in the *Queenslander* clearly shows: "Had it not been for the aborigines doing nearly all my work during the late rush to the Palmer ... my losses would have been ruinous".[18] But rogue attacks by native police detachments made it extremely difficult to retain Aboriginal workers and several pastoralists had to "arrange" that these law enforcers not "interfere" with "their blacks".[19]

The Aboriginal enclave established in 1870 by Mackay sugar planter George Bridgman brings together several of these themes. Partly as a response to a petition by Mackay residents demanding an area where their workforces could live untroubled by raids from native police, an area of 10,000 acres (4,000 hectares) was gazetted as an Aboriginal reserve. Bridgman spoke several Aboriginal languages, and was described as having great influence with the local tribes. He persuaded many families to live under his guidance on the reserve, which provided a secure retreat for the women and children of men working nearby properties. He encouraged hunting and also the cultivation of food so that people were not dependent on purchased food supplies, thus providing a constructive alternative for those who were otherwise reduced "to beg and steal about the townships and settlements".[20] With Aboriginal assistance, Bridgman built a school where writing, reading and counting occupied the morning hours, and gardening and oyster gathering, wood and water fetching, filled the afternoons.[21]

By the end of 1878, however, the government had thrown open 90 per cent of Bridgman's reserve for selection. The school continued with its 40 pupils for two years until funding for it, too, was cancelled. To understand this sequence of events it is necessary to situate Bridgman's humanitarian venture in the wider context of government responses to what was increasingly termed the "Aboriginal problem".

Political responses

In an attempt to counter criticism of a policy vacuum, the government had appointed an Aboriginal Commission in 1874 "to inquire what can be done to ameliorate the condition of aborigines and to make them more useful".[22] Submissions were invited throughout Queensland on Aboriginal employment as to numbers, condition and possible improvement in each district. Although it was soon described as "instituted for the purpose of shelving the question, and serving as a blind to the Home [ie British] Government",[23] the short-lived commission won an annual grant of £200 for the funding of areas reserved for displaced Aborigines.

A second proposal, that aggressive conquest of Aborigines in the northern frontier districts be replaced by a policy of "conciliation" through the distribution of rations and blankets, influenced police commissioner Seymour to trial the measures to good effect.[24] However, Seymour was less amenable to suggestions that native police detachments be replaced by "ordinary police".[25]

The major concern of the commission, and the most politically sensitive for the government, was the notorious reputation of the native police in the northern frontier districts. Conspicuous injustices exposed the uncertain status of Aboriginal testimony in courts of law where many were unable to take the oath. Arrests of troopers were infrequent because of problems in gaining convictions, and offenders were often captured and released without punishment.

So blatant were the abuses that attorney-general Samuel Griffith argued that all Aboriginal evidence should be allowable in cases relating to native police activities. Initially this was rejected by the legislative council, but finally in 1876 a Bill was passed to allow evidence to be taken on affirmation of truth, rather than on the Christian oath. Even so, as Aboriginal advocate Father Duncan McNab noted bitterly, many judges failed to utilise the provision.[26] In one case two men charged with shooting Aborigines were discharged by the magistrate after he refused a delay to allow interpreters to attend, stating "none of the aboriginal witnesses understand the nature of the oath".[27] At other times juries exonerated killers against both the evidence and the admissions of guilt.

Following the arrival in Brisbane of Bishop Matthew Hale, a man with long experience working with Aborigines in South Australia, the Aboriginal Commission was reactivated in 1876 and included Father McNab as a member. Directed to consider "the best measures of reclaiming and benefiting the Aborigines",[28] the commission was emasculated by political disinterest. "I trust we may be able to effect some good", wrote fellow commissioner W. Drew, "though I am not very sanguine".

Judicial arrogance made a mockery of legal redress for atrocities by the native police force. Police Inspector Wheeler, arrested for flogging an Aborigine to death, was granted bail and promptly absconded. "The papers just now teem with statements of cruelty to blacks by the Police", wrote Drew, "and altogether the condition of affairs gets worse and worse".[29]

It was not until the liberal government of John Douglas won power in 1877 that the commission gained formal gazettal of reserves for Aboriginal use — at Bribie Island, Durundur near Caboolture, Deebing Creek near Ipswich, Bowen and Townsville. The Durundur reserve of 2,130 acres was the outcome of assurances given to Father McNab by local elders that they would settle in the area provided they had official endorsement. In the early years two hundred people worked with McNab agisting and selling stock and renting out a paddock for police horses. White agitation against the community brought about the closure of the reserve in 1885.[30]

This ease of displacement prompted Father McNab to lobby for the right of Aborigines to purchase land, a cause opposed even by his fellow commissioners. "Many natives would occupy homesteads who will not live on a reserve", he argued. "They live frequently, not from choice, but by necessity, on reptiles and such food as men resort to only when reduced to the last extremity by siege or famine." Ownership would enhance Aboriginal conversion to the work ethic: "When once they learn that they can possess property, they are willing to labour for its acquirement, and wish to transmit it to their posterity".[31] He campaigned in vain.

As a retreat from the vices of Brisbane town the Bribie Island reserve failed to achieve its aims. "How far has it attained the purpose for which it was founded? In furnishing an asylum for the old, in breaking off the wandering habits of the young, and teaching them habits of providence and industry?" pondered Thomas Petrie, who managed the venture. "For the aged black, the settlement is decidedly a success. In breaking off the wandering habits of the young, the success is not so clear."[32] In an effort to encourage private trading the group was supplied with a boat, nets and harpoons. Petrie was disappointed that the men would not work without payment and readily drifted back to the towns. Two years later, following the election of the conservative McIlwraith government, this reserve was also cancelled, colonial secretary Arthur Palmer remarking of the destitute elderly, "Oh let them go and work like anyone else".[33]

Palmer was a pastoralist from central Queensland, and according to contemporary historian George Rusden his appointment presaged the end of the Aboriginal commission and cancellation of the reserves. Seeking perhaps to avoid public condemnation for such vindictive actions, the government instead starved the commission of funds and power.

The crisis peaked when, after the massacre of twenty-four Aboriginal men and women near Cooktown by sub-inspector O'Connor and his six troopers[34], the government immediately endorsed police testimony. With the *Brisbane Courier* running a vigorous campaign of conflicting evidence, Bishop Hale sought access to the records but was rebuffed by a scornful Palmer. McNab resigned in disgust, describing the commission as "a facade to mask government inaction". When Drew followed, the commission collapsed. The reserves at Mackay and Bribie Island, like that at Durundur, were thrown open to white settlement.

Police commissioner Seymour sought to deflect public acrimony, blaming "collisions" between native police and Aborigines on the failure of farmers to take "ordinary precautions" on newly settled properties. "The blacks are disturbed and prevented from obtaining their native food", he wrote, "small cattle stations cut them off from their hunting and fresh-water fishing grounds ... the natives are thus literally starving, and take advantage of the cover afforded by the scrub to make sudden raids on the cattle

and huts ... too much dependence is placed on the police".[35]

McNab was disgusted. Now free from the constraints of
the semi-government position, he challenged Seymour that
on his own admission seven out of ten raids by Aborigines
were direct responses to white provocation. The government, wrote McNab, was directly accountable for continuing atrocities because it maintained "a standing army of
native troopers under European Officers for the protection
of the Colonists, and of their flocks, by the destruction of
the Aborigines".[36]

Public opinion

It was precisely this official complicity which sustained a
long campaign in *The Queenslander*. "We are determined
that the public shall understand what they are doing",
thundered editor Gresley Lukin, "and that if no attempt is
made at reform the refusal shall come from people who
thoroughly understand their responsibility".[37] In a series of
articles headed "The Way We Civilise", for several months
The Queenslander detailed what they termed routine assaults
and murders by native police detachments around the
colony. White officers, they wrote, were complicitly guilty
of atrocities, either turning a blind eye or wary of exposure.
"Men are naturally reluctant to confess in public deeds
which, though sanctioned by our Government and Parliament, and by the public sentiment of a section of our
colonists, are yet of a nature which would, according to the
common law, bring them to the gallows."[38]

Station owners and miners despatched "tame" Aboriginal men and women as readily as "hostile myalls" who
crossed their path. The position of Aboriginal women and

children in occupied areas was particularly perilous. They were taken from their families "at will and unchecked" wrote one correspondent to *The Queenslander*. "It is an everyday occurrence in the north to meet travellers and teams accompanied by a black woman ... in a man's clothes and passing her off as a boy."[39] McNab also berated the practice: "... frequently the Whites seize the Black gins and after keeping and abusing them for a few days, let them go". Children were caught and traded like chattels. One man told McNab "he had seen a carrier run down a black boy, tie him in chains on his dray and after two days sold him to another carrier for two pounds ten shillings".[40]

But the police themselves were keen traders in children, offering "tame" youngsters as servants and companions. "This practice has been going on for years", wrote inspector Galbraith of Normanton at the turn of the century. "They change masters and mistresses, prostitution and disease follow, they can only speak pidgin English, and finally become pariahs among both blacks and whites."[41] Local justices were also participants in the culture of abuse. A traveller in the remote west urged the colonial secretary to act: "... all JPs should be struck off the rolls that are known to keep their black harems; this is a fine cloak to cover their licentious cravings ..."[42]

Demands in 1880 for a Royal Commission were rejected by Palmer on the grounds that it would "not find out anything they did not know at present".[43] Parliamentarian B. Morehead agreed: "The black race have got to go ... the appointment of a Royal Commission is unnecessary and useless". He was subsequently promoted to the ministry.[44] Only minor policy adjustments were made. In 1881 all police were ordered to submit estimates of Aboriginal numbers in their district. And in the public forum of the government gazette, a notice directed police and magistrates to "procure the arrest" of all half-caste children, "with a view to treating them as 'neglected children' under *The Industrial and Reformatory Schools Act of 1865*" so that they could receive "education and moral training".[45] But this instruction was quickly revoked by an internal police order: arrests were to be made only on the express authorisation of the police commissioner. In fact, facilities to handle "neglected" children were so inadequate that since 1880 jails were defined as "institutions" under the *Industrial and Reformatory Schools Act* to enable their accommodation of young "offenders".

One devastating consequence of the decades of widespread sexual assaults on women and children was rampant and largely untreated syphilis. Venereal disease was endemic also in the white population, but Aboriginal sufferers were not afforded the anonymity of private attention. And hospital treatment for paupers was dependent upon authorisation by a police magistrate. As private institutes, moreover, local hospitals were not compelled to accept paupers of any race and routinely refused them. Premier Samuel Griffith was challenged by his attorney-general in 1885 to legislate against such "objectionable" hospital by-laws, but he desisted. Although hospitals were formally notified that their pauper grant was "for the purposes of relieving the destitute and sick regardless of colour and sect", it was not until 1894 that the government confirmed it would cover costs of Aboriginal patients admitted by order of a police magistrate. Even so, it is clear from official documents that many hospitals continued to turn away coloured patients well into the twentieth century. Those few who accepted Aboriginal patients habitually housed them in outlying sheds.

Regulating labour

During the latter half of the nineteenth century a series of laws and regulations introduced at least the principles of protection for native labour. But these laws did not arise in the context of the Aboriginal workforce. They were a response to the internationally notorious trade in humans which flourished for the benefit of Queensland's sugar barons. Restrictions which controlled Aboriginal employment for much of the twentieth century had their roots in the perverse "Kanaka" trade.

As Queensland's sugar industry developed, it was to the Melanesian islands that entrepreneurs looked for the cheap "docile" workers vital for plantation profits. Many plantation barons doubled as ship owners, and within the first four years to 1867 more than two thousand Kanakas were "recruited" and shipped under conditions "almost too vile to put into words". Two parliamentary inquiries into the trade were held by 1869, but with most of the inquiry members and several parliamentarians either recruiters or profiting from the slave trade, it was common talk that the government was "winking at" the "slave trade in Queensland".[46]

Procedures to reduce abuses in recruitment and employment followed the inquiries, including witnessed work indentures, shipping inspectors, set rations and conditions, and the extension of the reception of "native" testimony in courts of law earlier alluded to. But atrocities and abuses continued unabated over several decades, facilitated because, as one historian noted, "administration appears to have been wholly in the interests of the planter-squatter class for whose benefit black labour was being imported".[47]

So notorious was the colonial Kanaka trade that when recruiters extended their operations to the New Guinea islands, Britain sent naval vessels to monitor transportation around Cape York. It was the British presence which finally exposed outrages committed upon Aboriginal workers conscripted to work the luggers collecting pearlshell and bêche-de-mer or sea slug.[48]

Estimates of Aboriginal and Islander divers working in these industries in the last quarter of the century have been put as high as one thousand per year.[49] Many were taken on board against their will or on the pretence that the journey was short and return assured. Reality spelt several months at sea with poor food, beatings for slow work, and frequent abandonment in hostile areas remote from home country.

But the system was also played from the other side. It was not uncommon for workers to sign on and jump ship further up the coast, and some groups bartered their women to the sea-traders for enough flour and tobacco to last the off-season. Often long-term reciprocal arrangements were made with particular captains, and in some localities tribal elders contracted out the young males as a tactic to advance control over the younger women. Even so, it was undeniably the case that North Queensland Aborigines were commonly victims of kidnapping, assault and murder.

In 1884 premier Samuel Griffith passed legislation to protect Melanesian and Aboriginal coastal workers, requiring return of all Aboriginal labour to home ports, inspection of boats, and introducing penalties for forcible seizure of Aboriginal women. Contracts had to be explained and witnessed by a shipping master, detailing the length of work period, wages, rations and clothing.[50] But the new regulations were applicable only within a ten-mile coastal strip, and inland workers remained defenceless against continuing exploitation and abuse.

There were employers who sought to place Aboriginal workers under contract to prevent the poaching of trained "boys" under false promises of greater payment. "Many of us that value and employ the [Aboriginal] labour would willingly subscribe to any regulations and supervision considered necessary", wrote one pastoralist in 1884. "It would be the means of making useful and prolonging the lives of a race that in a very short period of time will make their exit."[51] Assurances that all Aboriginal workers could invoke the protection of *Masters and Servants* regulations[52] were facile. Most employers had no intention of being tied to conditional contracts. And again, as with other "protective" legislation, proof of exploitation was dependent on the integrity of local justices. Since members of local judiciaries were often friends of, or related to, the regional squatter and pastoral families whose interests were best served by obedient servants, employee protection was unpredictable.

For many employers narcotic dependency was a far cheaper means of keeping a regular Aboriginal workforce. It was a common practice to entice men and women with bribes of tobacco, adulterated liquor or opium dregs.[53] Historian Geoffrey Bolton notes that this practice was entrenched also among the purportedly "respectable" class: "The men who put liquor and opium into Aboriginal hands ... included also respectable publicans of Cooktown, whose business friends on the local Bench would be sure to let them off with a nominal fine; [also] settlers around Atherton and Mackay who found these the cheapest means of paying Aboriginal labour ..."[54] As premier in 1884, Samuel Griffith accused his predecessor Thomas McIlwraith of stacking the magistracies with political appointments, many of whom he described as "the greatest ruffians in Australia".[55]

*   *   *

Nineteenth-century governments in Queensland were forced to respond to local and international campaigns demanding official interventions to bring Aboriginal/European relations under orderly control. The variety of recommendations, remedial programs and administrative responses suggests that the Aboriginal plight was a target for social change. Vigorous debate and practical adjustments in the legal domain and the field of "coloured" employment, and indeed the articulation of the Aboriginal dilemma *through* the prism of European reformatory rhetoric, run counter to the historical convention of a systemic racial exclusion.

That said, documents reveal the precarious position of Aborigines within colonial Queensland. At the local level, the arbiters and supervisors of protective provisions were often capricious in their application of available options. Outright collusion in exploitation and abuse, particularly in areas remote from official surveillance, was common. Early missions had not survived, and Aboriginal reserves had collapsed through white offensives or through lack of Aboriginal interest. During the 1890s, however, greater attention was directed to the seemingly intractable "Aboriginal problem".

3

Competing interests

In colonial Queensland the gap between law as written and law as executed remained wide. Networks of relatively unqualified agents were subjected to, and in many cases were themselves participants in, a range of interests which directly benefited from the exploitation of the Aboriginal population. This complicity effectively emasculated available legislative protections. The prevailing rhetoric of individualism and endemic financial stringencies also militated against concerted government programs of support.

As we have seen, early mission attempts in the "settled" south-east of the colony were unsuccessful. During the last two decades of the nineteenth century, however, a new wave of missionary activity saw the formation of a series of ventures in the north of the colony, most of which continue to this day as Aboriginal communities. The security of these missions was to some extent underwritten by comprehensive legislation in 1897 aimed specifically at the Aboriginal population. The emergence and operations of the missions and the new laws are the subject of this chapter.

"Missions to the heathen"

When the government produced a glowing report on the agricultural prospects of the Cooktown area speculators rushed to take up land. Aboriginal families driven from their lush country were directed to a pocket of sandhills and swamps reserved for them between the McIvor and Endeavour Rivers. People soon returned to scrounge a living around the new town.

In 1885 the Lutherans undertook to provide five years' schooling for children and a farm to occupy and provision the adults if the Griffith government supplied rations for the first year. When the funds ran out, families again went afield for food and work. It was not until the main mission site was moved to the fertile Hope Valley area two years later that a community was established. The new man in charge, Pastor Schwartz, was to maintain links with this mission for nearly fifty-five years.

Funding for missions was reliant on reports of local justices. The fledgling Cooktown missions were almost scuttled by the caprice of the police magistrate in 1893. Angry that the pastor of the McIvor River mission refused to send schoolgirls to do domestic work in the town, he counselled that government support was "unwarranted" while such revenue was ignored. Perversely, he advised cancellation of funding to Hope Valley because children would *not* remain at school, and refused the use of police to round up the truants arguing that it "would be contrary to the essentially voluntary principle of the scheme and would, moreover, inevitably break down".[1]

Missions were also vulnerable to local antagonism and impractical expectations. South of Cooktown a petition was raised against another Lutheran mission proposed at

Bloomfield River. Ration handouts, protested the locals, would enable Aborigines to evade "legitimate employment" and encourage them to "loaf about" the towns and nearby homesteads. Despite this opposition, two hundred and sixty acres was gazetted in the mid-1880s.

But local Aboriginal families exploited the rations and the farming programs, tolerating sermons only for the food which followed. The minister who ran the venture in its last years wrote in frustration that lack of Aboriginal commitment to mission objectives was typical of people who were "apathetic, insusceptible, defiant and lazy". As families maintained hunting and ceremonial practices and took occasional jobs with coastal luggers, numbers fluctuated between thirty and one hundred and twenty. These "nomadic habits" were condemned by the minister as both impractical and "morally wrong".[2]

Ultimately an adverse police report, in this case alleging continuing abuses of young girls by recruiters, caused the withdrawal of government funding. The few "converts", along with twenty-three from another abortive Lutheran mission at Mari Yamba near Bowen, were transferred to the major Lutheran reserve at Hope Valley.

Premier Samuel Griffith's aggressive reserve policy, underwritten by £1,000 per year with a further £2,500 for rations and blankets, captured the imagination of the newly federated Presbyterian Church in 1886. With several successful Christian night-schools operating for Melanesian plantation workers in Queensland, the Presbyterians decided to extend their "missions to the heathen" to the Aboriginal inhabitants of the colony.

Their attention was directed by Griffith to the west of Cape York, where recruiters were operating aggressively to replace workers lost after the Papua New Guinea labour trade was terminated in 1885. The government's man on Thursday Island was ex-premier John Douglas, long a campaigner against abuses in the pearling and bêche-de-mer trades. It was his ambition that a string of missions down the west coast would bring some semblance of control to operations in an area he described as being unsafe from both whites and blacks.[3]

Recruiters, as a matter of course, were bitter opponents of missionary intrusion. They saw the missions as rivals for Aboriginal labour, and their ministers as hostile critics of maritime work practices. Undeterred, and accompanied by native police protection, Douglas travelled in 1891 with Moravian missionaries Rev James Ward and Rev Nicholas Hey to select a site on the Batavia River opposite Cullen Point, positioned more for its defence potential than for its fertility. Here the new mission of Mapoon was granted temporary rations and the sum of £500 towards building construction. It was to survive until the 1960s, when it was sabotaged by government duplicity.

The early 1890s also saw the arrival in Queensland of Anglican missionary Rev John Gribble, a man with long experience among Aboriginal communities. Following a concerted campaign of vilification and persecution in Western Australia, Rev Gribble had fled across the continent to Queensland in fear of his life. His crime? The exposure and prosecution of police atrocities against Aborigines.[4] Gribble travelled to Cape Grafton near Cairns on the promise of official backing of £500 plus £240 per annum. By the time he selected the site for his Yarrabah mission, however, the colonial secretary had been briefed by his brother parliamentarians from the west and cancelled the funds. Undaunted, Gribble paid his own expenses, living on a diet of porridge and milk for several months until the Sydney-based Australian Board of Missions belatedly recognised his venture.

Gribble spent his time visiting local camps where the plight of the children caught his attention. Disease and starvation were common, and there were many orphans already addicted to alcohol and opium, a consequence of, and incitement for, juvenile prostitution. But Gribble's determination to deliver the young into a secure missionary environment was undermined by anti-mission agitators from Cairns across the bay. Jealously guarding their pool of cheap labour, townspeople warned local tribes that Gribble intended to kidnap their children and sell them into slavery.[5] Not one Aborigine had visited his mission when Gribble succumbed to fever after only eleven weeks and was evacuated to Sydney. He died soon after.

Gribble's son Ernest arrived in 1892 to continue the fledgling Yarrabah mission, maintaining a connection with the community until 1959. His early days were fraught with battles to protect the reserve from acquisitive white interests, including local timbermen who successfully petitioned the Land Commission in 1893 to have most of the area thrown open to logging.[6] In 1896 fifty Aborigines were reportedly working "well and cheerfully" at Yarrabah, and for several years mission men regularly worked the bêche-de-mer seasons to supplement meagre mission produce.

Near Brisbane an unofficial camp and school had operated for some time on an 80-acre reserve at Deebing Creek near Ipswich. To access government funding, the local Aboriginal Protection Association started an Aboriginal Home in 1893, run by a board of trustees. With £250 for a teachers' residence, and 1s 6d per head per year for rations, Deebing Creek boasted a settled population of sixty-two residents within two years, and a school of fifteen pupils. "Four hours' work is required per day from each able bodied male", reported the secretary in his petition for increased funding, "and the blacks are encouraged to build their own dwellings and cultivate their own plots of land for their own benefit". Supervision on the reserve was fairly tight, he continued, although restrictions "are not of such a character as to awaken that feeling of discontent with settled life, which has hitherto been almost universally proved to be the great obstacle in previous attempts to ameliorate the condition of the Aborigines".[7] Called to assess the situation, the local police magistrate testified that although the land was poor and not much progress had been made, the venture was "well worth a further trial".

Despite a greater commitment for funding and the positioning of several new missions well away from expanding white settlement, governments faced agitation against continued expenditure. In part this arose because too many sectors of the colonial population profited from the unpaid and unregulated labour pool: sea traders and pastoralists, employers of casual workers and domestic servants. But it also reflected frustration at the refusal of Aborigines to stay on the reserves, and the inability of officials to keep the children in schools. The question was, were current policies "worth a further trial"?

Reports and responses

At this propitious moment a treatise by ex-parliamentarian, erstwhile insolvent and showman Archibald Meston landed on the desk of the colonial secretary. In it Meston declared he had mixed with "tame and wild tribes" since boyhood, gaining "personal knowledge of their habits, customs, daily life, superstitions, inner life, and general character". Claiming to be a tribal initiate speaking several Aboriginal languages, Meston had toured widely with a group of "wild warriors" in exhibitions of strength and fighting prowess.

A boastful and erratic man, Meston favoured the concept of the "noble savage", and in his essay *Queensland Aboriginals: Proposed System for their Improvement and Preservation*,[8] Meston placed the decimation of the race firmly at the foot of governments. "Our own aboriginals", he lectured home secretary Sir Horace Tozer, "the people from whom we have forcibly taken this country, without payment, are wandering homeless through our settlements, clothed in rags and begging their food, perishing miserably from the vices which the white race has introduced, unnoticed and uncared for, except at the distributing food stations".

"Seventy years of scattered missionary efforts, isolated individual benevolences, and numberless good intentions of philanthropic statesmen" had not alleviated the suffering. Meston contrasted this policy vacuum with conditions for the eight thousand Polynesians who were "guarded by inspectors, stringent special laws and regulations, provided with medical attendance, hospitals, missionaries, and churches; well fed, well clothed, and well housed". What was needed, he concluded, was a concerted strategy like that of Victoria, New South Wales and South Australia where official Boards oversaw funded and closely controlled mission training stations and ration depots.

So impressed was Horace Tozer, that he commissioned Meston to travel the colony and make a full assessment of the Aboriginal conditions, particularly in the remoter western and northern sectors. Meston's report to parliament makes appalling reading.[9] Official response was delayed to enable police commissioner William Parry-Okeden to answer Meston's accusation that native police operations had decimated northern tribes by random shootings and habitual kidnapping of women and boys, leaving a legacy of terror. Not surprisingly, the two men produced contradictory observations and recommendations reflecting their differing preconceptions and status. Where Meston demanded that the native police should be abolished, Parry-Okeden insisted that an efficient, disciplined force was essential for the security of whites working in the north and could be used to mediate among dispossessed tribes in other remote areas.[10]

Meston lauded the vitality and expertise of the twelve thousand "wild" Aborigines north of Cairns who had not been contaminated by white contact. Arguing that the "treachery" of blacks was a "mischievous delusion", Meston excused the few cases of Aboriginal retaliation as "merely acts of justly deserved retribution". Five tribes numbering three thousand individuals between Newcastle Bay and Cape York had been reduced to one hundred survivors in only twenty-five years, said Meston, principally at the hands of settlers and native police.

This contrasted sharply with Parry-Okeden's characterisation of remote tribes as powerful, treacherous, and cunning "savages". Casting some light on the culture of police abuse, he insisted that "demonstrations of strength (of a character that they will respect) are a necessary prologue to gaining an influence over them for good". Strong native detachments "constantly patrolling among them" were essential for the required "control and punishment".

Meston also called for a complete ban on Aboriginal recruitment in the maritime trades. Cape York was so fertile that Aborigines gained nothing from maritime employment, he wrote. Constant abductions and sexual assaults by boat crews brought disease and death, hastening tribal extinction. Parry-Okeden, however, reminded his minister that the trade was completely dependent on Aboriginal labour. He proposed a government boat be made available for surveillance and pursuit at sea to enable more efficient policing.

Both men were appalled at the devastation and disease among tribes in the west and Gulf regions. According to Meston, people had been hunted from their tribal country "like animals" in "perpetual warfare with pioneers". Women and children were exploited like slaves by whites who were "responsible to no authority"; local groups were seduced by white men "of position and reputation" who used opium to snare servile workers and submissive sexual partners.

Once again the police commissioner insisted that increased native police strength was the key to apprehension of the "wretches who have wrought deeds of appalling wickedness and cruelty, and who think it equal good fun to shoot a nigger at sight or to ravish a gin". While conceding starvation was rampant, even among Aboriginal workers who were routinely fed "such pieces of 'junk' as have become tainted", Parry-Okeden characterised the sporadic killing of cattle as symptomatic of an Aboriginal "craving for animal food" and the "gratifying of carnivorous instincts".

Like Meston, Parry-Okeden was horrified at the ravaging effects of alcohol and opium. But he was not averse to manipulating addiction to his own ends. Taken aback by widespread terror and distrust of police, he suggested "confidence" could be bought through the introduction of tobacco, which he noted was so addictive that "even the wildest, when once they have smoked, try and become friends with and hang round the haunts of the whites". Such addicts, he reasoned, could prove very handy as police informers.

At base, Meston's recommendations reflected his preconceptions of "racial integrity". The remote northern tribes should be left untouched in their wilderness. But Meston wanted all fringe groups to be collected onto reserves and isolated from white contact which was "more degraded than any savage". Segregation, he argued, was the best option to save the Aboriginal race from plummeting to extinction and to secure the white race from "contamination" through mixed-race births and disease.

If those Aborigines who had been "crowded out by encroaching settlement" were to live productively it would be necessary to allocate large areas of good land in isolated locations, rather than the present infertile pockets upon which several missions struggled. Aware, perhaps, that segregation would not be a popular political option, Meston concluded that inter-racial associations would otherwise have to be controlled by legislation "comprehensive enough to provide for all contingencies attendant on aboriginal life in the settled districts".

The home secretary used the two reports to push for the formalisation of the reserve policy. With phrases rendered directly in reformatories rhetoric, he spoke glowingly to parliament of the benefits of compulsory rescue and retraining of this problem group. Of the reactivated Durun-

dur reserve, he reported enthusiastically that several destitute groups from the far west were now "kept clear of opium
and drink, restored to complete health, and gradually
initiated to industrious habits".[11] After a spate of deaths,
fifty-two people had been removed from Maryborough to
the sanctuary of Fraser Island under the control of Meston's
son Harold. Tozer reported proudly that in eight months
all had thrived: there was abundant local food and the
government had supplied fishing lines and a boat.

Children from the Aboriginal school at Myora on Stradbroke Island, closed in 1896 after a child was beaten to
death by the matron, had been transferred to Deebing
Creek. Now gazetted as an industrial school, Deebing Creek
took in "neglected" Aboriginal children from around Brisbane, and several from the white reformatory at Westbrook
— one a seven-year-old boy sentenced to three years' detention for larceny. Following a longstanding policy applied to
white children from orphanages and reformatories, youngsters from the age of twelve were sent out to work in menial
and domestic jobs.

Tozer assured parliament that the reserve policy had
potential at much more than the individual level. In protective enclaves such as missions, the race itself was regen-
erated: "The first change to be effected on these reserves is
the transition of all sexes into a healthy condition, and
restoring their proper sense of manhood and womanhood,
independence, and self-respect".

In their debates on the Aboriginals Protection and Restriction of the Sale of Opium Bill,[12] government statements belie the assertions of almost every historian to date:
that reserves were intended to facilitate wholesale racial
segregation and were set up to operate as "total institu-

tions". The colonial government had neither the manpower nor the means to martial nearly 20,000 Aborigines out of the general community to be supported and supervised on reserves. Their consistent failure to maintain even the odd small venture of fifty to a hundred people is testament to that.

Tozer clearly stated that the new law was aimed mainly at the 3000 to 4000 Aborigines living in the south of the colony, for whom the existing legal framework was patently inadequate. Like Meston, Tozer was well aware there would be no backing for a scheme which committed the government to the sustenance of the Aboriginal population. "If there are any people who have any idea that a large number of billets are going to be created they will find themselves mistaken", he admonished the House.[13] To placate fellow members who feared losing their "tame" workers, he stressed that "whenever existing conditions were in accordance with the laws of humanity, and some pretence at a home was provided, no interference would take place. But in places where opium was distributed they would have to be taken to reserves". The problem was: what regulations were needed and how would they be implemented? And who precisely would be subject to the new law?

Defining subjection

The provisions of the 1897 *Aboriginals Protection and Restriction of the Sale of Opium Act* clearly echo those of *Industrial and Reformatory Schools* legislation which had operated for almost half a century in the white community, targeting and removing those deemed to be "at risk" of abuse or neglect. Analysis of the terms of the Act confirm a primary concern with monitoring inter-racial relations rather than with racial segregation.

When the *Aboriginals Protection Act* became law in December 1897, the leading police officer in each district was delegated as the local "protector of Aboriginals", most of whom now became wards of the state. Protectors were directed "to see that they do not get any liquor or opium, that they keep their blankets, and are not injured in regard to their children and their wives".

Supervised work contracts enabled the vetting of employers to prevent assault, exploitation, and the manipulation of employees to gain access to wives or female workers "for immoral purposes". Tozer stressed that wages would remain a matter of discretion: "sometimes it may be clothing, sometimes food". Controls over maritime employment were deferred pending the findings of a parliamentary commission into the industry.

Importantly, the new law did not apply to all Aborigines as a *racial* group: rather people in specific *social* categories were now defined as "Aboriginals" and thereby subject to various supervisory strategies. Full-blood Aboriginals, whose status in law had proved particularly problematic, were now enclosed within the new protective network as wards of state. But only those half-castes living with, or as, Aborigines, or under sixteen years of age, were so designated. By their youth, or their persistence in traditional lifestyles, they were deemed vulnerable to exploitation. For these people, the state, through the local protector, would henceforth act as guardian.

The category which remained outside the legal definition of "Aboriginal" was that of half-castes over sixteen years and not living with, or as, Aborigines. Indeed it was strongly argued that this group should escape all official supervision. While males did remain free to negotiate their own employment, Tozer insisted that it was precisely the half-caste women and girls living with or working for *whites* who were at greatest risk. For these females a range of regulations was introduced, borrowing heavily from existing *Masters and Servants* procedures, as a protective cloak. To temper opposition, Tozer was forced to concede the exemption of those girls already living with "trustworthy" families. This loophole immediately proved problematic, as we shall see.

Aboriginal reserves now became strictly monitored areas, closed to public access, to which any Aboriginal "under the Act" could be transferred at the direction of the minister. Archibald Meston was named as Southern Protector in charge of all areas south of the Tropic of Capricorn and answerable to the home secretary. The position of Northern Protector went to Dr Walter Roth, who as government medical officer at Burketown had impressed police commissioner Parry-Okeden with his ethnographic studies of local tribes. As an indication of the "policing" dimensions of the new Act in the north, it was to Parry-Okeden that Roth was instructed to report.

Neither Meston nor Roth saw their brief as wholesale removal and segregation. "I do not see any clause in the Bill which says I am to put blacks into camps", wrote Meston in 1901. "If all the blacks were taken away they would be a heavy charge on the Government." Roth put it even more succinctly: "How can we keep 18,000 or 20,000 blacks on reserves?"[14] This may have been one of the only points on which they agreed. Their different approaches and simmering professional jealousies were soon to complicate the implementation of what was, in many areas, a most unwelcome intrusion into race relations.

Vested interests

Widespread evasions quickly made a mockery of "protection". In less than eighteen months an amendment Bill was before parliament, aimed primarily at countering the most prevalent sexual abuses, namely the violation of girl children, some as young as six, and assaults on "adopted" females. Under existing law, convictions of sexual assault were dependent on proof of age, a technicality beyond most Aboriginal parents. New home secretary Justin Foxton wanted the law changed to place the onus on the offender to prove that a girl was above the legal age of consent of fourteen years. Parliamentarians indignantly insisted that a man could readily mistake the maturity of "native" girls of nine or ten because they "ripened" much earlier in tropical areas.[15]

Foxton was forced to compromise: where medical proof showed a girl had not attained puberty an assailant could be charged. This was no comfort to Roth who, as medical witness in an assault case involving a girl of only "13 or so", lamented: "I know it is only one of hundreds that must continually be going on". The case was dropped because the girl could not prove her age as below 16 years.[16]

Roth had been horrified at the rush of applications from whites claiming Aboriginal girls had been "brought up as one of the family" and were therefore exempt from official controls. Many girls, he reported, were worked without wages and evicted "when they get into trouble". All female half-castes should be brought under the umbrella of the *Aboriginals Protection Act*; exemptions should only be granted where the girl clearly understood what that entailed. Otherwise, he wrote, "she would be denied the protection which the Act affords, and, not being able to look after her own interests, her condition would be nothing else than one of slavery". Using the provisions of the *Reformatories Act* Roth admitted he rescued such "little waifs and strays", sending many to the newly proclaimed reformatory school at Yarrabah.[17]

It was not until 1901 that an *Amendment Act*[18] extended the permit system to cover all females residing on any house or premises. This was a boon to Roth whose monitoring of rampant abuses in the sea trades had produced some fancy footwork on the part of boat owners and captains. These men disputed Roth's right to rescue abducted women and children from the boats, on the grounds that vessels were not "premises" under the original Act. Another scam, claiming females and boys were "passengers" rather than "workers" was now also blocked by a stipulation that all such travellers must have a permit.

A network of regulations was thrown around Aboriginal employment in the sea trades. In fact, John Douglas had set similar conditions in the 1890s — a six-month work period, contracts witnessed by the local missionary, and return to home country — but traders at the time had successfully lobbied the Justice department to have them overthrown as illegal and "confusing". Fixed-term contracts were now set by a protector, as well as a mandatory bond for safe conduct, intended to break the common practice of evading wage payment by dumping workers and claiming desertion.

Blatant abuses continued. Many magistrates imposed farcically low penalties. And recruiters pressured the government, claiming that the restrictions deprived the industry "almost to the last degree of labour".[19] This was belied by the protection at Thursday Island who reported that although 300 workers were still available, recruiters were soliciting boys of twelve and fourteen on cheaper rates. In 1902 Roth further reduced illegal practices in the trades by setting up the Aboriginals Protection Property Account to collect wages due to workers who allegedly deserted or died under contract.

Through his network of protectors Roth had quickly established that the "hands-off" approach to Aboriginal wages was a metaphor for slavery. Most Aboriginal workers were openly exploited and Roth argued that the *Amendment Act* should set a minimum rate. An added advantage, according to Roth, would be to encourage the work ethic through the "attractions" of spending power.[20] Horrified parliamentarians heatedly opposed any fixed payment as the thin edge of the wedge: governments might be influenced to insist on minimum wages for white workers also! "What a curious thing it is", mused the member for Clermont, that the minister believes in "a minimum wage for Aboriginal niggers ... but will vote against a minimum wage for white men like himself".[21]

With some Aboriginal workers receiving less than one-eighth of the white wage, there were also claims that cheap Aboriginal labour would undercut white employment. After much debate Tozer secured a minimum wage of 10s per month for boat workers and 5s per month for others in the *Amendment Act*.

It was on the matter of opium restriction that the fledgling Aboriginal bureaucracy faced its greatest challenges. Opium trading was worth over £30,000 annually to the government, and the records show that customs, treasury and justice personnel all conspired to sabotage the *Aboriginals Protection Acts*. Roth described the ignorance of police and justices as "astonishing", with many magistrates illegally reducing both prison terms and fines.

When Cairns police closed several opium dens, making the sale and consumption of opium "difficult if not impossible", the parliamentary Executive "bowed to vested interests", according to John Douglas, and ordered suppression of the restrictive clauses of the Act. More blatantly, customs agents along the coast had provocatively "invited applications" for opium sellers: within three years Cairns boasted two wholesale and eight retail dealers.[22] While the restrictive clauses "are neither enforced nor repealed", wrote Roth in his *Annual Report of 1902*, "this Department must be held morally responsible for all the abuses consequent upon the present practically promiscuous sale of the drug".

Meston was also disgusted. Arguing that the opium trade had cost a thousand Aboriginal deaths in ten years, he castigated treasury's excessive issuing of licences: "Had there been no interference by the Treasury, that traffic would have been stamped out in six months ... everywhere in the West opium is as common as sugar".[23] Even when charges were laid, magistrates routinely imposed nominal fines under the *Justices Act* when heavy penalties were available under the *Aboriginals Protection Act*. They treated the whole legislation "as a mere waste of paper", Foxton fumed.

A *Mining Act* passed immediately after the initial Aboriginal legislation had also deliberately subverted restrictions. Invalidating tight anti-trespass directives for Aboriginal reserves, it allowed anyone a cheap permit to prospect on Crown land, a clear motive "to consort with the aboriginals", according to Foxton. The 1901 *Amendment Act* plugged this loophole, making access dependent upon the permission of the local protector.

So the radical legislation of 1897 and 1901 did not operate to facilitate wholesale removal of Aborigines from colonial society, nor were its provisions smoothly exercised to regiment racial interactions. This glimpse at the early records shows immediate distortions of the capacities and objectives of the regulations as a range of vested interests — even among government departments — jockeyed to maximise their own advantages. Where do the two men charged with implementing the new protective strategies fit into these power struggles?

Power and influence

When the home secretary had praised the Fraser Island mission he was only telling part of the truth. Behind the scenes the Mestons senior and junior had lurched from one public relations disaster to another. Within three months of the official gazettal of the settlement as an Aboriginal reserve under the 1897 *Aboriginals Protection Act*, Archibald Meston was charged with assault by several Maryborough men who had been forcibly ejected from the restricted area. Then the Mestons were jointly charged with harbouring a deserter from hired service; and after Harold was moved to Durundur a scandal arose when the (illegal) liquor supply of the replacement superintendent was pilfered by reserve residents. Each row went to court: Meston defended his management and the government carried the legal costs.

Foxton made his own inspection of Fraser Island in 1899 and discovered simmering discontent and violent control. He approached the Anglicans who agreed to take over.

When Meston protested furiously against the handover to "some religious denomination", the church leaked information detailing routine ill-treatment, malnutrition and a high death rate. With the mission in church hands, Meston deployed his options as southern protector, defiantly sending men and women from Fraser Island out on work agreements contrary to mission policy.

When the superintendent charged a group of absconding mission residents with boat stealing, Meston, in his capacity as magistrate, found the men innocent, bought them new clothes, and paid their passage back to the island. Furious with these disruptive tactics, Foxton directed Meston to stop interfering in the church's management of Fraser Island, suggesting he should pay more attention to widespread abuses prevalent elsewhere in his protectorate. Dogged by opposition and interference, the mission was closed in 1904, 117 residents were transferred to Yarrabah, and 35 others to Durundur.[24]

Meston was also ordered not to meddle in the operations of the Aboriginal Girls Home at West End. Started in 1899 and managed briefly by Meston's wife in her capacity as protectress of Aborigines, the hostel was controlled by a Mrs Frew. As a base for local domestics and women travelling through Brisbane or visiting for medical treatment, it operated to keep girls off the streets and out of disreputable hotels and boarding houses. By 1901 seventy girls were working in the city and suburbs of Brisbane, forming a small part of the domestic workforce at a time when most upper-class homes averaged four servants and most middle-class homes at least one.

The Aboriginal Girls Home facilitated close monitoring of the girls' movements even though females in employment when the 1897 *Aboriginals Protection Act* came into force were legally immune from supervision. And Roth had also conceded that the girls' financial status as wage earners meant he could not invoke the *Vagrancy Act* to bring them under official control.[25] Instead, as he candidly admitted, he resorted to "moral suasion" and "bluff" to order the girls to accept management by the protectress.

Meston frequently clashed with Mrs Frew. In 1903 he complained officially that she was too eager to move girls out of the Home and into employment. The girls also resented her methods. Several of the 121 girls working around Brisbane lodged objections with their member of parliament in 1905, alleging also that she was defrauding their accounts with fictitious deductions. An auditor-general's inquiry found their claims proven. Mrs Frew was forced to resign and the Home was closed.

The closure of the Girls Home, and the demise of the Fraser Island mission, are in part traceable to sharp funding cuts imposed in 1903. With an eye, no doubt, to minimising political as well as financial damage, the incoming Morgan government set up a sub-department of Native Affairs. To quarantine government ministers from the conflicts and scandals of Aboriginal administration, the position of Chief Protector was created. And it was Roth who was elevated to the post: Meston was retrenched. Describing his dismissal as a "damnable injustice" Meston sent a bitter protest to premier Arthur Morgan. "But for me there would be no mention of Aborigines in the Statute book of Queensland, no Protectors and no Act. I am a year senior to Roth. All practical work has been done by me. He does nothing but write reports and advertise himself to make the Minister believe he is a marvellous man." [26]

With the restructuring came a range of tighter regulations. All wages of female workers were to be paid directly to the local protector who would act as trustee on the individual accounts. This was despite such widespread unreliability among protectors that a system of thumbprints was also initiated to certify their dealings on Aboriginal monies. The Aboriginals Protection Property Account, started by Roth in Cooktown for receipt of unclaimed wages, was extended to cover all Aboriginal workers in Queensland, with proceeds disbursed to relatives or "for the benefit of Aboriginals generally". All protectors and superintendents of missions and reserves were required to lodge detailed annual reports, and yearly inspections were initiated.

Antagonism towards Roth was immediately inflamed by the tighter controls. Vested interests in the north who, as Roth later wrote, were no longer able "to do as they please about recruiting, paying off and returning or not returning natives" launched a concerted campaign of destabilisation. Through Cooktown MLA John Hamilton they lodged a petition alleging Roth's strict surveillance was jeopardising government revenue. Roth countered that two of the signatories had recently been prosecuted for illegal recruiting, trade had actually increased, and all boats were fully manned. It had been necessary for Roth to appoint a separate protector at Thursday Island to bypass a perverse shipping officer. One trader, debarred from recruitment after a series of regulation breaches, complained direct to Foxton that such "arbitrary conduct ... inflicts great and undeserved hardship on myself and my family".[27]

Photos from Roth's 1897 *Ethnological Studies* were circulated by Hamilton in parliament in 1904, and were de-

scribed as "grossly indecent" and "conniving at immorality". Under Hamilton's successor, a protest meeting at
Cooktown submitted allegations of official obstructionism
and medical negligence by Roth. Twenty-four of the signatories were directly involved in what Roth described as the
trade in the "flesh and blood of the native". All charges were
dismissed after a government inquiry.

Roth faced resistance even from within his bureaucracy.
He was furious when he discovered that information he
sent to head office from Cooktown had been passed on to
the local police sergeant "for report and comment". Increasingly, police protectors bypassed him to report directly
to the police commissioner, a procedure Roth failed to
reverse despite appeals to both the police commissioner
and his own departmental head.[28]

Roth fought discriminatory and collusive government
policy aggressively and publicly. As state schools, government reformatories and orphanages, charitable homes and
fostering families increasingly refused to accept part-
Aboriginal children, Roth berated the government over
what he termed the "false 'White Australia' policy".[29] He
challenged ministerial directions that set the subsidy for
white reformatory children at 7s per week from the Home
department budget, while the 2s 6d per week allocation for
Aboriginal children was deducted from the general grant
for Aboriginal relief. He publicly accused the government
of directly sabotaging opium restriction provisions, finally
taking his case to a federal Royal Commission on Commonwealth tariffs which prohibited all permits for opium sale
from June 1906. When state member for Clermont Joe
Lesina spearheaded a vicious campaign in parliament and
through the press, alleging Roth had sold over 2,000 "speci-

mens and curios" which rightfully belonged to the state, Roth handed in his resignation after nearly ten years' service.

Acting chief protector Richard Howard stepped into the breach. According to his telegram of acknowledgment, he had "been with Aborigines since a child in Victoria and since 1865 in Queensland". An outstanding horseman and bushman already in his mid-fifties, Howard's northern career had included droving, coach-driving, horse-breaking and station management. A census supervisor since 1881, he was promoted to registrar-general, was subsequently a member of the Land Court, and later an inspector for the State Agricultural Bank at Roma where he also held the position of protector. "What he did not know about bush and black's lore is not worth going out of one's way to enquire", observed a reporter in 1906, helpfully adding that at 6 ft 2 in "in his stockinged feet", Richard Howard was known to his acquaintances as "Long Dick".[30]

Howard believed that the complexity and endurance of Aboriginal culture was indicative of the adaptability and intelligence of Aboriginal people. Rejecting Roth's protectionism he advised against "entirely isolating these people from contact with the white population". They "become more quickly civilised", he advised parliament, if allowed relatively free interaction with "the right class of whites".[31] Northern traders welcomed the change: "He has years of bush experience and knows the natives — their vices, and virtues, if any — he will never photograph them ... he intends to provide against the raiding by the niggers of white men's property in this district, if the Government will give him the chance to do so".[32] Missionary authorities were apprehensive. Howard was seen to be far less committed to protecting Aboriginal interests.

God or mammon?

It is often asserted that church missions acted simply as agents of government policy, operating to strip Aboriginal people of their culture and turn out the cheap labourers upon whom the pastoral and sea trades depended. Do the linkages between governments and missions in the early days support this view? Is it even useful to discuss missions as a uniform category?

For Rev Hey of Mapoon the differences between the state and the missions were significant: they were "at cross purposes", being concerned with "two entirely different objects", he wrote in 1897. Catering to the hearts and minds of mission populations was the duty of the church, while provision for physical well-being devolved to the government. In order "to feed the Aboriginal as cheaply as possible" or "to get as much as possible out of his labour" the state readily relocated Aboriginal groups for greater expedience: the church, in contrast, placed itself *among* the people to work for a different kingdom.[33] Hey resented the state's emphasis on productivity, arguing that his mission "is not to soils; it is to men". At Mapoon the site was swampy and the soil poor. And scant funding forced the missionaries to spend most of their time and energy developing the foodcrops essential if regular contact with the five hundred local people was to be achieved.

Seventy miles (112 kilometres) south of Mapoon a more fertile area was discovered on the Embley River, home to a similar number of Aborigines. The Presbyterians obtained government backing in 1898 and started the Weipa mission. Areas were soon cleared for crops, and a school catered for 78 children. But the government cut promised funding, rations ran out, and the locals dispersed to hunt for food.[34]

When the Anglicans opened a mission in 1905 on the fertile Mitchell River near the base of Cape York, government input was less than one-third of requirements. With reference to the proposed mission, the Normanton protector had written to Roth expressing the hope that "all local aboriginals will come under its control". Around Normanton and the gulf regions Aboriginal families had long remonstrated with Roth over the casual kidnapping of their children. According to the Normanton protector, whites commonly "have an idea that they can trade an aboriginal as they would a horse, or bullock". Roth insisted that restrictions over trespass onto the reserve land would be tightly policed. As the protector noted, the mission "will act as a deterrent in preventing some white men, with black boys under them, from rounding up small mobs of wild natives and despoiling their women".[35]

The pattern of financial starvation was common to most missions and government settlements. When a third Presbyterian mission opened in 1905 at Aurukun on the Archer River, the government grant did not even cover the cost of the huts. In the first year the mission struggled to survive. A drought dried up the main lagoon and crops were ruined. Malaria, and the recruiting legacy of syphilis, decimated the population.

In fact, the dormitory policy — whereby most young children were confined to church care — was a direct consequence of underfunding. Lacking rations or crops to feed a fixed population, the missions concentrated on the children. This had two advantages: it allowed provisioning of the key mission constituents; and it assured the involvement of the adults. "I can only feed fifty or sixty people half a day, or twenty-five or thirty people daily", wrote Rev Richter from Aurukun. "These daily rations would suffice for about forty children if I keep no men at the station working, but ... without men I have no children. Knowing this, we have hastened to make arrangements to take children in as boarders."[36] Sickness could also be treated quickly; at Mapoon Rev Hey reported that daily sea baths had all but eradicated fever epidemics among dormitory children.

At the Presbyterian missions, as at the Lutheran mission at Cape Bedford, native languages were the basis for schooling and church services: "They learned to read and write in their own language, Christian doctrine, Bible history, as well as sewing and housekeeping for the girls and station work for the boys".[37] Vegetable gardens were laid out, bark huts soon constructed and repaired by the men, and, as Rev Hey wrote, the native camps gradually turned into a village.

On the more "settled" east coast, Yarrabah mission, also severely underfunded, laboured under additional difficulties. This facility became the unofficial reception house for government removals in the north. Proclaimed an industrial school, Yarrabah accepted most of the "neglected" children, although Mapoon took in several from the Gulf area. Family groups were also relocated, some sick and starving, many defiantly resisting deportation. Unlike the Presbyterian missions of the west coast, therefore, Yarrabah's population was overwhelmingly displaced and often incompatible.

Proximity to Cairns undercut mission authority: people

commonly walked off the mission in protest at Gribble's work regime or deserted to return to home country. Frustration intensified when local police informed Gribble they had no powers to arrest and return those transferred under departmental regulations rather than on a specific ministerial order. Unwelcome trespassers, preying on groups living away from the main mission station, presented a further vexation. Partly to occupy a greater reserve area and thus minimise the risk of land excisions, and also, as with other missions, to utilise scattered fertile pockets of land, Gribble had always encouraged outstation communities. Fitzroy Island was even under lease to Gribble from the Lands department, and here several ex-Fraser Island people, seeking detachment from the main station, persuaded Gribble to allow them to farm.[38]

Inadequate government funding took an unremitting toll on Aboriginal health. The rationale of "health and welfare" which underlay the cavalier removal of families was not substantiated by a financial commitment to secure well-being on the institutions. At Yarrabah, where inmates suffered high levels of fever and venereal disease, and the Fraser Island arrivals sickened from the change in climate and an addiction to "earth eating", Gribble's plea for regular visits from the government medical officer at Cairns was turned down in favour of the cheaper option of £3 of medicines.

Even on the state-run settlements, documents show a similar disregard for basic health needs. The early days of Barambah (later renamed Cherbourg) are a case in point. Initially operating as a grazing outstation of the Deebing Creek mission, Barambah was established as a government settlement in 1906 following the closure of the Durundur reserve. But no access to professional medical care was organised for the community of over two hundred people. It was left to superintendent Bertram Lipscombe to dispense medicines and attended to all medical crises in addition to his duties with stock, agriculture and "controlling the natives".

Howard's boast, made in his 1909 *Annual Report*, was that the Barambah settlement "cannot be considered other than a most successful undertaking". But there is a damning letter on file warning of "the danger of allowing the Superintendent to have anything whatever to do with the medical treatment of the natives". The Barambah official continued: "Altho" he <u>has not</u> the most elementary knowledge of medical treatment or diseases he <u>has</u> conceit & assurance enough to treat the whole department".[39] This condemnation in 1910 did prompt the appointment of a trained nurse to the staff, and a local doctor was commissioned to make weekly visits.

In an attempt to rein in escalating expenditure the government extracted "contributions" from the wages of employed Aborigines living on its settlements, and sold settlement produce. But missions generally discouraged external employment as a risk to health and morals. And by maximising the mission labour force they could also increase agriculture and building programs.

To force the missions into greater accountability, Howard now advocated a single annual grant to each mission to replace the yearly subsidy which swelled erratically to cover costs of teachers, school needs and medicines. The missions, he said, should match "£ for £, by agriculture, stock raising, fishing and other pursuits" the government input.[40] The Presbyterians declared themselves quite willing to commercialise the missions even to the extent of paying wages to mission workers. But they were wary of financial commitment without tenure after a protracted though ultimately successful two-year battle to prevent the government from excising 5,000 acres from the Weipa reserve for trading interests.[41] Any investment of church monies in the industrial development of the reserves, they insisted, would require the "undisturbed possession of the reserves". This proviso was dismissed by the government, which described existing tenure arrangements as affording "adequate security for the work proposed to be done".

The narrower parameters of mission funding are certainly linked to a crisis at Yarrabah at this time. The mission had run at a loss for many years, indebtedness to local stores was substantial, and in 1909, with the major supplier owed £1,000, several refused further credit. In response, the Board of Missions' head office in Sydney cut staff, closed two outstations, and set a limit of £70 a month for food. The horrified Bishop of North Queensland, George Frodsham, warned such ruthlessness would bring starvation to Yarrabah's population of over three hundred: he threatened to disperse the people and close the mission.[42]

Called to make an official report, the police magistrate was highly critical of the lack of productivity. There was a large number of "almost white" youngsters, he observed, who should be sent out to work. Frodsham angrily retorted that the many "diseased girls" transferred to Yarrabah were proof that domestic service was detrimental to their welfare. Mission families used a visit by Howard to complain bitterly about lack of food and clothing. Overall, as Howard recounted, there was "a general desire by natives to get away from the mission".

The tenor of the mission changed dramatically when Mr Ivens took over from Gribble, who had succumbed to a nervous breakdown. Howard was enraged when Ivens refused to accept any further "removals" from north Queensland, and one group of people from Ayr had to be transported at considerable expense down to the southern settlement at Barambah. One consolation, Howard informed his minister, was that in contrast to the missions the group would now be separated: "... the children would be compelled to go to school and the parents to accept healthy employment".[43]

To bring the Anglicans into line, the government threatened financial penalties. But the Board of Missions stood firm, insisting they would not be held financially accountable for indefinite numbers of distressed and diseased people. "So far as food and clothing are concerned it is the Government's business to support the natives: the Missions are responsible for their moral and spiritual welfare." They backed their stance with statistics: Queensland's 10s per head per annum for Aboriginal relief compared poorly with Victoria's £14, New South Wales' £4, and Western Australia's £1 10s.[44]

Minister John Appel now made a brief visit, accompanied by Howard and government medical officer Dr Tyrie. It was a public relations disaster. Superintendent Ivens was accused of insulting the minister, of denouncing Howard for being "openly and avowedly hostile to the Mission", and of questioning the intelligence of Dr Tyrie who had described the duckpond as a malarial breeding ground. Bishop Frodsham defended Ivens, and informed his Archbishop in Brisbane that the minister was "intent on destroying Yarrabah" by turning it into a labour depot like Barambah. Ivens was subsequently sacked on the "expressed wish" of the minister.[45]

Yet another damning ministerial report three years later provoked a furious reply from Rev Needham, briefly in charge of Yarrabah. "How Appel can criticize Yarrabah in view of conditions at Taroom passes my comprehension." At this reserve west of Maryborough, already home to over one hundred people, the government had taken the cheaper option in 1911 of appointing a superintendent rather than enforcing mass relocation. Needham accused the government of hypocrisy, noting sarcastically that the daily journey of men to do farm work was a farce, that teenaged girls were in moral danger living unsupervised in the camps, and that the men passed the day gambling and playing cards.[46]

If Taroom was a "travesty of good management" as Needham described it, then Barambah was an outright scandal. This settlement of over five hundred and fifty people was blighted by an excessive death rate. In 1913 there were only sixteen live births, and many of the fifty-nine deaths occurred among "young and apparently strong people". In a surprise visit Howard discovered a filthy hospital and dying pneumonia patients unattended. His internal report condemned the lack of interest and outright neglect of the settlement nurse, and also of visiting medical officer Dr Junk, who attended the large and debilitated community only half a day each month.

For public consumption, however, Howard offered a more politically expedient explanation. Impugning both Aboriginal conduct and mission practices, Howard was dismissive of the disgrace at Taroom and Barambah where "the death-rate greatly exceeds the birth-rate". "This is explained", he wrote in his *Annual Report*, "when we remember that our own Settlements are used as a dumping-ground for cases that the charitable Missions are not always eager to receive". Blithely ignoring his own observation of fatalities among the young and strong, Howard now alleged: "... delicate children born of parents whose constitutions when they were sent there were undermined with disease, drink, opium, prostitution, &c., form the majority of the patients who increase the mortality record".[47]

Howard had neatly blamed the victims rather than deadly conditions and official negligence. What credence, then, can be placed on his representation of missions and settlements as merely "dumping grounds" for the diseased and degraded? Did other factors operate to motivate the relocation of Aboriginal groups from rural independence to institutional subjection?

Manipulating the options

The extensive powers of the chief protector spawned autocratic, and at times idiosyncratic, decision making. The removal of people from Ayr to Barambah in 1910 shows how easily local knowledge was subverted by head office. The seventy-five people living on the town reserve at Ayr supported themselves through local farm work, and were described as "well behaved" by the local protector. But he could not prevent white trading of morphine and alcohol, and for several years called in vain for the gazettal of an Aboriginal reserve with its severe limits of trespass. The local council ordered him to evict the families and burn the humpies, an order he ignored. He appealed to Howard: "[Their] depravity has been largely brought about by white people, [and they] have more right to the land than the

Shire Council has". Howard opted instead to remove the "troublesome", but by the time the paperwork reached Ayr everyone had moved out to work except three pensioners. It was several months before a removal order was effected against fourteen adults and eleven children. Within four years of their arrival at Barambah five had died.

At other times, hardships for country workers were increased by Howard's laxness in enforcing available regulations. "The practice of allowing camp natives to take casual employment is still followed and found to work more satisfactorily than the strict letter of the Acts", he noted approvingly during a tour of the state in 1911. But the effect of this casual non-enforcement of wages seemed unremarkable to Howard: "They are mostly paid with old clothes and broken victuals, besides getting two or three good feeds while at work". For many, he conceded, this was "a more or less precarious existence" only mitigated by Aboriginal readiness to share food and money among those too old or ill to work.

Even a formal contract was no guarantee for Aboriginal wages, Howard observed. Wages functioned more often as book entries than as cash, particularly in western areas. Here many pastoralists had "a deep-rooted objection to paying the aboriginals anything for their services, unless it is coming back again through the station store". So common was this dodge that the Hughenden protector demanded direct payment of half the wages, which he then deposited in workers' savings accounts. Even so, no guidelines had been set for Aboriginal withdrawal of their own savings through local protectors. Some protectors arbitrarily rejected requests by workers to spend their own money, while others took a lax approach. As Howard noted: "This frequently led to trouble when the natives concerned met and compared notes".[48]

Howard retired in 1914 after several bouts of ill-health. As early as 1911 Rev Hey had been canvassed to replace him, and Rev Gribble was approached two years later. One volunteer for the job was Archibald Meston who declared, with typical modesty, "I have superior claims to any other person who may apply". He was passed over as being "a most difficult officer to control",[49] and the job of chief protector went to John Bleakley. Bleakley had already served in the Aboriginal department for six years, two and a half of those as deputy to Howard. He was to run Aboriginal affairs in Queensland for nearly three decades.

A committed Anglican, Bleakley was of the opinion that Aborigines were a child race which needed to be "socialised" in order to be "christianised". "To make good Christians of the natives", he wrote in 1961, "they must first be made good citizens and taught the sound doctrine of self-respect and self-reliance". In contrast to Howard's relatively "hands-off" approach to inter-racial encounters, Bleakley never altered his conviction that missions and settlements formed a vital buffer zone: "Not only do they protect the child races from the unscrupulous white, but they help to preserve the purity of the white race from the grave social dangers that always threaten where there is a degraded race living in loose conditions at its back door".[50]

The Presbyterians declared themselves very pleased with the new management: "we believe that ... we have men who understand the problem of the native race, and also can appreciate missionary work".[51] Their confidence was confirmed when Bleakley overrode agitation by anthropologists against the Presbyterian push to start a mission on

Mornington Island in the Gulf of Carpentaria. Anthropologists, Bleakley later wrote, saw Mornington Island as "the only remaining chance for studying these people in their primitive unspoiled state". Scoffing at the "absurdity of this claim", Bleakley argued that "blackbirders" were habitually "kidnapping the men and defiling the women".[52] His contempt for the intellectual learning of anthropologists, in contrast to the practical experience of administrators, would serve to reinforce his authoritarian approach to Aboriginal affairs.

Shortly after his arrival on Mornington Island, superintendent Robert Hall reported that 160 Aborigines had gathered around the new mission and "they all seem friendly. I hope your government will treat us as generously as the other mission stations". But with wartime shortages the promised £500 was cut back to £300. Undeterred, Bleakley drew money for fencing wire from the Aboriginal Protection Property account, the trust fund set up to dispense unclaimed earnings to relatives. He was to demonstrate an increasing propensity for raiding Aboriginal trust monies to offset shortfalls in state funding.

The relative closure of departmental operations from outside scrutiny suited Bleakley's interventionist approach. His actions at Kuranda exemplify his wilfulness. When the Seventh Day Adventists took up over 400 acres (160 hectares) near Kuranda in 1913 Bleakley nurtured the Monamona mission as a compliant alternative to Yarrabah. He relocated family groups from Bowen, Mareeba and Mt Carbine to ensure mission numbers. But Kuranda businessmen lobbied against any removal of local Aborigines, declaring them to be a "wonderful little tribe of niggers ... a strictly moral tribe pure blood and on a fair increase". The proprietor of the Barron Falls hotel informed lands minister Edward Theodore: "They are very interesting to tourists ... of great service to the inhabitants & give no trouble to the Police". More revealing was his deprecating remark that the Aborigines would probably be of "great commercial value" to the mission which he described as working "in open competition to the whites in the district".

It was easy enough for Bleakley to claim "destitution and starvation" and present a ministerial removal order to the local protector. So confident was Bleakley that he assured mission staff they would soon receive "about fifty from a district near you which for diplomatic reasons we will not name at present". But the Kuranda protector baulked at the removal, sending the men out on work contracts. And whereas mission crops had been wiped out by a crippling drought, the protector wrote emphatically of the Kuranda locals: "... the drought is not affecting them in any way ... they can obtain plenty of native food and ... they can also get plenty of fish". It took a further twelve months, but by the end of 1916 Bleakley marshalled sixty-four local Aborigines at Monamona. Belying the "destitution" and "starvation" listed on the removal order, documents reveal only fifteen described as frail, ten were in work, and forty-nine were said to be "strong".[53]

The "impossible task" of policing employment and abuses on the east coast, and the need for a government-run institution in the north, prompted a settlement to be started in 1914 at Hull River near Tully. With four hundred occupants in its first year, Bleakley envisaged "practically the whole of the native population of that and neighbouring districts" would be contained here. Most men worked under contract on local properties, but a "sufficient number" were kept on the reserve for developmental work.[54] Produce from plantations of tropical fruits and root crops was supplemented by catches from fishing boats. But the settlement was plagued by multiple desertions as people found easy refuge in surrounding ranges. In March 1918 the whole venture was demolished in a vicious cyclone which killed fifteen Aborigines and also the superintendent and his daughter. Within three months the government opted to establish a replacement institution on Palm Island, where physical isolation would prevent desertions.

A major factor of Bleakley's long administration was his manipulation of financial options to consolidate control. In his dogged pursuit of increases in Aboriginal wages, and in his readiness to exploit trust monies to departmental (rather than Aboriginal) advantage, his authority brooked no question. From 1914 Bleakley increased the scale of minimum wages, now directly payable through local protectors for all workers. In one year, Aboriginal savings controlled by the department jumped £12,475 to £56,855. Workers' access to their own savings was restricted to items which were "in keeping with the objects for which the system was established". Although Bleakley maintained that the "nest-eggs" were to sustain workers through droughts or off-seasons, this pool of private wealth was exploited by the government. Bulk trust monies were invested to produce interest, which was used to reduce state allocations for items such as rations and blankets.

Bleakley rejected the allegation that workers were thus stripped of about £29 a year. "The policy of the Department", he argued in the *Annual Report*, "is not to pauperise or spoonfeed the aboriginals, but to educate them and raise them to higher planes on the social scale". To increase "social responsibility", Bleakley called for a tax of 10 per cent on the bank portion of individual savings in 1915. On Bleakley's figuring, the "benefits" of such a scheme would net £1000 per annum *more than* the current outlay of £1,500. Keen to centralise control, Bleakley drafted new legislation for a state takeover of full physical and financial control of the ten missions. This would have cost the government an estimated £15,000 to £18,000. With current mission funding at only £3,700 per annum, the government declined to finance Bleakley's empire building.

During the First World War Bleakley demanded trustee powers over the wages of nearly two hundred men who volunteered for active service after the lifting of initial restrictions by military authorities.[55] Ultimately the Army pay of eighteen soldiers went directly to the department and spending was tightly vetted. This "friendly restraint", said Bleakley, was necessary to prevent "these lads ... from wasting their savings in drink, prompted by the loafers and parasites anxious to relieve them of their money".

Aboriginal labour was at a premium during the war years, but the McCawley Station Hands Award, brought down in 1918 by Queensland's Arbitration Court, was silent on these vital employees. Although the Australian Workers' Union had lobbied for equal wages for Aborigines, they were specifically excluded from the register of pay and conditions. Bleakley was adamant that full Aboriginal employment depended on their wage advantage in comparison with whites: he argued that they could not compete equally, being inferior workers and lacking responsibility. A deal was struck for the department to bring in a separate scale of pay. The rate was set at two-thirds that for whites doing the same tasks. For the first time, conditions for Aboriginal workers in the pastoral industry were set down, covering clothing, food, work hours and accommodation.

Station owners howled in vain that the new requirements made Aboriginal labour unviable, and surveys showed demand had not been affected. Bleakley later boasted that these 1919 *Aboriginal Employment Regulations* controlled rural employment "practically without a hitch" for the next twenty-six years.[56] "Most of the idle labour was, in time, absorbed by others quite satisfied to pay the price", he reported at the time. He also noted approvingly that "a number of old people and very young children, who were being exploited as cheap labour", were subsequently transferred to missions and settlements "where they would receive proper care".[57] The cost in fractured families was not tallied.

In 1919 Bleakley also implemented a levy on wages of all those not living on missions and settlements, set at 5 per cent for single workers and $2^1/_2$ per cent for married men. This windfall, channelled through the new Aboriginal Provident Fund, was designated for workers and their dependents when ill or out of work. Documents show Bleakley also tried to seize control over *all* wages and savings. Settlement officers "have not been competent to directly manage their institutions",[58] he told a royal commission into the public service. The logical solution, he assured his minister, was the centralisation of all accounts at head office. Once again this inflation of authority was refused.

Bleakley's masterminding of Aboriginal employment provided much more than financial advantage: it also enabled the manipulation of social conventions. The accelerated uptake of young girls and women "rescued" from camp environments in turn exacerbated perceptions of "inappropriate" sexuality on the settlements — whether through voluntary liaisons or the practice of promising little girls to older men according to tribal custom. Whenever possible, decreed Bleakley in 1916, all girls between school and "marriageable age" should be hired out as maids on outback properties.

But such dispatch of young girls came at a cost. Bleakley himself conceded two "grave dangers" — the moral danger of falling "prey to unscrupulous men", and also the probability that familiarity with a white lifestyle would "unfit them for their only legitimate future — marriage with men of their own race".[59] Documents reveal additional penalties for Aboriginal social relations. As Bleakley's evacuations removed eligible women, protectors and pastoral employers frequently applied to the department for partners for rural workers. And within a few years the settlements and missions also complained of "an insufficiency of wives for the men needing them".[60]

The yearly increase of illegitimate births to domestic workers bore testimony to the failure of the department to discharge its guardianship role. It was common practice after confinement for girls to be hired out again with their children at a reduced rate; others married settlement men and returned to the workforce with their husbands. Protectors were frequently loathe to risk removal of a good domestic on the basis of pregnancy to station workers, and some white owners sought to adopt such babies as a means of maintaining staff and gaining a potential servant.

In fact there were no provisions under the *Aboriginals Protection Acts* to allow for adoption by white parents, but it was not uncommon for protectors to dodge this restraint by signing up children at token wages. Bleakley denounced this "absurd" device, declaring that "the motives of such people are probably often open to suspicion".[61] It was not until 1919 that regulations forbade employment of children under the age of twelve without permission of the chief protector.

The government's economic determinism, which predicated social policy upon the exploitation of Aboriginal wages and savings, was savagely attacked by a council of prominent church, business and union leaders, formed in 1919 to consider an "Aboriginal Betterment Scheme". The push for such a scheme emanated from the Social Workers' League at the newly formed University of Queensland. As fellow members of the council, Bleakley and his minister were nonetheless implicated in accusations that the state entrenched Aboriginal destitution by its policy of manipulating Aboriginal savings for the reduction of government outlays on Aboriginal welfare. "In spite of the faithful and conscientious efforts of the Aboriginal Department", Archbishop Donaldson reported in his presidential address to the Anglican community, "the system is a disastrous failure ... the Government's expenditure of £30,000 per annum ... is in a sense thrown into the sea".

Tapping in to this indictment of financial waste and unproductive policy, Bleakley argued for a new direction. The archbishop was right, he said. Even with a network of seventy-five protectors inter-racial relations could not be controlled. Furthermore, the one-quarter of the Aboriginal population in supervised work were "social outcasts", and the remaining 13,000 "remain destitute and degraded and no social improvement is possible". What was needed was new legislation to concentrate Aboriginal labour within missions and settlements. "In spite of being for years starved and crippled for want of adequate funds", wrote Bleakley,

the missions had achieved "spectacular" results. By minimising outside work, family life was preserved intact, pro-
ducing benefits far in advance of the government
settlements.[62] Self-sufficient communities should be developed to trade among themselves; a "native currency" for
workers would eliminate the "degrading effect of ration
issuing or 'working for tucker' ".

But these changes were dependent upon parliament
granting "sufficient funds", costed by Bleakley at only £50
per head over a seven-year period. When premier T. J. Ryan
moved into federal politics, the scheme lapsed without
trace.

*   *   *

Legislation introduced at the turn of the century defined
and targeted particular categories of the Aboriginal population for administrative attention. But regulations encompassing a range of domains — labour exploitation, sexual
assaults on women and children, the vulnerability of working women, the security of families in rural and remote
areas, the operations of Aboriginal communities — were
subverted by vested interests, unsuitable personnel, and the
private agendas of diverse authorities.

The economic impetus of government, the financial
factor which minimised expenditure on Aboriginal needs
while at the same time maximising exploitation of Aboriginal earnings, served only to entrench social destitution and
increase social distress. The very comprehensiveness of
departmental powers and fields of authority all but effaced
effective challenge of departmental practices. Public campaigns were too easily neutralised and discarded. Even with

the backing of the chief protector, it seemed no agency could force change upon an inflexible government.

4

The health dimension

Little can be learned from history books about the operations of Queensland's Aboriginal department for the first half of this century. The few historians who venture into this area, having defined the 1897 *Aboriginals Protection Act* as an instrument of racial segregation, await in vain for the overturning of the reserve policy as an indication of administrative reform.

From a perusal of parliamentary debates between 1915 and 1939 Raymond Evans detects "a predominant mood of political indifference and neglect", indicative, he says, of the "very low priority" of Aboriginal affairs in Queensland.[1] New Acts in 1939 and 1965, according to race relations analyst Frank Stevens, merely reproduce the prevailing mentality of racial exclusion. "The fundamental basis of Queensland administration remains unchanged from the 1965 legislation, which in turn was based on the 1939 Act, conditioned as it was by the ordinances of 1895."[2]

Did the assumptions and procedures of Aboriginal affairs really remain constant over that period? Do the documents still support the premise of a fifty-year period of inactivity and indifference if reformatory strategies rather than racial exclusion motivated administrative attention?

Critical conditions

As the sub-department of Aboriginal affairs lurched to the end of its second decade, internal reports continued to expose the pathology of the institutions under its control. Even in 1918 there were few houses for the almost six hundred people living at Barambah: most families made do with bark gunyahs which freely leaked rain and frequently iced over internally in winter. Almost as soon as they arrived at this southern settlement, families transported from Ayr and Springsure succumbed to the appalling conditions. Only one blanket per person was allocated. In that year alone, twenty-six people perished from influenza.

Called to report on the punitive death rate, visiting medical officer Dr Junk described conditions as "most conducive to sickness". Uncovered latrines invited typhoid. The "hospital" was grossly overcrowded, with a tiny badly smoking kitchen: it was so tainted with death that people feared to go near it. No beds were provided for ailing venereal disease patients at the "lock hospital", and infectious patients were confined in an open-sided shed. Even children in the dormitory had to sleep on the ground, their single blanket, meagre clothing, and scant and inferior diet contributing directly to endemic skin diseases.[3] Yet there is no hint of these fearful conditions in Bleakley's official account. Health at Barambah, he declared, "generally has been fairly good".

The departmental policy of sending all possible inmates out to work brought financial benefits from income generation and from reduced dependency. But it also provided a ready conduit for relayed infections into the settlement communities. When the influenza pandemic of 1919 hit Queensland, 15 per cent of affected Aborigines, or 298 people in all, died of the disease. Bleakley later claimed credit for this "low death toll", citing his decision to close the settlements and stockpile blankets and medicines.

Contemporary records give a dramatically different version. It was the visiting doctor at Taroom who initiated quarantine restrictions in the face of what he described as "an explosive outbreak". So furious was Bleakley with the doctor's "arbitrary action", which he alleged panicked the inmates and severed supplies, that he demanded the doctor be reprimanded by the hospital board. In disgust, the doctor resigned his appointment. Within twenty-four hours almost the total population of two hundred persons at Taroom fell ill and thirty-one died, including the superintendent Charles Maxwell.[4]

At Barambah the rate of attrition was so relentless there was no time to build coffins or dig graves. People were sewn in blankets and buried five or six to a trench. Mrs Ettie Meredith later recalled nurses went days without sleep and the matron spent the nights crawling into the humpies by lamplight to check the sick.[5] Eighty-seven died. With cavalier disregard for the internal damning report of the previous year, Bleakley claimed publicly that inmates had "succumbed, principally in sheer superstitious fright".[6] But the full death rate for 1919 reached 120 people. A further twenty-nine people were treated for the vitamin deficiency disease of beri-beri. There were only twenty-six births.

According to Archbishop Donaldson of the Anglican church, the department's outlay of £75,000 during the epidemic was largely "useless" in its effects. Although local protectors were directed to locate influenza victims in rural areas, sufferers were not brought to towns and hospitals for medical attention. Rather, isolation was enforced, with sympathetic protectors providing food and medicines during the crisis.

The Archbishop complained bitterly that the missions received no funding to fight the epidemic. Two hundred people were afflicted at Yarrabah, the worst affected of the missions; but only one person died. "Unlike the rest of the State", wrote the Archbishop, "we prepared for the visitation ... there was no panic: aborigines who fell ill reported at once and received immediate treatment".[7]

Departmental records of the 1920s show a continuation of defective management, financial privation and pathological conditions. The northern government settlement at Palm Island, started in 1918 to replace the ruined Hull River venture, was placed under the control of ex-army captain Robert Curry, a man with no administrative experience. Animosity between Curry and storekeeper Ernest Tedman, said to have German sympathies, was so acute as to impede operations, and a police magistrate was sent from Ingham to investigate.

Reporting on Curry's administration, the magistrate stated that most men regularly took mainland work to support their families and supplement meagre rations. "Unfinancial natives", in contrast, were desperately deprived: many of the women and children "have only what they stand up in". Forced to stand naked when clothes were washed, they redressed before clothes dried "thus leading to colds, pneumonia, and other chest complaints".[8]

Overwhelmingly, it was the unemployed, the destitute or those in "moral danger" who were removed to missions and settlements. Superintendent Lyon of Yarrabah described many arrivals as "dull, miserable looking, prematurely old", often needing months of careful nursing. Unable to make themselves understood either to staff or to other Aborigines, many promptly absconded to find casual or regular work around Cairns.

People "cleared" from the Atherton and Yungaburra districts after the 1919 pay rates came into force demonstrate this ease of departure. The protector had urged the removal to Yarrabah of the "hundreds" who would be thrown out of work and "will soon become a nuisance". His successor had no such problems with the workforce although one group was sent to Yarrabah; of these, fourteen Atherton people immediately walked off. Ultimately they were recaptured and sent to Palm Island.[9] Lyon privately admitted his official population figure of four hundred in 1921 was overstated by nearly one-quarter: a considerable number of inmates, he conceded, had been "at large" for more than three years.[10]

With the annual grant fought out over mission dependents, Lyons' inflated count is an understandable ploy: the government grant met only one-third of running costs. Despite a cyclone in 1920 which destroyed most of the native huts, the bishop of North Queensland described Yarrabah homes in 1921 as of high quality and spotlessly clean. Vital statistics attest to health standards, showing fifteen births and only ten deaths, of people "all quite old". Yarrabah residents regarded Mrs Lyon as a very good nurse, and serious medical cases were immediately despatched by boat to Cairns.

The mortality figures for church missions and government settlements are indices of the differing living and medical conditions. For the 1922 year ninety-three people died on the three government settlements whose populations totalled 1,634, whereas the death toll for the ten missions, with far greater numbers, was only fourteen. Bleakley was well aware that most illnesses derived from substandard shelter and defective basic amenities. "Where it has been possible to improve dwelling conditions a notable improvement in health has resulted". Replacement of "the old camp gunyah" with small "wooden, mudbrick, or thatch cottages", wrote Bleakley, lifts the whole social tone and makes one "wish that funds would allow the progress to be more rapid".[11]

Called to account

Bleakley's ambitions were severely checked by the meagreness of government allocations. The trust funds under his control, on the other hand, had swollen with the re-setting of Aboriginal wage rates. A public service inquiry into the operations of the Aboriginal sub-department in 1922 detailed gross misappropriation of Aboriginal trust funds to cover departmental expenses.[12] Country workers were levied 5 per cent for single and 10 per cent for married workers to cover lean periods, netting the Aboriginal Provident Fund over £3,000 in 1922 alone. Of this considerable sum only £253 had been allocated for rations, despite the widespread distress of families in the drought-decimated cattle industry. From the Aboriginal Protection Property Account, which held unclaimed wages for workers' dependents, nearly £1,700 had been diverted for capital improvements at Barambah and £950 to cover mission shortfalls. (Two years later £500 per year was routinely diverted to keep Yarrabah operating, and a further £1,426 financed the new dormitory at Barambah.)[13]

The operations of police protectors on the savings accounts of rural workers were found to be so unreliable that the public service commissioner insisted Aborigines be given the right to appeal dealings on their accounts. This was ignored. It now transpired that there was no departmental surveillance of the network of protectors who supervised nearly 8,000 rural Aborigines. Bleakley himself was criticised for official negligence in failing to carry out mandatory annual inspections of the missions: most had not been visited for six years. Bleakley had, in fact, spent only four weeks outside Brisbane in the previous four years. No official had yet inspected Palm Island.

Ever attuned to new avenues of income, Bleakley targeted the commonwealth maternity bonus, payable to all "half-caste" mothers. Bleakley advised impoverished mission authorities how to tap into the windfall. The money order, he informed superintendent Lyon at Yarrabah, will arrive at your office. "As Superintendent you have authority to open the inmates' letters and the woman could be sent for to sign the money order, so that the money when cashed could be placed to her credit in your books, to which the expense for her confinement could be charged". This policy, he confirmed, was followed at all government settlements and also "in the Maternity Homes where white girls go as well as black".[14] The practice of plundering private pensions for general expenses was to become common.

The multiple levies, taxes and penalties which drained the already low earnings of Aboriginal workers further entrenched poverty on missions and settlements endemically destitute through underfunding. When Queensland's governor Donald Thatcher visited Palm Island in 1923 he was besieged by hungry residents who protested they could barely survive on 1lb of flour a day, and 1lb of meat and one issue of sweet potatoes a week. Thatcher agreed. He informed the minister of the particular hardship for ex-pastoral workers who were heavily dependent on meat: the meat ration was subsequently doubled, temporarily. Thatcher also questioned the wisdom of sending more than a hundred of the best workers to the mainland to work while building and agriculture on Palm Island stagnated. Surely, he suggested, it would make more sense for men to earn wages working to develop the settlement?[15]

Bleakley was hurriedly despatched to assess the situation. Extolling the settlement's "industrial development", he moved to retrieve his reputation. We have here, he enthused, a "tastefully laid out ... well-disciplined community of 800 natives" thriving on plantations of coconuts, pineapples and bananas, and a citrus orchard. School for 112 children comprised an open shed under the tutelage of "a couple of intelligent halfcastes", he noted approvingly. He glossed over the seventy-six dormitory girls lodged in two sheds, and the thirty-seven boys in another. Offhand, he mentioned that the sewing mistress acted as nurse, the hospital was a small thatched building, and the Ingham doctor's monthly visits had been terminated. Assessments of health and housing were not included in his report.

Although necessarily brief, this overview of the Aboriginal institutions in the early 1920s reveals the precarious state of living, food, and even basic medical needs. Adverse reports from health professionals seemed to have little impact on departmental priorities. What was the relationship between the two sets of administrators? Did the medical profession abdicate its responsibility for social health to the untrained appointees of the Aboriginal department?

The clinical approach

Interesting correspondences can be drawn regarding the relationship between medical and Aboriginal authorities and the earlier emergence of health professionals as accredited supervisors of local government practices. During the nineteenth century, and despite recurring epidemics of typhoid and dysentery, matters of public health were handled by local authorities, specialists in drainage and engineering who fiercely repulsed any encroachment by the new experts in medical science. It was only after a public outcry over the exclusion of medical expertise, and an outbreak of the plague in Brisbane in 1900, that a state department of Health was finally established, headed by a medical practitioner with experience in "sanitary science".

In general, epidemic diseases were seen as air-borne products of squalor and filth. The father of bacteriological research in Queensland, Dr Joseph Bancroft, first identified mosquitoes as carriers of parasites in 1877. His work on the causes of leprosy led him to convince the government to remove victims to Stradbroke Island to prevent cross-infection, although it was not until 1892 that the government legislated to legalise such medical segregation. Only in 1900 did bacteriologists receive official sanction for their research under the newly formed department of Health. Their studies into the transmission of typhoid, dysentery, smallpox and the plague confirmed the new focus on the *body* as the site of disease, and prevention became the key policy. The field of public health now included experts on the characteristics of disease. Notification of infectious diseases was made compulsory, and officials were despatched into the community to police drains, dwellings and offensive trades.

In terms of Aboriginal health, the significant event in Queensland was the establishment in 1910 of the Australian Institute of Tropical Medicine (AITM) in Townsville. One of the early targets of AITM research was hookworm, widespread in tropical areas, and found commonly among Aboriginal people coming before medical personnel. It was Dr Thomas Bancroft, son of Dr Joseph Bancroft, who suggested infection occurred through the tran,fer of hookworm larvae through the soles of bare feet walking on contaminated faeces of other sufferers. Lodged in the gut, hookworm brought on severe debilitation and critical anaemia.

Federal campaigns to identify and eradicate hookworm ran from 1916 but were actively resisted by several states, including Queensland, which resented the implications of Commonwealth intrusion in state matters. Only in 1918 did Queensland participate in the hookworm campaigns manned by personnel from the federally funded AITM. It was through these campaigns that federal health professionals were accepted into, and reported on, the communities controlled by the department of Native Affairs.

Hookworm personnel were merely one body of clinical assessors in what has been termed a "new-hygienist" movement of inspection and education in the general community. Sanitary inspectors were part of this push, as were school nurses, public health officers and maternal and infant welfare instructors. Pathological environments were now seen as reservoirs of potential health problems relayed into the social sphere through uninformed or unresponsive individuals. Head of the Commonwealth department of Health, Dr John Cumpston, described the health professional's task as "the moral equivalent to war". Health assessment had moved from environmental to individual. But had the department of Native Affairs in Queensland moved with the times?

When an epidemic of fever broke out along the Cairns coast in 1916, the finger of blame immediately pointed to Yarrabah mission. Their sanitary habits are appalling, said the rumour mill. But a public health inspector, after careful consideration, disagreed. There were thirty sanitary pans, he noted, all emptied daily, and the people appeared well and happy, with little sickness. In his opinion, the system was "far ahead of some of the Northern Towns". But a hookworm survey the following year identified an infection rate of 80 per cent in the north Queensland Aboriginal population, compared with only 22 per cent for Europeans.

Did the health inspector perhaps miss something at Yarrabah? Indeed he did. He was attentive to the physical but oblivious to the pathological. There were thirty pans, but the community numbered 300 persons. Pans were emptied daily, but they were tipped into an open cart and returned unwashed; effluent was emptied into an open trench but it was only a few hundred metres from the village and covered over only once a week.[16] Public health practices obviously bore no relation to clinical hygiene. Archbishop Sharp declared himself puzzled: "Considering the general healthy appearance of the people, the report of the visiting representative of the hookworm campaign was disconcerting. Over 90 per cent of the people were found to be infected and were treated by Dr Charlton".[17] Declaring himself in favour of "proper sanitary systems", Bleakley forwarded a further 60 pans, courtesy of the Aboriginal Protection Property Account. But by the early 1920s, when superintendent Lyon pleaded to replace leaking kerosene tins, his request was annotated "No further action".

This is reprehensible given critical hookworm results, bad enough to prompt the state government to participate in a five-year national survey from 1919. It was learned that although Europeans generally recovered quickly from infection, Aboriginal sufferers showed severe anaemia after prolonged infestation, resulting in measurable physical and mental retardation.[18] In fact, Bleakley had access to Lyon's own comments at Yarrabah: "comparing the general intelligence of the people since [the hookworm treatments] with that of previous years, one is forced to admit that the result in mental improvement has been very considerable".[19]

Despite his knowledge of the critical links between effective sanitation, hookworm and chronic debilitation, it is clear that Bleakley continued to address community priorities in economic, rather than in clinical, terms. This is again apparent in the case of the near-Brisbane reserve at Myora on Stradbroke Island. Here the director of the hookworm campaign notified Bleakley in 1921 that almost all the community were infected and waste-disposal methods were "most primitive". Rather than provide the necessary amenities, Bleakley sent advice about flyproof pans, bark closets and beach burial of waste at low tide. Stung by a rebuke from the commissioner of Public Health after a second survey revealed continuing mass infestation, Bleakley blamed the residents, "mostly old people who have not the means for providing better structures". Belatedly he sought £25 from the Aboriginal Protection Property Account, but was directed by the undersecretary to scavenge material from the deserted St Helena penal station. Four years later nothing had been done.[20]

By the early 1920s state-wide campaigns by hookworm specialists were cataloguing the extreme pathological conditions on Aboriginal communities under departmental control. Just as medical authorities at the turn of the century fought to move from exclusion to centrality on matters of public health, these clinical experts had created a toehold within the discourse of Aboriginal health as accredited appraisers. But they were toothless. Files show that critical information was registered with head office, and that Bleakley continued to quantify, rather than qualify, Aboriginal health needs. Improvements on church missions were dependent on allocation of government funding. Effectively, any responses to the new clinical register of health needs were thereby mediated through the department.

Health on a shoestring

Defective sanitation was only one of several factors jeopardising health on Aboriginal communities. Head office was well aware that food, water and shelter were also dangerously substandard. Testing on the Presbyterian missions had exposed critically high rates of hookworm, with Mapoon registering 75 per cent infestation. The committee on Heathen Missions (so-called until 1931) had also reported a noticeable improvement on all missions following treatment and advice from hookworm personnel. The mission committee, however, was in no position to implement vital changes. Droughts in the early 1920s brought the missions close to defeat. At Aurukun the water supply failed and people were "sent bush" to survive: only school children remained, depending precariously on an emergency well. The bêche-de-mer trade had partially collapsed and sandalwood was almost logged out. Rations were reduced "to the lowest minimum". Finally the cash crop of coconuts was sacrificed for survival.[21] Epidemics of whooping cough and influenza swept the missions.

Mapoon was also devastated by a lack of bêche-de-mer work coupled by the failure of the copra market. So desperate was the committee it even contemplated a campaign to contract their men into the sea trades. As conditions deteriorated, controls tightened. Superintendent Love refused any rations for seasonal workers or for any able-bodied men who would not work the required twenty-four hours per week on the mission. Several men complained directly to Bleakley that their children were starving since seasonal earnings were insufficient to cover the lay-off. Called to account, Love justified his policy on the grounds that the manipulation of rations was a useful means of "finally enforcing authority", and that hungry children could blame their lazy fathers.[22] In letters to the mission committee, however, Love admitted that off-mission earnings were far too low to support families. There were simply not enough rations: only potatoes and coconuts with occasional pumpkin, melons and bananas. "I cannot do enough", he admitted, "and I have no means of buying tea, sugar, jam and medicines that are necessary for growing children".[23]

Against this background of deprivation the mission committee was incensed to read publicity on the new Barambah dormitory "which must have cost £1,000", when their own desperate pleas for funds were rejected. Again they sought a grant of £350 to cover deficits on the four missions. Second and third generations of mission inmates, they argued, are housed in derelict dormitories of leaking iron sheets. There was no way mission crops could support the large influx of aged and infirm to Weipa and Aurukun, and families were routinely sent into the bush for food. The department made an emergency allocation of £500 but refused to consider increasing the annual grant.

Industrial self-sufficiency was always a hollow pipe-dream for the remote missions. "We have nothing at all at Weipa by which we can earn money", wrote superintendent Mayer despairingly in 1926, "no marketable sandalwood, no bêche-de-mer". Native foods were non-existent, "no fish, no birds, no ducks, no nothing. The people walk twenty-five miles down to the beach for food, and the mission exists on the government grant". Cattle, goats and horses were dying in the drought. The mission and dormitories survived on a small quantity of water from the well, and "the lagoon water which the natives use is both filthy and dangerous". Not surprisingly, malaria and blackwater fever were rife. Crops failed entirely in the droughts of 1927 and 1928, when a cyclone wrecked nearly every building. In 1930 it was decided to relocate the mission nearer the beach.

Much of Yarrabah was also destroyed by the cyclone including the hospital and all beds in it. Schooling stopped as all hands were put to rebuilding, but replacement wards of old iron and palm fronds leaked badly in wet weather. A devastating influenza epidemic swept through the mission "probably due to exposure during the cyclone and the general damp conditions following", wrote superintendent McCullough. Destitute locals were refused access because the mission lacked the money for provisions.[24]

Crisis conditions on the government's own settlements could not be attributed to natural disasters or church "inefficiency". Rather they were perpetuated by gross negligence in areas such as planning, provisioning and personnel. Woorabinda's early days are a case in point. Started south of Rockhampton in 1927 to replace the Taroom settlement, and despite four years' forewarning, it appears that Aboriginal welfare was barely considered. When more than two hundred people arrived at the site there was no doctor available, no sanitation facilities, and no timber for houses. It was superintendent Colledge's opinion that people were "very comfortably housed for the winter" courtesy of some sheet iron and plenty of "free bark". But within a month the waterholes had dried up, there had been a fatal epidemic of influenza, and he reported sanitation remained "in a deplorable state".[25]

Twelve months later the dormitory children were still sleeping on damp ground in a bark and iron shed without mattresses or stretchers. There was no money for beds or buildings, said Bleakley: perhaps the girls could make beds from saplings and flourbags, and perhaps a section of the kitchen verandah could be screened off as a dining room. Colledge was sweating on the impending visit of the bishop of Rockhampton, remembering the bishop of North Queensland's caustic criticisms at Taroom. He urged Bleakley to keep the bishop away from the eating area. Conditions were worse than the sleeping quarters, he confessed, and children ate with their hands because there was no cutlery.[26] Bleakley responded soothingly, "there is no need to be ashamed of Woorabinda so why worry about the opinions of visitors … it will take some time to get the needed improvements".

Indeed the Anglican hierarchy was highly critical of government practices. They were frustrated with the futile timewasting in "continually badgering the Government" for their annual grant, with officers paying "as many as twenty visits to the Government" before funds were released.[27] In the meantime, as McCullough pointed out from Yarrabah, underfunding invalidated the very basis of the mission as a protective environment. Shortage of food in the dry season meant girls as young as thirteen were walking over the hill to Cairns to get cash "in a very questionable manner". There had been a dramatic rise of 34 per cent in the mission population between 1925 and 1930, nearly all "derelicts and helpless children", but since all able-bodied men relied on off-mission work for their subsistence no development was possible, making "the problem of coping with the increase very serious".

At this time Rev Kernke was sent to Yarrabah to assist at the mission. He was horrified at the conditions endured by the inmates, and wrote a bitter critique to his archbishop. It is worth quoting at length:

> Twice a year, they are purged with hookworm treatment, while all the year the disease is spread along the roads by a sanitary system, which would disgrace a wild blacks' camp … The night soil is dumped in trenches within a stones throw of the houses at the end of the Village and left there to be scratched about by the fowls … it is a crying shame that there is not a certificated Nurse in charge [of the hospital] … nine out of every ten confinement cases, have to be rushed off to town after the baby is born … As perhaps you know, the natives have had a frightful skin disease for months, it starts with a small itchy water blister and turns into large running sores like boils. These Mrs McCullough says are caused through filth, considering the provision made for cleansing of these people, I am amazed at their cleanliness. How many white men would walk from half a mile to a mile before breakfast, to have a bath in a creek, and not only that, they are expected to be in Church by

6.45 am, carry their wives' daily supply of water and chop the wood, and be at work by 8.30 ...[28]

Within two months Kernke had been withdrawn from Yarrabah. And three years later the bishop of North Queensland was still urging appointment of a qualified nurse to replace Mrs McCullough: "The care of the sick at Yarrabah is most inadequate and there have been cases of cruel neglect. Since Mrs McCullough is not a Nurse and has had no training of any kind, this might have been expected".

The tragedy is that on all the missions and settlements Aborigines suffered similar deprivation of basic amenities. Medical personnel continued to denounce pathological conditions: their progressive surveys created a clinical classification of missions and settlements as incubi of disease and as communities of individuals untutored in social hygiene responsibilities. Despite this, departmental assessment and management of endemic ill-health in the late 1920s remained steeped in the rhetoric of nineteenth-century environmentalism. Even in those terms — sanitation, drainage, adequate food, safe water — Aboriginal institutions were defective. Was there no way to enforce vital changes in departmental policies and practices?

Raphael Cilento

Internal correspondence from the mid-1920s to the mid-1940s shows a protracted and increasingly acrimonious battle of wills between Bleakley and Dr (later Sir) Raphael Cilento. Indeed, prior to Bleakley's resignation "on health grounds" in 1942 he bitterly denounced Cilento's appointment to the tribunal which was to assess him as incapacitated, declaring he would not get a fair hearing. Analysis of Aboriginal departmental health practices in this period is inextricably tied to Cilento's movement into Queensland's health portfolio.

In 1926 Raphael Cilento published a treatise called *White Man in the Tropics* detailing how healthful working conditions could be secured to enable the development of the "empty" north. As head of the AITM since 1921 Cilento had redirected clinical research in pursuit of a distinct sociological and preventive objective. The federal hookworm surveys were part of a concerted campaign to "Clean up the North" through an emphasis on education and environmental cleansing. Also targeted were industrial hygiene, sanitary engineering, venereal disease, tuberculosis and tropical medicine.

Venereal disease or the "red plague" was prevalent in the white community. During the first two decades of the century a wide-ranging discourse centering on concepts of "social purity" and "moral and social hygiene" resulted in the introduction of laws in all states by 1920 (except South Australia) for compulsory notification and treatment, funded by the Commonwealth government. But identification and management of VD among Queensland's Aboriginal population was arbitrary and erratic. Although the government medical officer at Thursday Island estimated up to one thousand sufferers in the Cape York and Gulf areas in 1920, the local protector only eighteen months later considered that the disease was not endemic and advised no action was needed.[29]

Until the mid-1920s VD patients on missions and settlements were treated spasmodically by visiting doctors, and chronic cases were occasionally sent to local hospitals or to

Palm Island. Evidence from 1925 shows that twelve patients were confined in the old Cooktown Gaol, and seventeen others were lodged in a shed in the grounds of the Normanton Hospital. When hookworm personnel advised the Commonwealth health department that VD was again increasing, the Aboriginal department declared itself unable to fund inspections, and requested that AITM personnel researching malaria on the northern missions should also identify and treat VD sufferers. On Bleakley's own admission, "at most of the mission stations no medical advice was available". It was not until 1926 that the state decided to open a "lock hospital" like the segregated facilities that had operated in the white community for nearly thirty years to halt cross-infection. Building was commenced at Fantome Island near Palm Island to receive long-term Aboriginal patients, thus relieving "the mainland hospitals of the obstinate cases requiring lengthy segregation and care".[30]

Between 1923 and 1928 Raphael Cilento was seconded to New Guinea, and in 1929 he resigned from the AITM, sensing the imminent transfer of the financially crippled institution to Sydney. He and his wife Phyllis, also a doctor, settled in Brisbane where he was determined to maintain momentum in three crucial fields of tropical health: Aboriginal health, tropical fevers and residual hookworm infestation.[31] It was in his capacity as director of tropical hygiene with the Commonwealth Health department, from 1928 to 1933, that Cilento made extensive inspections and reports on Aboriginal health in north Queensland. In his travel diaries, in letters, in professional reports and in newspaper articles he wrote continually of the link between Aboriginal morbidity and substandard housing, poor diet, endemic parasitic infestation, early ageing and infertility in women, all stemming from ignorance, poverty and dirt, and therefore, in Cilento's eyes, all preventible. When a major, and very public, scandal erupted at Palm Island in 1930, it was to Cilento that Bleakley turned for expert advice.

Cilento had been most impressed in 1923 with superintendent Robert Curry's "sheer grit and personality" in carving the Palm Island settlement out of jungle and scrub. By the late 1920s, however, essential work was crippled by a bitter feud between Curry and Dr Pattison, the settlement doctor. Cilento described Pattison as "a drunken sot" who "won his fatal following among the lowest of the aboriginals by gifts of chlorodyn for which the abo [sic] man or woman would sell his soul or body, if he is an addict".[32] Repeated requests by Curry to Undersecretary William Gall, a friend of Pattison's and in Cilento's opinion "the worst of Undersecretaries to the Home Department", led to a public campaign of character assassination of Curry, ending in a gutter fight in Rockhampton between a "drunken" Gall and Curry over "a point of administration".[33] After his wife's death in 1929, and with an inquiry under way over a punchup between himself and Pattison, Curry went berserk on Palm Island in February 1930. He killed his two children, shot and wounded Pattison and his wife, rampaged through the settlement with a rifle, set fire to several buildings, and finally took to sea in a small boat. Returning the next day, he was shot dead by an Aboriginal man acting on the orders of settlement officials.

The replacement superintendent was Edward Cornell, a former prickly pear inspector "owed one by a super sympathetic Government" and with no experience in "handling men", according to Cilento. Pattison resigned, his position now filled by the ageing Dr Thomas Bancroft of hookworm research fame. Described by Cilento as more interested in "queer zoological freaks" than in Aboriginal health, Bancroft reportedly spent only a few minutes a day attending patients. Despite Bancroft's persistent claims that the settlement was free of leprosy and VD, both diseases were rife. Cilento was appalled. "The natives are unsettled, gambling and opium eating are extraordinarily common ... Old Dr Bancroft is about 70 and gave up active medical reading and practice ten years ago ... he cannot refuse the most obvious blackguard of a native whatever he wheedles for. At present this is opium, no less! ... Twenty or thirty of them are getting a bottle of mixture daily ... and more and more are sharing it, clamouring for it and even stealing it. The place is becoming a drug paradise."[34]

In his time at Palm Island, Bancroft lodged several highly critical reports centering on the appalling death rate of over six per cent, mostly from malnutrition and chest infections. Deaths were excessive among the elderly, alcoholics, and those suffering opium addiction and VD. Nearly every baby died who was not breast fed, a direct outcome, in Bancroft's opinion, of economising with a mix of condensed milk and arrowroot. "The question arises should these infants be properly fed on peptonised milk? the expense would be considerable; is it worth while trying to save them?"[35]

Healthy "half-castes" did quite well with dugong and turtle, Bancroft reported, but the ill and aged got nothing. As a consequence, most of the "full-bloods" were starving and children suffered chronic skin diseases. Bancroft urged an increase in the current diet of 1 1b of meat and 6 lb of flour per week for adults (less than the 1923 ration criticised by Governor Thatcher), but this was rejected by Cornell. Further condemnation of meagre rations was recorded by the public service inspector in 1932. His report, commissioned by the Presbyterian committee, also condemned the matron's habit of ordering goods from Townsville and charging them to inmate's accounts without their knowledge. Inspector Bradbury was disgusted that sacks of meat shipped to the Island on boat decks exposed to the sun were used as seating by VD patients rejected from the body of the boat.[36]

The first Fantome Island patients arrived in 1928 under the attention of Dr Pattison at Palm Island. There were 28 patients in 1930, 73 in 1931, 156 in 1932 and 227 in 1933, reflecting an increasing utilisation by the Aboriginal department of medical personnel rather than unqualified police officers to identify and report on VD. In 1931 hookworm inspectors were asked to examine also for VD and leprosy. And the following year Cilento acquired a grant of £70 from the Aboriginal department to survey the Cairns district and the Atherton tableland. He wrote of the fear and reluctance of people to submit to inspections which could lead to their abrupt removal from family and country. Most camp people, he told his wife, "broke for the bush when we appeared anywhere and though we got the majority or perhaps 55 per cent I am confident that all those who knew they were sick lay 'doggo' ".[37]

On revisiting Palm Island, Cilento reported that the drug addicts had been weaned and the hospital was well run, although VD was still rampant. Cilento urged Bleakley to appoint a medical superintendent to oversee both Palm and Fantome Islands. Cornell's management of the Islands was inept, he wrote. "The outstanding industry of the island is gambling and from money they go on to gamble clothes, other possessions and women. The superintendent takes the easy course of ignoring the problem." Conditions at Fantome Island were also deplorable: the 140 sufferers had neither adequate medical wards nor proper domestic shelter. Syphilis treatment was successful but gonorrhoea patients "remained apparently fixtures" because there was no nurse to treat the female patients. Bleakley ignored Cilento's recommendation.

Fantome Island had already emerged as a key component in an increasingly interventionist strategy of medico-hygiene policing. Cilento wanted all patients "worked through Fantome" and back to Palm Island, with the exception of the incurables. After processing, he suggested, workers could be returned to the mainland, to work on Palm Island, or be placed in semi-official postings on other settlements.[38]

Conviction that such screening was imperative was a direct outcome of the fanning out of medical researchers across the remoter northern areas of Australia. Here horrific patterns of appalling sexual ignorance among European males and habitual abuses of Aboriginal women were uncovered. The scarcity of white women and isolation from scrutiny fuelled the culture of the "gin-jockey". Cilento's diary reveals his disgust. "Their whole talk and thought is about women and their great quest in life is to get a 'young gin'. Abos trade girls of 10–12 as a valuable asset at 10/- a time … Typical conversation, 'Say Doc if you got a coupla quid I'll let you have two bonzer young gins'." Cilento despaired that VD would ever be eradicated among either blacks or whites: it is "too widespread to make a campaign, too chronic to cure … No one cares whether he has it or not". Among the Aboriginal population leprosy also was endemic. "A sweep would show hundreds", he lamented, "but what would one do with them?"[39]

Cilento's notes of his 1933 medical survey paint a damning picture of police calibre and commitment. The Cooktown sergeant, "apparently a drunken and venal incompetent" anxiously stressed that he would be out of town when Cilento visited; at Coen the local protector, a "Sgt on verge of DTs, eyes propped out, face lean but purple dewed with constant sweat", had failed to organise an assembly of local Aborigines for Cilento's inspection. The protector at Laura, although "sober on this occasion", had also neglected to organise the health check. What use were police, fumed Cilento, when what was obviously needed was men with expert knowledge. "Is it that the Govt does not really care at all so long as the native farm work is done without expense?"[40]

In fact, it was precisely because "previous inquiries through the police had been without result" that Bleakley had enlisted Cilento to investigate activity in the Bloomfield River area.[41] He was well aware that his network of police protectors were often indifferent or inept in controlling prostitution and in stamping out sexual abuses. Cilento soon detected routine prostitution of girls as young as twelve to Japanese seamen along the coast, fostered by addictions to opium and tobacco. The result was a big percentage "of natives half cast white, half caste asiatic".

Ultimately, wrote Cilento, Aboriginal women had little hope of escaping VD because of the large numbers of "coloured" foreigners in northern coastal areas "unprovided with women". Documents show that a full survey of VD in northern Queensland was only aborted because of cutbacks in Commonwealth funding. At the same time, it was openly admitted that the Fantome Island facility would have been totally incapable of coping with anticipated numbers.

Medical and moral policing

One effect of the clinical regime of identification of sexual diseases was an intensified focus of official attention on women. Sexual interference and "uncontrolled promiscuity" were regarded as key components of the VD epidemic. "Normalisation" of sexual relations, it followed, was the key to familial responsibility and social health. Documents show that department officers arbitrarily manipulated sexual unions to foster "normalisation", even where this directly flouted state laws and precepts.

In the early days of Palm Island, for instance, superintendent Curry had devised a sham ceremony as a means of "legitimating" unions and promoting monogamy. This entailed reading part of the official marriage lines and having the parties sign an official record. Curry assured couples such marriages were legal. Privately, however, he confided to Bleakley that "should any of the officials enlighten them on the subject my marriage laws would be of no use".[42] Bleakley willingly condoned such "ceremonies". They have used one at Yarrabah for years, he told Curry, where the seriousness and binding nature of the commitment was stressed and a written register kept. "To insist upon the registered legal marriage for all natives would be unwise and unfair", he continued, "as many are too primitive to understand the legal side of the ceremony". It could also create a legal minefield: "Divorce, where such became necessary, would be quite beyond them".[43]

"Settlement marriages" had no legal status nor could they be retrospectively recognised. But the registrar-general did advise in 1928 that no court would rule them null and void, nor interfere in any inheritance to wife and child, and all children could be registered as legitimate. Bleakley's main preoccupation, however, was to legitimise his own authority. He urged superintendents to continue the deception. If "married" people realised they were "living in immorality" this might "sow distrust in the Department's administration".[44]

The central purpose of the department's control of marriages was to foster "appropriate" unions. Permission was often refused if one party was deemed to be a "waster" or "immoral", and sexual disease was taken as proof of the latter. On Palm Island, however, such social engineering proved unworkable. In the mid-1930s there were 235 more males than females, and all young girls possible were sent to domestic service on the mainland "before reaching marrying age, and very few show any inclination to return and settle down to camp life".[45] Most Palm Islanders were thought to be affected by VD and it was reported that "control and care of the health of the Palm Island natives is in a state of chaos". This made a mockery of attempts to regulate sexual activity in terms of "healthy" unions. Refusing marriage on the grounds of VD infection was futile when nearly every applicant expected a negative blood test, the Catholic priest conceded. It only provoked applicants into "either commencing or continuing a life of immorality because of their inability to marry".[46]

It was not uncommon for both tribal and legal marriages to be fractured by administrative deportation from towns and rural areas. Inevitably new commitments formed in church and settlement communities. Departmental records reveal that de facto relationships were often given official status even when a prior marriage was known to exist, on the assumption that breaking these "sinful unions" would invite promiscuity.

Bleakley endorsed unions of mutual consent as a lesser danger to community control, although he was acutely aware that church objectors might expose the department's hypocrisy. On Fantome Island, where many VD sufferers were confined without their partners, the problem of response to "immoral" unions seemed insoluble, as Dr Julian observed. "Of the natives at Fantome quite a number are married or drifted together casually or by tribal custom, prior to admission ... there are frequent attempts at sexual intercourse and a number successfully so ... Under present conditions one has to either condone with or punish and such a position is most unsatisfactory."[47]

The Catholic priests acknowledged the inevitable, and readily married all people possible under church sanction. "Their attitude to the unmarried living together is: Not to break good faith unless there is hope of better things. They respect the validity of mutual consent ... They regard the tribal marriage as a correct one."[48] But James Feetham, the Anglican bishop of North Queensland, deplored official endorsement of "sinful" relationships. He demanded the scandalous situation be cleaned up, even threatening to expose the government in parliament "with regard to the evil state of things on Fantome Island, which has absorbed a great deal of public money and which is actually a hot-bed of disease". Several Palm Island superintendents, he claimed, including the present one, drank heavily and had sexual liaisons with young Aboriginal girls. Feetham was sure Home department personnel were well aware, but he doubted action would be taken: "they keep great quantities of white-wash on hand for their officials".[49]

Strategies were canvassed to regularise new unions. A "native" divorce was proposed by superintendent Bill MacKenzie of Aurukun who objected to the "cruelty" of forcing wives to accompany husbands removed to Palm Island for violent behaviour. Superintendent Colledge at Woorabinda suggested the Justice department be formally approached regarding a special divorce category. Bleakley's department did request the power to annul legal marriages in 1934 but this was refused as an infringement of state laws.

While sexual unions on missions and settlements could be subjected to varying degrees of official manipulation, the plight of women in rural areas remained intractable. Indeed Cilento's 1933 report was entitled "The Condition of Women in the Coastal Areas", and Bleakley had for several years been working up amendments to legislate "for the more effective check on moral offences against aboriginal females". Wholesale segregation of females in institutions was impractical, he concluded, because of prohibitive costs and also because of "the social dangers should the males be deprived of their women". Existing regulations were aimed "at moral control of women in employment", but Bleakley admitted "the indifference of many of the employers renders it ineffective".[50]

Cilento's extensive reports of 1932 and 1933 had focused critical attention on the large number of sexually active females beyond the range of departmental controls. Bleakley was keen to extend his authority over the many part-Aborigines of Malay or Pacific Island extraction not living as or with Aborigines and thereby not subject to the *Aborigi-*

nals Protection Acts. This was achieved by the *Amendment Act* of 1934 which greatly widened the scope of official guardianship and intervention. In a clear indication of the medical/moral policing rationale, Bleakley explained that departmental jurisdiction would now include "the illegitimate children of half-caste mothers, the children of parents both halfcastes, and the crossbreed element of aboriginal or Pacific Island strain which were reported by Dr Cilento to be living in low conditions and a menace to health and discipline".[51]

"Greater control over the health and social conditions of the half-caste element" and over "certain alien coloured people" presently a "disturbing influence upon Aboriginal people" would now be possible.[52] All "half-castes" under twenty-one now came under departmental attention (increased from sixteen years), and individuals could now be transported "for disciplinary reasons". To prevent "undesirable marriages being performed by irresponsible persons" all marriages of people of Aboriginal extraction now required permission from the chief protector.

It has been argued that the *1934 Amendment Act* was devised as a response to moral and social problems arising *within* missions and settlements, problems deriving ultimately from the government's "segregationist" policy.[53] But Bleakley himself stated that the main purpose was to target those previously *exempt* from departmental intervention. By broadening the categories to include everyone of Aboriginal and Islander extraction, a "big proportion" of the coloured population of north Queensland who might be "a menace to health and morals because of their low caste condition and association with Aboriginals" were brought under surveillance. This would enable supervision and control over "their conditions of living and associations in the interests of health and morality".[54] To facilitate this social survey each protector was to make a list of all persons "whose breed brings them within the Provisions of the Amending Act", detailing living conditions, associations and "need of protection".

The medical/moral objectives of the new regulations were aimed at processing disease, "to facilitate the discovery and treatment of disease" as Bleakley put it. He demanded that all members of the police force be vigilant and assist the network of protectors. Bleakley was well aware that many people would be caught unnecessarily in the new net: exemptions would be issued readily *after* a medical examination had shown an individual to be free of contagious disease. The medical rationale of the new regulations is further underlined by the mechanism which saw all existing exemptions temporarily cancelled until these people also produced a clean medical report. Bleakley soon boasted that "a good deal of cleaning up has been done" of people "previously beyond our reach" but "a source of danger and infection to our own wards". Palm and Fantome Islands now operated as "medical clearing Stations", he wrote, linked in a "medical drive" to sweeping inspections on the mainland.[55]

By the mid-1930s, then, medical expertise was impacting intensively on departmental policies and procedures regarding moral and sexual conduct. The dramatic leap in numbers confined on Palm and Fantome Islands attested to the department's commitment to the war against VD. Were changes also enforced in other areas of Aboriginal health and welfare?

Diet and disease

It is clear from Bleakley's letters that as late as 1933 he still manipulated ration issues as a mechanism to engineer social responsibility. In fact it was Bleakley's defence against claims of starvation on the communities that "the aim has been to avoid pauperisation and only supplement the efforts of the inmate to raise his home consumption needs ... care has been taken to avoid creating any inducement for the ablebodied to loaf in camp on the dole". In general, he assured his minister Edward Hanlon, inmates appear "well nourished and content".[56]

The reality, of course, was horribly different. Clinical tests at Cape Bedford had exposed major health problems deriving directly from malnutrition. Here the Lutherans had lobbied in vain for ten years for a grant of farming land. The government subsidy was nowhere near enough to keep families alive and church donations only provided "the bare means of existence". Pastor Thiele deplored the culture of dependency: "You will admit that it is not the ideal to feed the aboriginals like so many animals kept in a Zoo".[57] Cilento also wrote scathingly of the barrenness of most of the northern missions, and in all his surveys he took every opportunity to examine and criticise dietary deficiencies, but with little effect.

It is important to realise that until 1934 it was from a base in Commonwealth health institutions that Cilento had mounted his campaigns to force changes in Queensland's handling of Aboriginal health. In 1934, however, courtesy of an offer from home secretary Edward Hanlon, Cilento accepted the newly created position of director of Health and Medical Services, and was thereby in charge of public health in Queensland. For Hanlon, this very much in-

cluded the vexed area of Aboriginal health. As an adviser
on medical aid for Aborigines, Hanlon anticipated Cilento
would be a "tower of strength to the government". With the
amalgamation in 1935 of the health and the home departments (of which Native Affairs was a subsidiary), Cilento's
inspectorial rights over Aboriginal health intensified.

Cilento's more direct leverage can be detected in the
innovative instructions emanating from the office of Native
Affairs. Whereas in 1933 Bleakley still justified meagre
rations in terms of averting "pauperisation", after 1934 he
was finally forced to incorporate Cilento's guidelines.
Cilento's surveys, he informed his network of protectors,
had revealed that "foodstuffs issued from most Protector-
ates to indigents are not as useful from a health point of
view as they possibly could be". Commonly "large quantities
of flour are issued" but potato, onion, vegetables and meat
were rarely supplied. Bleakley now issued Cilento's revised
ration scale but he cautioned his officers to keep costs "as
low as possible": "hunting facilities" would enable the department to save paying out for meat.[58]

Bleakley boasted in 1936 that Cilento's campaign on
malnutrition had changed the emphasis from quantity to
quality in terms of "the best nutritive properties". But his
rhetoric was not matched in practice. On checking rations
at the Monamona mission, Cilento reported a lack of meat
and deficiencies in iron and protein. Even so, wrote
Cilento, "the diet is on the whole better than that seen in
any other aboriginal institution".[59]

Missions at this time received only £5 per person per year
(or 3 pence per day) in government support, far below
allocations to government settlements. Palm Island, for
instance, was funded at £16 per head, but even here a

dietary survey identified gross deficiencies in protein and fats, and a meat ration at only one-third Cilento's recommended amount.[60] Allocation for "daily maintenance" at Fantome Island was also around eleven pence per person. For many years, and quite illegally, the department deducted *more than twice that amount* per day from the savings of patients until accounts were all but cleaned out. Bleakley justified this rort on the grounds that most patients "are admitted to Fantome Island through their own fault".[61]

A second crusade of Cilento's, also directly impacting upon Aboriginal health, was the detection and treatment of leprosy. Frustrated with state indifference, he had persuaded the federal Health Council in 1933 to fund a five-year study of leprosy in the tropics. Cilento was disgusted to discover that no medical expert administered leprosy management in Queensland, and there was no leprosy specialist at the Peel Island leprosarium near Brisbane. Internal records show that when it came to Aboriginal sufferers, Bleakley openly opposed identification and treatment at the Peel Island sanatorium because "once aboriginals had been declared to be lepers they were legally out of my control".[62]

Cilento had for many years made submissions to the Queensland government for a campaign against leprosy, and although he finally secured an in-principle joint state–federal program, nothing eventuated. In 1937, however, when the National Health and Medical Research Council (NHMRC) was established to pick up the mantle of the long defunct AITM, Cilento secured the first major project as a survey of leprosy in the Aboriginal population. In the same year, a new *Health Act* in Queensland specifically empowered Cilento, as department head, to "enquire into all matters affecting the medical welfare of Aboriginals".

Only after "further emphatic representations" did Cilento manage to wheedle £500 out of Hanlon in 1937 for a study of leprosy in the Monamona mission population. The study confirmed his suspicions. Out of just on two hundred people, thirteen tested positively to Hansen's disease and a further twenty-five showed latent symptoms. Cilento now ordered Bleakley to close the mission to outside access, and to retain and segregate leper suspects within the mission, regardless of the costs of extra facilities.[63] Bleakley passed on the instruction, but not the enabling finances. When a doctor visited two months later, he reported all crops had died in the drought, cattle were too thin to be killed, and the people had been sent bush to survive. The superintendent pleaded that without farming land or funding for food, he could do nothing else.

Cilento wrote a furious letter to Hanlon. "If an investigation was made with the same care at other aboriginal settlements", Cilento reported, "doubtless other leper centres would be discovered".[64] Queensland's Aboriginal population was dying out because of defective medical care in diseases such as leprosy, malaria and tuberculosis, he remonstrated. Wretched diet was the root cause of Aboriginal debility. "Diseases that flourish during conditions of food deficiency continue to threaten the survival of the race and to fill the Lazaret … No measure of improvement is of any value if he is to die of malnutrition." Ultimately, wrote Cilento, as he had argued since 1924, "the medical problem of the aboriginal is at present his only problem".[65]

*   *   *

There may well have been a dearth of parliamentary interest in Aboriginal affairs in the 1920s and 1930s, but the files show this in no way reflected activity at an administrative level. These two decades saw the emergence and consolidation of a range of clinical professionals as investigators, exposers, critics and challengers of Aboriginal health policy and practices in Queensland. In general the official response was one of irritation, reluctance and miserly inflexibility.

The most strident critic and agitator of this period was Raphael Cilento, whose specialties of Aboriginal health and tropical diseases led him to concentrate much of his energy in Queensland. When Cilento took over Queensland's health department in 1934 and shortly after acquired authority over all Aboriginal health matters, he traced a similar path to that of the nineteenth-century medical experts who had also battled recalcitrant bureaucracies before finally asserting the centrality of clinical expertise in public health administration.

In view of the common assertion that Commonwealth involvement in state Aboriginal affairs commenced only after the 1967 referendum, it is important to note that these surveys and treatments derived from Commonwealth interventions rather than state programs. Acknowledged authority to monitor and direct Aboriginal health practices was one thing. But upgraded medical services and amenities, or even standard quality nutrition, were inextricably tied to the financing of the Aboriginal sub-department and to the deliberations of its chief bureaucrats.

5

The new "experts"

The monopoly of public administrators over all aspects of Aboriginal health and welfare was finally fractured in the early 1930s by health specialists whose initial brief had been limited to the identification and treatment of disease. But these were not the only "specialists" during this period causing political embarrassment and alarm in Queensland's Aboriginal affairs. Anthropologists were emerging to claim authority as expert spokespersons on matters of Aboriginal culture and as definers of Aboriginal interests. How did politicians and bureaucrats respond to this body of intellectuals? Did their activities impact on policy and practices at state or national levels?

Unwelcome observers

The Anthropological Society of Australasia was founded in 1890 at a time when ethnologists were primarily compilers and collectors of photographic and material evidence of rapidly disappearing "child races". It was a bitter dispute over ownership of the considerable collection of artefacts of the first chief protector of Aborigines in Queensland, Dr Walter Roth, which provoked his resignation in 1906. As early as 1911 a deputation from the Australasian Association for the Advancement of Science called for an inquiry into "the native obligations of the Commonwealth". Two years later they urged a Permanent Native Commission be formed of state and federal representatives. Both proposals were ignored.

A redirection of interest from evolutionary to environmental factors early in the twentieth century focused attention on the structure and social cohesion of "primitive" societies. Bronislaw Malinowski and A. R. Radcliffe-Brown were key proponents of the new theory of structural-functionalism and both men attended an international scientific conference in Sydney in 1914. Here it was decided that anthropology should be taught at Sydney University. Deferred during the war years, the school finally started in 1923 under the auspices of Alfred Radcliffe-Brown.

Radcliffe-Brown had never worked among people in their tribal setting. He was primarily interested in refining and expanding scientific principles and in publicising research in public and political forums. But he saw no advocacy role to change administrative and missionary practices in line with these "scientific principles". His preoccupation with theoretical rather than applied anthropology accentuated the assumption that Aboriginal culture was pristine and timeless and at the same time precarious and vulnerable to collapse upon "contamination" by a dominant European culture. It also sidelined analysis in Australia of the ongoing impact of administrative policies, especially with regard to enforced social change.[1]

Such academic detachment was anathema to A. P. Elkin, who took over the chair of anthropology in 1934. A prolific writer of journal and newspaper articles, and a committed agitator and lobbyist for Aboriginal interests, he was considered the expert spokesman on Aboriginal matters. It was Elkin's thesis that the drastic decline in Aboriginal numbers was a direct outcome of a critically accelerated pressure to adapt on a race which had stagnated for millennia in equilibrium. The Aboriginal problem was therefore one of adaptation. And it was up to scientific experts, namely anthropologists, to oversee the critical interface between Aboriginal and European cultures in order to minimise the detrimental effects of the culture clash.[2] Elkin urged field workers to inform "both missions and administrations" of the "systematised knowledge of the essentials of native social and cultural life, and of the principles operating in the contact situation".[3] Such professional guidance was at the core of Elkin's conviction that Aboriginal people were capable of social improvement and could reap the benefits of a civilised lifestyle.

The bureaucrats and politicians, however, were not so convinced. Although all administrators sent to work among the natives of Papua New Guinea were trained at the new school of anthropology, no such instruction was mandatory for those working among Australian Aborigines. When the federal government commissioned a survey of Aboriginal employment and institutions in central and northern Australia in 1928, it was Queensland's long-serving key administrator, John Bleakley, who was appointed to the task. And when his highly acclaimed report was discussed at the national conference of interested parties — from government, pastoral interests and missionary bodies — anthropological representatives were pointedly ignored.

The fieldworkers fanning out of the new department from the late 1920s were abruptly faced with the moral, social and political implications of Aboriginal living conditions, and were immediately implicated with regard to professional ethics. Should they merely record with scientific detachment? Or should they speak out as informed observers? Ursula McConnel, invited by Bleakley to provide a "scientific" assessment of Aurukun in 1927, took the latter path. Correspondence reveals Bleakley had expected professional endorsement of his stewardship. Stung by her vehement condemnation of the cruel practices of superintendent Bill MacKenzie, regarded as a fine example of firm management, the administrators closed ranks. The local protector branded McConnel as "objectionable" for having made "damaging and disloyal statements";[4] Bleakley impugned her professionalism, describing her as "very eccentric and somewhat hysterical";[5] and MacKenzie said she would never set foot on his mission again.

The unprincipled nature of these character attacks is betrayed by evidence that the department was well aware of ill-treatment of mission inmates. McConnel's accusations had been corroborated by a detailed letter to Bleakley from the Aurukun people. This six-page protest catalogued a culture of abuse: disobedience or brawling led to whipping, chaining to trees, imprisonment without food or water, or banishment from the mission. It was alleged MacKenzie fired shots over people's heads and on occasion threatened them directly with the gun. And married men were prevented from taking up employment off the mission. The community demanded Bleakley organise MacKenzie's dismissal.[6]

Forced to validate his "protectorship", Bleakley travelled to Aurukun, where, after private discussions with the complainants, he conceded that most of the charges were true. MacKenzie had indeed exceeded his authority in meting out punishment of "undue severity", but, he wrote, reprisals were warranted to maintain social discipline. Most of the aggression was triggered by assaults on women who subsequently welcomed MacKenzie's interventions, Bleakley informed the undersecretary, and it was because men working the boats commonly prostituted their wives to crew-members that this avenue of employment was closed. Beyond a letter of disapproval no official action was taken.[7]

MacKenzie's authoritarian regime was also endorsed by mission committee convenor Rev Kirke, who held his own investigation. Again the emphasis was on the imperative to normalise social relations rather than on the drastic punishments. "Many of the people who come in from the bush are still dominated by tribal law and custom", Kirke reported, "particularly in regard to marriage, death (*pourri-pourri*) [i.e. sorcery] and the right of the husband to abuse his wife. It is in regard to wife beating, the procuring of abortion and the selling of women for immoral purposes that the Missionary has his greatest difficulties".[8] It can fairly be assumed that neither of these key officials would have bothered to inspect Aurukun had the community's petition not tallied so closely with McConnel's exposé. Yet to cover their default they subsequently maligned her as disloyal and eccentric.

Ursula McConnel was not the only anthropologist in the area. It is scarcely a coincidence that the Aurukun petition landed in head office when Donald Thomson was doing his field research on the reserve. Funded by the Australian National Research Council, Thomson spent four years in Cape York meticulously cataloguing Aboriginal languages and customs. He was appalled by MacKenzie's punitive regime which included head shaving, flogging, chained work gangs, and confinement in a small iron shed.

But it was atrocities well outside institutional "authority" which sickened him most: like watching MacKenzie round up two women and three men at gunpoint and chain them together for the 240 mile (380-kilometre) walk across the peninsula to Laura for transportation to Palm Island.[9] This practice was not uncommon. A year previously another group were force-marched a distance of 145 miles (230 kilometres) in twenty days. They were beaten by police before they left Aurukun, flogged several times along the way including one woman who was six months pregnant, and the women were sexually assaulted. This could not be dismissed as a "beat-up" by anthropologists. Deputy chief protector Cornelius O'Leary found sufficient evidence existed to take action against one police officer and to demand explanations from the other two.[10] There is no record of such action being taken.

Thomson, a devout Presbyterian, held his counsel, preferring to take his accusations directly to the mission committee. He met a stone wall. Like the department, the committee also spurned the new order of "specialists" as both ideologically eccentric and administratively naive. Increasingly bitter at his rejection, Thomson finally went public in 1947 with a series of damning exposés.[11] Official records show the same propensity to slander and ridicule Thomson's pro-Aboriginal observations as had occurred with McConnel. The disrespect was mutual. Thomson later wrote: "Trained scientific observers all agree that the aborigines could be saved if the Governments really wanted to save them".[12] "Queensland native policy, if it could be called a policy", he declared in the context of further Cape

York scandals, "was such that Queensland had become
notorious. It was doing much to debase and discredit Australia in the eyes of the world".[13]

The government and the mission committees predicated
their "protective" policies on social control. Anthropologists, they decided, were a disruptive influence on the
previously insulated communities. At Mapoon, for instance, a resurgence in *pourri-pourri* was directly linked to
Thomson's enthusiastic inquiries into "old" tribal customs.
The pitching of tribal lore above occupational expedience
was seen as provocative. Thomson was never allowed to
return to the area. And Rev Kirke argued that, in view of
"the high handed demands made, and the superior airs
affected by certain anthropologists", all anthropologists
should be banned within a 15-mile radius (24 kilometres)
of the missions.[14]

The qualification was an oblique reference to Dr R.
Lauriston Sharpe. His "loyal co-operation and assistance"
during anthropological studies on Mornington Island
earned the respect and gratitude of mission officials.[15]
"Perfect harmony prevailed", MacKenzie observed approvingly, perhaps if we cultivate Sharpe it would provide "an
excuse to keep other less desirable anthropologists out".[16]

Selling the science

As mentor of anthropological advance in Australia, Elkin
was acutely aware that open conflicts with government and
mission authorities could provoke a marginalisation of the
new expertise. He distanced himself from the more abra-
sive of his colleagues, even to the extent of freezing them
out of National Research Council grants. On file there is a
letter from Elkin to the Presbyterian mission committee in

which he requests the names of those "who have caused such an unhappy situation, so that we should know how to act in case they applied for grants in the future".[17]

The marriage of anthropology with Aboriginal administration was Elkin's ultimate aim, and to this end he worked assiduously behind the scenes, applying discreet pressure to people of influence. He lobbied home secretary Edward Hanlon in 1934 with the suggestion that superintendents who had been anthropologically trained at the university would be "more efficient". Officers who undertook courses in administration, tropical hygiene, criminal law and geographical mapping would "understand the aborigines, and there are very few men or women who have this understanding apart from special training".[18] Rev Hey, the man who had established and run Mapoon for over twenty years, was in full agreement. At least one year's study in anthropology was essential "to gain an insight to the mind of primitive man". His affirmation betrays the presumption of dealing with an anachronistic curiosity: "Teachers of backward races must have or should have a thorough training in heathen psychology otherwise the greatness and importance of the task is only partly understood".[19]

The following year Elkin floated a new scheme. In return for a regular grant to the anthropology department from the Queensland government, training would be provided free of charge for officials. Asked for his opinion, deputy chief protector Cornelius O'Leary was dismissive. Trained scientists, he said, are "not inclined to practicability". And capable officers with field experience among Aborigines should not be debarred from employment just because they lacked university training. According to O'Leary, none of the superintendents on government settlements were interested in such training, and most mission personnel could not spare the time or expense.[20]

For Bleakley it was a matter of pragmatics. Anthropologists lacked any practical experience in "the social and physical welfare of the native races" and Queensland's Aboriginal population had not benefited from the new science. It was the general consensus among officials, he declared, that anthropologists were impractical, and that theoretical learning was no comparison to knowledge of behaviour and customs gleaned by long years working in the field. Missionaries "have come nearer to an understanding of the native psychology than many of those claiming scientific knowledge", he averred. "I doubt whether even Scientists can plumb the depths of the native mind in a short space of one or two years."[21] The nub of Bleakley's repudiation, however, was overtly political. "There was little to show that such work was undertaken with any object of assisting the Department in its difficult task", he protested.[22] And anthropologists were "too prone to criticise ordinary safeguards for the preservation of order amongst the natives".[23]

Ultimately, he added disingenuously, it was up to the government to make funds available if it wanted its officers to be trained in the new "science". He was on safe ground here. Hanlon was furious at the continuing highly public embarrassments which anthropological researchers had brought upon his department. Raphael Cilento himself lobbied on behalf of Elkin's proposal that a government anthropologist be appointed in the Cape York area, but Hanlon was adamant. The government's job, he stated, was to feed Aboriginal people, not to waste money on the "fairy stories" of anthropologists.[24]

In hindsight, Bleakley was to concede that blame for the initial "deplorable absence of cooperation" between the two bodies lay primarily with the administrators who looked on the new teachings "as a museum science".[25] But in rendering the tactics of the time as a matter of misconception, Bleakley was effectively papering over both bitter politics and public condemnation. As the new spokespersons fought to establish their credentials in the previously closed field, the entrenched authorities bluntly disparaged any critical disclosures. Only those who appreciated the department's "difficult task", like Dr Sharpe, were deemed to be suitable advocates of their profession.

Indeed, as Bleakley observed after yet another anthropologically-induced crisis, the department's experience of "the activities of women Anthropologists has not been a very satisfactory or harmonious one".[26] This exasperated reference was to Mrs Caroline Tennant Kelly. Her sojourn at Cherbourg, sanctioned by Bleakley after an approach by Elkin, had exposed the government in the national forum to charges of massive exploitation of Aboriginal earnings.

"Social anthropology"

Why did Elkin's testimonial for Tennant Kelly succeed where other eminent appeals over two years drew a blank? Perhaps it was the assertion that "Mrs Kelly is possessed of plenty of common sense and tact and will not cause any implications on the settlement".[27] Tennant Kelly arrived at Cherbourg in March 1934 to make investigations "of a scientific nature into the social anthropology of the aborigines". A letter from her to Bleakley in late May expresses appreciation for his interest in applied anthropology and thanks him for permitting her to meet Queensland's governor on his visit to the settlement. Bleakley would have been unaware he had received a ticking bomb.

On the sixth of June Governor Leslie Wilson wrote to the acting premier, Percy Pease. The visit to Cherbourg was most hospitable, and the settlement, so he was informed, was "growing in numbers". Unfortunately, he was also informed, most of the births were of "half-caste" babies to the many girls sent out to farms and stations as domestic help. "Ninety-five per cent of them return to the Settlement, either about to have a child, or who have had a child, the father of which is a white man", the governor disclosed in alarm. Obviously the girls were at fault. "One may deprecate the fact that white men become fathers of these half-caste children, [but] the blame must rest, to a very large extent, on the native girls, who, by temperament, and a desire to have a child by a white father, encourage white men in every way." What action did the government propose to stem this explosion? he demanded. Perhaps all girls should be imprisoned on the settlement under close guard. Or should the settlement be moved to a more isolated location, since proximity to Murgon and Wondai was conducive to misdemeanours? A solution must be found to the question, he concluded, "before matters, as regards the half-caste problem get worse".[28]

Who gave him this information? Bleakley demanded furiously of W. Porteus Semple, superintendent at Cherbourg; certainly such material never came from head office. I have "grave suspicion", responded Semple, "that it was Mrs Kelly, the woman sent up by The Sydney University and who was on the Settlement at the time of his excellency's visit ... I am very sorry that this woman was ever allowed to come on to this Settlement and your Department should think in allowing a similar privilege".[29]

Called to account, Semple and Bleakley quickly compiled a detailed analysis of births at the settlement over the previous five-year period which showed nearly all "half-caste" births on the settlement were to legally married couples living at Cherbourg.[30] Only eleven of the 353 girls "sent out to service" had fallen pregnant to white men, and no illegitimate children had been born of white men near Cherbourg. The "moral welfare" of working women was important, but, as Bleakley cautioned his superiors, there were vital economic considerations. Over £1,460 in wages flowed into the settlement from domestic workers. To retain the girls at Cherbourg would cost the government at least £478 more per year.

There was also a practical *caveat*: "... an equal if not greater danger exists from the temptations to immorality on the Settlements themselves". Superintendents routinely sent girls to other settlements to prevent "jealousy and quarrelling". And since 1925 all unmarried females at Cherbourg had been strictly segregated in dormitories behind barbed-wire fences. Despite these stratagems there had been several births to "half-caste" men on the settlement, many of whom were already married.

In an address to the anthropology session of the Science Congress in Melbourne in January 1935 Tennant Kelly amplified her observations. People of many different tribes were "herded together" on the settlements in Queensland, she reported, and old customs were subject "to the ridicule of missionaries and the prohibitions of officialdom". Her statements were gleefully circulated by the newspapers.

Semple was furious that his management had been so

publicly maligned. She is "a liar and a mischief maker" and "states a great deal of rubbish", he protested. In fact, her close association with the "natives" rather than with the authorities had dismayed Semple who was repulsed by her familiarity. "It is no wonder that she was taken for a half-caste", he told Bleakley. "She dressed like a Native, sat under the trees with natives, often with her arms around them, her hair was always untidy." She discussed with people the continuation of customs and ceremonies, on one occasion, according to Semple, ridiculing missionaries officiating at a funeral service. He described her claim that missionaries interfered with native customs as "a beastly lie".[31]

It was Tennant Kelly's interference in money matters which most exasperated Semple. She asked about rations and wages received, he related archly, and had the audacity "to bring one Native into the Office and demand Free Issue for him by the way of clothes". On another occasion she marched into the office and exclaimed, "Natives should be allowed to draw money from their accounts whenever they wished and how much they wished". She seemed to "revel in intrigue", particularly any squabbles among officials, and "paid undue business to the administration".[32] "It is my opinion that your Department should force an enquiry with regard to this woman's statements and expose her as a lying Charlatan."[33]

But it was the department which was subjected to "enquiry". Its manipulation of Aboriginal wages and savings was exposed to national debate when Tennant Kelly accused Queensland of blatant exploitation of Aboriginal labour. Some domestics hired out from Cherbourg rated a pitiful 5s per week, she reported, of which they were only allowed 6d for their own spending. Her indictment was wholeheartedly supported by Rev W. Morley, secretary of the Association for the Protection of Native Races (APNR). Aboriginal workers, he told the conference, were "induced to bank their meagre earnings, and then, in some instances, were refused permission to withdraw the money".[34] And this system put over £300,000 of Aboriginal earnings in the government's hands. "Manifestly the aboriginal labourer in Queensland is a very satisfactory asset to the State finances", wrote Morley in the APNR annual report, "but there is little satisfaction ... in the fact that in a British State a population of 17,000 voiceless and voteless fellow-creatures are held in conditions of economic slavery".[35]

Morley had in fact for several years been trying to extract information from Bleakley's department on the setting of Aboriginal wage rates, the handling of Aboriginal savings accounts, and the government's dealings on the accumulated trust monies. When Queensland's premier, William Forgan Smith, attempted to divert censure following Tennant Kelly's bombshell at the Science Conference by offering to respond promptly to any legitimate complaints, Morley was quick to give him an extensive list of correspondence from the APNR which both the Native Affairs department and its minister had disregarded. We are grateful, wrote Morley, that you are now dealing with the matter. Perhaps you should appoint a Royal Commission or a Board of Enquiry, so long as "no person however highly placed, who is associated in any way with either the Aboriginal Department or the Police Department, should be appointed a member".[36]

Bleakley was horrified at the new crisis. He fired a letter off to Rev John Needham, chairman of both the APNR and the Australian Board of Missions which managed Anglican missions in Queensland. Morley, he wrote, seems determined "not to be convinced" that Queensland's regulations acted to protect Aboriginal interests. Needham duly concurred. Morley is a good chap and "really keen about obtaining justice for the aborigines", Needham explained. But he is an old man "really obsessed with the wrongs of the blacks, and this obsession warps his judgement".[37] With the benefit of a crash-course in Native Affairs accounts from Bleakley, Needham declared in the Board of Missions annual report, "the native is not an economic slave, but most truly a cared-for ward of the State". Quoting the latest annual report from Bleakley, Needham confidently declared that all Aboriginal earnings went to the workers, and that the government "did not receive one penny of revenue from native taxation".[38] But was this the truth?

Economic slavery?

Analysis of internal documents held by the department reveals a complex web of negligence, fraud and misappropriation in the official handling of income generated by Aboriginal workers. Financial abuses occurred at several points: non- or under-payment of wages and "pocket money", fraud by police protectors, unofficial departmental appropriations, and official government confiscation. So undisciplined was the system that Bleakley had to exhort police protectors not to subject Aboriginal workers "to suffer loss and deprivation through the neglect of officials who are supposed to protect him". Frequently, Bleakley cautioned the protectors, employers were "allowed to neglect payment of wages due to aboriginals for several months and then create trouble trying to evade payment or pledging inability to pay. In some cases these arrears have not been recovered".[39]

This was more than simple negligence. All too often the police connived with employers. In a later directive to police Bleakley condemned those who issued work agreements at illegally low rates of pay, waived the statutory provision of clothing for youths below eighteen years, and acquiesced to piecemeal work schedules to maintain availability of favoured workers at the whim of particular employers. This practice kept prized workers "unemployed for various periods to suit the convenience of such employers", who should, instructed Bleakley, "be prepared to employ him permanently and not merely when it suits his convenience".[40]

Perhaps the 1927 Wrotham Park incident best demonstrates the extreme vulnerability of Aboriginal labour to police abuse. Here, with £199 13s owing in back pay, workers refused to re-sign. It is on record that the local constable went out to the station, terrorised the men and women, plied them with alcohol, threatened to have them all removed to a government settlement, and finally locked them in a poisons shed overnight to break their resistance.[41] An internal police inquiry found the constable guilty on all charges, but gave him "the benefit of the doubt" on the assaults and ultimately fined him 10s for filing a false report. In disgust, the home secretary leaked details of police corruption to the press, causing the *Police Union Journal* to claim police were being falsely victimised.[42]

In fact, there had been a series of inquiries over the years into police corruption, by police inspectors and by government auditors who were appalled that offenders continued to operate. The sergeant at Longreach, for instance, deducted from Aboriginal accounts excessive amounts for clothing and goods which he had acquired second-hand. He also colluded with the local storekeeper in charging "exorbitant amounts" for goods sold to Aboriginal workers; he was remiss in chasing unpaid wages; and several receipts in his hand for outlays on workers' accounts lacked both signature and thumbprint of the account holder but nonetheless had been "witnessed" by a third party.[43]

Entrenched police fraud and pilfering from Aboriginal savings was confirmed in 1932 by a public service inspection. The latter practice, concluded the inspectors, was common and invariably executed in small amounts on doctored receipts over a long period of time. Official policy which denied workers the right even to see their wage forms or passbooks only compounded the difficulty of detection. "As the native could not, in many instances, check his own earnings and spendings", observed the inspectors, "the opportunity for fraud existed to a greater extent than with any other Governmental accounts".[44]

In defence of his management, Bleakley suggested he had little control over police dealings on Aboriginal accounts and many protectors had no training in clerical work. Significantly, he did not tighten supervisory procedures. But he successfully proposed the centralised control of the savings pool, swollen to £265,000 after a series of wage increases through the 1920s. Only a £15,000 working balance would remain in country accounts,[45] a strategy that Undersecretary William Gall declared "will go a long way to minimise fraud by members of the Police Force who are Protectors".[46]

With around £40,000 held operational in the department's main trust account, the government acquired the tidy sum of £200,000 for investment in Inscribed Stock. This followed the practice since 1926 of investing the "idle portion" of the Aboriginals Protection Property Account and of the Aboriginals Provident Fund to achieve an interest bonus to offset departmental expenditure. Bulk amounts from settlement trust accounts, comprising accumulated levies on all inmates for general maintenance, were also invested to create revenue. No authorisation existed for such revenue raising, and the records show frequent illegal shuffling of cash around various trust funds as settlement accounts or the Provident Fund ran into deficit.[47]

When the world-wide depression impacted upon Australia in 1929 the Queensland government cut funding to all departments by 20 per cent. Bleakley was directed that "as far as can reasonably be expected, the aboriginals under care of the Department should, from their own funds, meet the cost of relief and protection".[48] Although a proposal was floated to garnishee 50 per cent of all Aboriginal trust monies, Bleakley opposed this grab, managing to retain the bulk of the money in departmental, rather than in treasury, hands.

To reduce costs and raise revenue, Bleakley compiled an inventive range of new deductions and charges. All Aboriginal savings accounts were hit with an extra tax of $2^1/_2$ per cent, disguised as an "administrative charge" to avert protest, and all settlement inmates with accounts over £20 were levied 5 per cent of their income. Money was taken from the accounts of Fantome Island patients to cover treatment, and 50 per cent of unclaimed accounts of missing or deceased persons was diverted to the department's standing account. Revenue created through the investment of bulk trust funds, "diverted towards the cost of maintaining the Aboriginal community, as a whole", was calculated to relieve state finances of nearly £15,000 per annum.[49] The government was well aware that appropriation of the interest component on Aboriginal savings, over the base Commonwealth Bank rate paid to account holders, was "not in accordance with Regulations".[50]

In 1935 the Labor government led by William Forgan Smith sought to make political mileage from the punitive creative accounting practices of Arthur Moore's Country-National Party coalition, in government for the 1929–1932 depression years. The coalition had milked Aboriginal savings for revenue, claimed government members, and raided trust funds to cover maintenance and administrative costs. In his defence, Moore sought evidence of all Aboriginal savings "appropriated for departmental purposes in each of the last ten financial years".[51] Briefing documents for minister Edward Hanlon's reply reveal that amounts totalling £18,960 from personal accounts and £72,032 from trust funds were diverted to offset government revenue between 1925 and 1935.[52] But Bleakley deviously advised his minister to deny any appropriation for departmental purposes: the above amounts, he prompted, "although withdrawn from deposits were actually deductions from earnings" and not from savings.[53]

With his own party so heavily implicated in the protracted misappropriation of funds, Hanlon took the dishonourable option floated by Bleakley, and further avowed that the interest bonus from Aboriginal accounts, yielding about £9,000 per annum, was used "solely for the benefit of destitute aboriginals, and not in any way for departmental purposes". But this was also untrue. Bleakley had explicitly informed the undersecretary that the bonus was pooled into the standing account which also paid out for mission assistance, and industrial improvement and development on settlements. Either Hanlon was lying to parliament, or his undersecretary did not fully disclose the unauthorised usage of Aboriginal monies.

Tennant Kelly's agenda to expose Queensland's handling of Aboriginal wages and savings to national scrutiny brought varied responses from her fellow academics. Ursula McConnel, with an eye it seems to her own professional future, distanced herself from both Tennant Kelly and Rev Morley, "neither of whom are fully qualified Anthropologists",[54] and suggested to Bleakley she could act as a consultant on "any project concerning anthropological co-operation in aboriginal affairs".[55] Elkin, in contrast, supported Tennant Kelly's activism: "We are up against vested interests", he told reporters, "and cannot hope to obtain any desirable reform without drastic change in Government policy".[56]

Government policy at state level was, as always, the province of politicians and bureaucrats. The uncompromising directness of the emerging "experts" on Aboriginal affairs was matched by the slamming of doors as career administrators defended their domains against the nonconformists. Tennant Kelly, advised Bleakley in a confidential reply to a request for his opinion from the Aborigines Protection Board in Sydney, "is not a suitable person" to carry out anthropological investigation on a government settlement. She interfered in administrative matters, gave ill-conceived advice, and her familiarity with "the natives" was subversive to discipline.[57]

The anthropologists, meanwhile, pursued their campaign to secure a pre-eminent position in Aboriginal policy formulation in the national forum. By the mid-1930s they were insisting that the plight of Aborigines was a national problem requiring a national solution. Would they infiltrate state practices from the springboard of federal agencies, as had their medical colleagues before them?

National forums

By the mid-1930s a second set of intellectual technologies was also operating to make population groups accessible to government attention and response. The activities of the Bureau of Census and Statistics, started in 1921, were building a separate national picture of the "Aboriginal problem". Research by the new body of specialists not only exposed differentiations in racial numbers, but also brought state practices under the eye of the national statistician. A 1925 conference of statisticians resolved to make annual surveys of Aborigines to ascertain "their numbers and the extent to which they enter the economic life in Australia".[58] Detailed information on location, employment, institutionalisation and housing in each state accumulated on federal files. By comparing figures from year to year, the Commonwealth statistician could, and did, demand explanations for variations in numbers. Administrators such as Bleakley were required to account more accurately for movements of people between districts, for mission and settlement numbers, and whether inmates were in "supervised camps" or in "regular employment".

Annual censuses also gave a clear indication of the changing demography of "full bloods" and "half-castes", highlighting the increase of the latter group. Between 1901 and 1911 the "half-caste" population grew by 3.2 per cent, double that of the non-Aboriginal population. In the following decade the increase was marginally greater, but by the mid-1930s the rate had jumped to 4.1 per cent, as against a growth rate of 1.5 per cent in the white population.[59] The figures bespoke the problem: what should be done about this mixed-race group?

In Queensland Bleakley had for several years pushed the idea of a separate "half-caste" colony, where technical training and citizenship education would equip individuals to "successfully make their way in the industrial world".[60] But his application for funds to develop the small Salvation Army mission at Purga near Brisbane was rejected. The negative attitudes of his superior, Undersecretary William Gall, were probably behind the scuttling of his plans. In a rambling epistle to Queensland's governor in 1934 Gall canvassed what he saw as the official options to deal with "the half-castes on the different Settlements". Side by side with the white race, he declared, "they will be undesirables". Marriage with "all blacks" would only result in "the breeding up of an inferior race", and marriage with whites would have the same outcome. Economic independence for this growing social group was severely limited by the priority of protecting white employment. Gall's ultimate suggestion to prevent "half-castes" becoming a charge on the state? "Governments, sooner or later, will have seriously to consider the question of sterilization". "Inferior races", he concluded, "will have to go".[61]

It was within this discourse of interracial sexual and labour "concerns" that Queensland's 1934 *Amendment Act* was debated and passed. This law dramatically expanded the net of official controls: new categories of mixed-race families now fell under departmental supervision; and existing certificates of exemption were initially revoked. While, as I have argued, the purpose of the changes was primarily to implement a program of medical and moral policing, the annulment of exemptions and the wider entrapment of state "wards" effectively stripped a large number of individuals of long-held political and social rights.

This was no oversight. Queensland's 1930 *Election Amendment Act* had already removed the right to vote at state elections for all those defined as "half-castes" under the Aboriginal Acts. Now all mixed-race individuals, their exemptions newly revoked, also lost voting entitlements at state level. This disenfranchisement was thrown into stark relief by the operations of Commonwealth electoral officers who recognised no such exclusions, and were pushing nationally to fill voting registers. Bleakley opposed this differentiation in eligibility. It caused "much confusion and discontent" among mixed-race voters, he protested, most of whom lacked either the interest or the intelligence to exercise their electoral prerogative, in his estimation. The prime minister, Joseph Lyons, refused to bring Commonwealth registration into line with Queensland. No other state had indicated any problems, wrote the prime minister, primarily because no other state had such restrictive eligibility.[62]

The removal of rights proved the catalyst for a highly public campaign, centered on Thursday Island. Nearly 240 Thursday Island residents, many of them returned soldiers, protested they were at risk of being defined as "Aboriginal" under the new legislation and would subsequently lose all control over their lives. The *Courier-Mail* ran emotive stories under such headings as "Whites become Blacks", suggesting that white men with Aboriginal wives could now be arbitrarily removed to Aboriginal settlements.[63] Furious with the unwelcome spotlight on departmental procedures, Bleakley attempted to downplay the dissent as merely an aftermath of the latest census, taken "to enable the coloured population to be correctly tabulated". So strident was the uproar that the attorney-general was sent to Thursday Island to meet a deputation of protesters and accept their petition to the home secretary.[64] The files show Bleakley immediately had every member investigated and passed this information to Gall.

The government line was that there had been no disenfranchisement of mixed-race citizens, merely a procedural reshuffling. But the Anglican bishop of Carpentaria, Bishop Stephen Davies, whose province extended across the whole of northern Australia, publicly refuted this. The government's own assertions that exemptions would be reinstated after medical clearances proved that "full rights of citizenship have been temporarily withdrawn", he told the *Courier-Mail.* "This latest legislation helps to confirm our view that in Queensland the tendency of policy in dealing with the weaker race is to restrict their freedom and even to lower their status." It was morally wrong, he continued, that the whole population group should be penalised because of the health problems of a few "delinquents".[65] He urged the Commonwealth government to take full control of Aboriginal affairs throughout Australia. Bleakley sourly observed that the Bishop was "in the business too" of maligning his administration.

There is evidence on file that in 1936 Bleakley drafted a new Amendment Bill to relinquish departmental controls over "quarter-castes", and to free children of exempt "halfcastes" from departmental dominion. In an attempt to mollify irate Thursday Islanders it was also proposed to transfer discretionary powers over assessment of liability of mixed-race individuals to state control from the chief protector to the law courts. But action on this draft Bill was delayed continually through 1937 and subsequently dropped.[66]

On the national front the federal government was also under fire after several highly publicised atrocities, and outrage at the questionable application of "justice" in the Commonwealth-managed Northern Territory. Bleakley's comments at the time give an indication of administrative attitudes to such exposure: "It is unfortunate that the Commonwealth Government has had to suffer considerable annoyance and inconvenience because of the garbled and often mischievous stories which have been circulated through the Press".[67] In an exercise in political face-saving, federal Cabinet declared it would heed a resolution passed by the Science Congress that a national plan be formulated for the "care and development of the aboriginal race". As a preliminary step Dr Donald Thomson was appointed by the Commonwealth to "study the natives in their natural conditions" in Arnhem Land and advise on policy direction.[68] And in 1936 the conference of Commonwealth and state ministers voted to initiate a national Aboriginal Welfare Conference the following year.

While the anthropologists lobbied vociferously for a nationalised Aboriginal administration, the states had no intention of submitting to federal interference. Centralised control, argued Bleakley "would prove far too costly".[69] Undersecretary William Gall was also less than enthusiastic. Who would act as protectors since all existing officers — teachers, police, and public servants — were state employees? And what if the Commonwealth demanded land for reserves which the states might be loathe to commit? When the inaugural national Welfare Conference got under way early in 1937, bureaucrats and politicians abounded. Excluded were representatives from missionary boards, from Aboriginal Protection organisations, from the press, and, most pointedly, the most senior anthropologist in Australia, Professor Elkin.

As senior administrator, Bleakley submitted an eleven-page agenda suggesting a standard policy to safeguard nomadic tribes in their development towards self-dependence, to control and protect the "detribalised", and to "uplift" "superior crossbreeds".[70] But it was quickly apparent at the conference that the states had widely differing views on long-term policy: proposals by Western Australian that the "Aboriginal race" should be gradually "absorbed" into the white race through interbreeding were opposed outright by Queensland and the southern states. Aboriginal people should be allowed to retain their "racial entity", insisted Bleakley, adding that there would be absolutely no public support even for "constrained intermarriage". He also opposed a modified proposal that "half-castes" could be "bred out" through intermarriage: only "low whites" entered such unions, he argued, and the marriages were rarely successful. Ever the pragmatist, Bleakley concluded that such a policy would "not meet the difficulty of otherwise providing for the lawful mating desires of the men folk thus deprived of their potential wives".[71]

Although many historians have argued otherwise, Bleakly was quite explicit that there would be no "breeding out" of "half-castes". Rather, his assimilation policy centred on the "socialising in" of individuals trained to take their

place in the white community.[72] Queensland's policy of
self-supporting communities to provide education and vocational training for placement in local industries was held
as a model for such assimilation. It was also generally agreed
that "primitive natives" needed protection on inviolate
reserves in their local areas. Here Queensland came in for
criticism. The strategy of settlement and simple agriculture
on remote missions "was received dubiously as only encouraging herding into Compounds to depend on white man's
foods and expose them to epidemic diseases", he reported.[73]

Well-pleased with their frank exchange of views, the
administrators proposed a series of rolling conferences.
Again "humanitarian organisations" would be excluded
because their lack of practical experience and "divergent
views" would only "confuse the issues". But the meetings
never eventuated and Bleakley later remarked bitterly that
the initial conference had probably "fulfilled its purpose as
a piece of political window-dressing, and ceased to be a
matter of interest".[74] There were no national conferences
for more than ten years.

Although Elkin had been excluded from the conference
of state policy-makers, he continued to influence federal
directions from behind the scenes through his close friendship with John McEwen, minister for the interior from late
1937. The federal government had been subjected to a
barrage of critical publicity from anthropologists on the
international stage after a series of scandals in the Northern
Territory. McEwen delegated Elkin to investigate and report, and the outcome was a declaration by the federal
government of a "New Deal" for the nation's Aborigines.
Launched by McEwen in 1939, and closely reproducing an

earlier treatise by Elkin, the federal policy stipulated a redirection from negative protection to positive training.

At the same time, a federal department of Aboriginal Affairs was established under anthropologist E. W. Chinnery, former director of Native Affairs in New Guinea. The stated aims of the department were to raise the status of Aborigines to qualify for the "ordinary rights of citizenship" and to help them share in the opportunities "available in their native land". Elkin wrote approvingly that Chinnery brought "both anthropological knowledge and much administrative experience to bear on the problem".[75] Bishop Davies was also impressed with Chinnery's dual qualifications: "I have seen the result of giving full control of Aboriginal affairs firstly to an anthropologist then to a medical man, the first was the late Professor B. Spencer, the second Dr Cook, both excellent men in their own spheres but great failures in administrative positions".[76]

Queensland, however, had no time for the new experts. Aborigines have become "fashionable" in recent years, minister Edward Hanlon remarked sarcastically to his colleagues, and "all sorts of people have sprung up with ideas as to what should be done with them". After a "short, crammed course in anthropology in the wild outback of Sydney" the "new race of anthropologists" were now "demanding appointment in the department" insisting they were the only people qualified to handle native affairs. Hanlon scorned any suggestion that long-serving administrators should "make room for these experts".[77] Nearly twenty years later Cornelius O'Leary, then director of Native Affairs in Queensland, recalled Hanlon's attitude to federal control: "When the Commonwealth Government gets rid of its cranks and Anthropologists I will give consideration to the matter".[78]

An *"uplifted status"*

Queensland's rejection of anthropological counsel did not denote a policy vacuum. Bleakley was a committed and ambitious public servant, constantly seeking greater efficiency in his management of the Aboriginal population. In a detailed report submitted in 1938[79] he called for a radical restructuring of policy and practices. The missions, he wrote, were characterised by missionary despair and financial wastage. Under the present system, poverty was so entrenched that government grants intended for community development went to rations. Even so, mission inmates spent so much time foraging for bush foods that building and agricultural programs stalled. None of the missions had medical facilities and most lacked trained teachers. There should be a formal division of responsibility: the churches should provide all missionary needs, and the state subsidy should cover food, health, education, building and industrial needs.

The wayward network of police protectors had also exercised Bleakley's mind. Inevitably, he noted, the conflict of interests between policing and protecting occurred "frequently ... and the second has to be subordinated to the first". Police could not act as defenders of Aboriginal interests while at the same time they prosecuted as police. Most police were not qualified for their Aboriginal duties, argued Bleakley, citing the several cases of "dereliction of duty and abuses on the part of a number of Police Protectors" as evidence. The rapid turnover in rural areas meant most men were neither familiar with their duties nor trusted by local Aboriginal people.[80] Bleakley urged that police be replaced by civil protectors, and all aspects of Aboriginal management in rural areas be supervised by two trained travelling inspectors.

The third aspect of Bleakley's restructuring proposals was aimed at "uplifting" the "superior cross-breeds" to allow absorption into the white community. Minister Edward Hanlon had argued enthusiastically in parliament in favour of such social progress. Treating "half-castes" as Aborigines, he told his colleagues in 1937, was "retarding their progress". What was needed was new villages with "proper homes", an "ordinary school", and private enterprise shops and industries.[81]

But the government declined to bankroll any of Bleakley's reforms; and there was no intention of supporting the many "intelligent half-castes" on the settlements. On the contrary, it was argued that the government should implement measures "that would mean their gradual decontrol". Such "decontrol" would not only benefit Aborigines. Bleakley later observed: "In political quarters some advantage was seen in the fact that numbers of such half-bloods, previously made subject to the Act, would, if free, be entitled to the franchise".[82]

The *Aboriginals Preservation and Protection Act* was introduced late in 1939, "to achieve the desired emancipation", as Bleakley phrased it.[83] "Half-castes will be free to earn their own living and live their own lives", exulted Hanlon, "unless a court places him under the control of the Chief Protector of Aboriginals".[84] In a none-too-subtle jibe at those who condemned deprivation of rights under the previous law, Hanlon now boasted that 2,400 half-castes had already been exempted from total control. The new emancipation would, as Bleakley later admitted, repair political damage and lighten the financial load.

A much narrower category defined those who would remain under departmental control. An Aboriginal under the new Act was someone having a preponderance of "Aboriginal blood", one declared by a court to be in need of care and protection, a resident of a reserve, or the child of an Aboriginal mother on a reserve. The term "half-caste" was now replaced by "half-blood", and applied only to a person of Aboriginal/European parentage, or a person of part-Aboriginal parents who had between 25 per cent and 50 per cent "Aboriginal blood".

Children over sixteen of "half-caste" parents were now swept into Bleakley's dominion: he was nominated legal guardian of every Aboriginal child in the state under the age of twenty-one *even when the parents were living*. In such a role he could authorise marriage or adoption. This resolved a significant anomaly. Previously the Native Affairs department had no power to sanction adoptions of Aboriginal children despite countless requests from white "benefactors". In principle the department denounced such adoptions, arguing that children were likely to be exploited as free labour and were often rejected on adulthood. In practice, however, there is evidence on file of cases where small boys were left with pastoral families on condition that they received some schooling and were not overworked. The department was well aware of the child labour aspect of "adoptions". With reference to small girls, deputy chief protector Cornelius O'Leary remarked: "The general training of an aboriginal child in a white home makes it difficult for her to enter an aboriginal camp later should the adopted parents leave the district or decide they will keep her no longer".[85]

On the other hand, on government settlements officials routinely applied pressure to "induce the mother of a child showing marked European colouring" to relinquish the baby for adoption to white parents.[86] Such light-skinned "wards of the state" were processed through orphanages until passage of *The Adoption of Children Act* in 1935 authorised the State Children's Department to handle Aboriginal adoptions.[87] In an illuminating aside, in Bleakley's 1937 application for salary upgrading (one of a stream of frustrated approaches) his comparison of his position as equal to that of the better-paid director of State Children was disputed on the grounds that "care of an aboriginal child would not be as important to the State as that of its white child". Bleakley vehemently disagreed.[88]

Under the 1939 *Aboriginals Preservation and Protection Act* Bleakley's position was recast from chief protector to Director of Native Affairs, a title encompassing his jurisdiction over people of the Torres Strait Islands, for whom parallel legislation was enacted. Bleakley's authority was considerably enhanced. He took over previous ministerial powers regarding forced removal of individuals to missions and reserves, the issuing and cancelling of certificates of exemption, the prosecution of "moral offences", and the control of mining on reserves.[89] His empire at this time covered nearly 3,000 settlement inmates, around 3,500 each for missions and the Torres Strait Islands, and a further 7,000 people listed as in "supervised camps" in rural areas.[90] He commanded nineteen staff in Brisbane and a further ninety-two on the Torres Strait Islands and government settlements.

But how well did he run his empire? A 1941 public service investigation into the operations of the department revealed extensive negligence.[91] And Bleakley was singled out for particular blame — he could not answer questions correctly, was unaware of official incompetence and failed to discipline careless officials. Head office was overstaffed, yet filing was haphazard: for many months it had been common knowledge that records were hopelessly muddled. Accounts were improperly kept, no internal checks were in place to detect fraud and error, and Bleakley failed to make proper inquiries for the disposal of savings of dead or missing workers to their relatives.

Administrative malpractice was particularly costly for Aboriginal workers. It was blatantly illegal, declared the inspectors, to use interest earned on combined private savings accounts to offset government expenditure. By law, all accounts over £50 should have been individually credited with any interest due, a distribution they calculated at £5,882 on the total of £190,489. The practice of loading retail store prices above purchase and transport costs on the settlements was also condemned as "making a profit out of the aboriginals". Neither the "collection" of interest revenue from the Property Account and the Provident Fund, nor the extra tax on settlement workers, were judged to be legitimate, and the inspectors argued that the standing account, through which these monies were laundered, should be abolished.

Under normal circumstances, the commissioners advised the minister, Bleakley would be charged under the *Public Service Acts* with incompetence and inefficiency. But on the premise that the situation had resulted "from causes outside his control" Bleakley was summoned to appear before a medical tribunal to assess his fitness to continue. When he learned Dr Cilento was to be one of his examiners, Bleakley protested, "I cannot, with confidence, look upon him as an unbiased referee".[92] The commissioner was unmoved. Bleakley was judged unfit for administrative responsibility due to "nervous debility suggestive of cerebral arterio sclerosis"[93] and offered the choice of dismissal or retirement. He took the latter option and was granted nine months' sick leave of absence on full pay, after forty-one years with the native affairs department.

Bleakley's position was filled by Cornelius O'Leary. Born in Murwillumbah in 1898, O'Leary was the son of a railway worker. At only 15 years of age he joined Queensland's Native Affairs department and by the age of 26 held the key position of Thursday Island protector. He was only 32 when he was sent to restore order on Palm Island after Curry's death in 1930, and was promoted to deputy Chief Protector five years later. A 1952 article in *People* magazine described him as an "explosive and go-getting" man with "a nominal *kingdom* of 22,000 subjects". After ten years as chief protector it was said his "dogmatic" and "bombastic" attitude "toward the natives, whom he wants to integrate into the community as useful and respected citizens" had attracted bitter criticism.

O'Leary inherited a most irregular set of financial practices, as the public service commissioners had disclosed. And government auditors also challenged the legitimacy of departmental authority, pointing out that the 1939 *Aboriginals Preservation and Protection Act* had repealed all existing regulations, and no updated regulations had yet been finalised. Therefore, noted the auditor, there was effectively no authority covering deductions from Aboriginal wages, transfers of deceased accounts to the Aboriginal Protection Property Account, or transfers of trust funds to the departments standing account. Further, he declared that reduced wages on settlements and charges levied for settlement maintenance were illegal even with respect to the previous regulations.[94]

Operations on the standing account, which merged several disputable levies on Aboriginal wages with outlays which were strictly government obligations, had been condemned in successive *Audit Reports* over many years. O'Leary was keen to clean up the transactions, urging the government to budget for the extra £19,000 per annum it was currently "saving" through the laundered levies.[95] Ultimately the government created the Aboriginal Welfare Fund in 1943, framing the regulations specifically to legitimise its customary diversion of trust moneys to cover administrative costs under the euphemism of "providing benefits to aboriginals generally".[96] Started with an injection of £50,000 from consolidated revenue, the Welfare fund received all interest on invested funds, the 5 per cent levy on savings accounts, and proceeds from settlement stores and cattle and produce sales. The fund was *not* authorised to finance operational grants to missions, the cost of relief to indigent Aborigines, or forced removal expenses. Levies on rural workers into the Provident Fund were reduced to 5 per cent for single men and $2^1/_2$ per cent for married men. Settlement workers were still taxed 5 per cent for single and 10 per cent for married men towards amenities and maintenance.

*   *   *

In the national forum the 1930s were a period of high

profile and ultimately high achievement for anthropologists as emerging authorities in Aboriginal affairs. Elkin's close association with the Minister for the Interior, John McEwen, had cemented a new national approach and was certainly a factor in both the launching of a federal department of Aboriginal Affairs and in the placement of an anthropologist at its head. At state level, however, the exclusion of anthropological expertise from practical administration was almost absolute. Horrified by unwanted publicity and allegedly unwarranted attacks on procedures of control and "protection", state administrators closed ranks to ban the new "experts" from the national Aboriginal Welfare Conference. Welfare, it seemed, was not just a matter of Aboriginal requirements.

In tandem with anthropological advocacy for policy redirection from negative protection to active promotion of Aboriginal advancement, research from the new science of census-taking gave measurable content to the "half-caste problem". Comparison of numbers confined to settlements at government expense could be made with the considerable population in employment and in residence in the wider community. The push to reduce dependency in Queensland by narrowing the categories of control had the added benefit of repairing some of the electoral damage arising from the previous *Amendment Act*. And by the early 1940s restructured departmental accounting practices theoretically rectified malpractices exposed by internal investigations and reports.

6
National priorities

Authority for Commonwealth leverage in state Aboriginal affairs is generally thought to have originated in the 1967 national referendum, but records show federal penetration since the 1920s. Activities of specialists in disciplines such as epidemiology and statistics had to be accommodated by state administrators. Anthropological inquiry, although incorporated at a federal level in the late 1930s, continued to be ostracised by Queensland government personnel.

The 1940s were to be a period of intense federal involvement in Queensland. With the outbreak of war, national priorities took precedence over state sanction. Manpower and matériel were mobilised; northern areas were perceived as under imminent threat of invasion; thousands of troops poured into Queensland's coastal towns. What impact did these activities have on the Aboriginal population in the cities and in remote north Queensland? What measures did O'Leary's administration put in place to maintain control during this time of flux? What were the effects of wartime rationing and shortages on Aboriginal communities habitually on the brink of collapse? And how were the broader social pension schemes, also a feature from the 1940s, applied to Queensland's Aboriginal population?

War services

Prior to the outbreak of hostilities there were no formal restrictions to enlistment and many "full-blood" men, Torres Strait Islanders and part-Aborigines volunteered. In May 1940, however, the army decreed that non-European volunteers were "neither necessary nor desirable", but soon backed down after considerable pressure, including calls from anthropologists and lobby groups who highlighted the proud service and sacrifices of Aboriginal and Islander men in World War I. A deputation of Brisbane men had called on Bleakley to argue their case with the army, and O'Leary later wrote approvingly that despite the early sanctions several men "managed to get into the forces".[1] Over eight hundred Aboriginal and Islander soldiers throughout Australia fought in the services.

If the possibility of equal pay was a factor in the enthusiasm to enlist, the men were soon disabused. Aboriginal and Islander soldiers received only one-third the white pay rate, rising to two-thirds in February 1944.[2] Bleakley demanded control of the wages of more than two hundred Aboriginal soldiers from Queensland, but was granted management of only sixty-two accounts, and kept a tight rein on withdrawals.[3] It was official policy that all returned soldiers were entitled to exemption, but in practice this was conditional on "their conduct etc. [being] reasonably satisfactory".[4] Exemption, of course, meant expulsion from missions or settlements. Many men did not take up the option.

The war effort presented a boon for Aboriginal employment which Queensland's administrators were quick to exploit. O'Leary unsuccessfully proposed that three hundred men could be consigned to the army as scouts and trackers. Instead, an army of Aboriginal and part-Aboriginal workers from the government settlements were transferred around the state to replace white workers in the peanut, cotton, maize and arrowroot industries.

The manpower programs were a federal initiative, so full wages were paid to all workers. And the Australian Workers' Union forced Queensland's native affairs department to concede that all Aboriginal men would be *temporarily* unionised and would *temporarily* enjoy the same rights as other workers, except the right to drink at hotels.[5] By August 1942 more than 550 men, including groups from Mapoon and Yarrabah, were bringing in £46,680, all streamed through departmental control. By 1943, when over 700 men were so employed, revenue rose to £61,790.

Aboriginal women were also pressed into service, harvesting crops in the absence of men. On the settlements they also produced large quantities of clothing for departmental wards, filling the dire shortage of ready-made wear. O'Leary had rejected the option of ration books, available under the federal clothing ration scheme for all institutional inmates, on the grounds that Aboriginal clothing needs were much less than for whites, and that Aborigines were likely to traffic in the coupons since they would not "appreciate the seriousness of the breach".[6]

Workers remaining on the settlements were under intense pressure to increase the production of vegetables for the benefit of army and allied personnel as well as for factory workers. This raised the problem of enforcement. At Woorabinda superintendent Colledge bemoaned the lack of "drastic measures" for those who "will not go to work". All the best men, he complained to O'Leary, are out on manpower schemes. "We are left with a lot of wasters" and "we cannot find any punishment severe enough for some of them".[7] Men with holiday breaks from defence work often collected their wives from domestic positions organised by the department, contravening the hated work agreements in order to spend time together as a family on the settlements.

The greatest surveillance of the war years was imposed on Aboriginal women and girls, even those not officially under departmental control. As the presence of allied soldiers in towns and cities fuelled an obsessive preoccupation with moral and medical scrutiny, police and native affairs officers colluded to investigate any claims of consorting. Complaints from an army camp on Brisbane's outskirts that the presence of women in nearby huts was encouraging sexual promiscuity were investigated by police and found to be groundless. Even so, removal of the women to a settlement was recommended and approved on the grounds that they were living in a lonely area and without male relations. The women returned to New South Wales before the order could be effected.[8]

Police admitted that the mere presence of "coloured" girls in the city provoked groundless allegations of prostitution: paranoia peaked when black American soldiers were involved. "Streams of black soldiers" are visiting "three coloured prostitutes" day and night, wrote one "concerned neighbour" who lodged a formal complaint of police inaction. Inquiries revealed three "highly respectable" girls employed in a city shop, but living in a house where the owner did laundry for black servicemen — hence the streams of black soldiers!

All males and females under departmental control were "rounded up" by Brisbane police and sent to settlements or to contracted rural work. Public antagonism to Aboriginal men drinking in hotels prompted the department to arrange for a young Cherbourg man to act as a "native policeman to assist in investigations" in South Brisbane, an area of cheap lodgings and favoured by Aborigines. It was found that none of the men were subject to departmental control. Two returned soldiers interrogated by police declared that they had as much right to drink in hotels as the whites who had not seen army service.[9] When the *Courier-Mail* ran an article in 1945 featuring the extreme hardship and poverty of families living in this area,[10] O'Leary was able to detail for his minister the "breed" and sexual history of each complainant, even though no names and addresses appeared in the article and most were not under departmental control.

Military mentality

Irrational exaggerations over the incidence and dissemination of venereal disease triggered punitive and often illogical sanctions against local Aboriginal populations, particularly where the large troop movements in north Queensland were concerned. When two suspected cases of VD were identified at Yarrabah, it was suggested that infection may have originated with manpower workers returning to the mission. Correspondence from Palm Island, with a far larger contingent of men out on manpower programs, did not support this theory, and subsequent clinical tests on the suspects proved negative. Nevertheless, because of the army camp at False Cape on Yarrabah's boundary, both the superintendent and the protector enforced a virtual curfew to put Cairns off-limits to all Aboriginal women for the duration of the war.

Given the considerable level of veneral disease in the

armed forces, the military hierarchy was particularly extreme in its haste to apportion blame. When a large camp was set up near the independent mission of Cowal Creek at the tip of Cape York, army authorities wanted the mission population removed, claiming that infection among the troops was "traced to the native women". Although a check by health professionals revealed no infected women at Cowal Creek, the whole community was banished to a previously abandoned settlement site.

Army command consistently alleged that venereal disease "is so widespread among natives of the peninsula as to constitute a menace to troops stationed in the vicinity".[11] Infuriated by this spurious maligning of mission populations, Rev David Galloway, moderator of the Presbyterian Church, remonstrated with both the Minister for War in Canberra and the Minister for National Security. Weekly inspections prove there have been no cases of VD on the Presbyterian missions for several years, he wrote, and the allegation was both false and malicious.[12] All other Cape York missions reported similarly.

Military authorities also cavalierly impugned Aboriginal loyalty. National security officials had questioned Rev Galloway, alleging that men from Mapoon had worked closely with Japanese boat-crews in the past and "would not hesitate to sell us out if the opportunity arose". No Japanese had been on any of the Presbyterian mission stations for over a generation, he retaliated, and it had never been departmental policy to sign Aborigines or part-Aborigines with Japanese crews, whose poor treatment was well known. "Further", continued Galloway, "the allegation so frequently made by ill-informed persons, that an aboriginal will sell out at any time for a stick of tobacco, is a libel on an already much maligned race".

In an interesting variation on this theme, anthropologist Donald Thomson, now an RAAF flight lieutenant, was asked to use his earlier contacts with Aborigines in Arnhem Land "to re-establish friendly relations ... and to undermine any sympathy for the Japanese which [they] may have harboured". Thomson recruited forty-nine men for a special early warning unit but had difficulty convincing them that it was now desirable to shoot disembarking Japanese on sight, because three men had been imprisoned ten years' earlier for just this action.[13]

Acting on "information" from several sources, a special army intelligence investigation concluded that less than 1 per cent of the 10,000 Aborigines on Cape York could be relied upon to be loyal.[14] Although this was quickly discredited as a gross distortion, and despite opposition from both mission and departmental authorities, plans were made to transfer most of the Aboriginal population south to Townsville where they could be more closely watched. Evidence in the Presbyterian archives provides an alternative insight: "It is unofficial, but we understand that this is done not because of any expected invasion, but to keep them from contact with soldiers who are apparently expected to be in that part of the world ... of course the Army has the last word".[15]

Arguing that it would be "against their best interests" for Aborigines to be evacuated, the Presbyterian mission committee insisted "if the people keep hidden I do not think they will be molested". No doubt with an eye to logistics and costs, the minister concurred. Ultimately only one mission was evacuated to the south: the circumstances and consequences of this action will be discussed below. But, with invasion deemed imminent in 1942, defence strategies drastically affected the Aboriginal institutions of the north — institutions already labouring under severe privation.

Under threat

As the Japanese pushed towards Australia, all female staff were evacuated from Thursday Island and the Torres Straits, and the wives of missionaries were also sent south for safety. Contingency plans developed by superintendent Bill MacKenzie at Aurukun were adopted by all Presbyterian missions. In the event of a Japanese landing all the "biggest dormitory girls" were to be "married off", and the smaller children returned to their parents where possible. People would take to the bush and swamps where canoes and dinghies had already been hidden. Emergency caches of food, clothing and medicines were secreted at designated spots around the reserve and a scorched earth policy would be followed with regard to property and stock.[16]

Mornington Island staff were notified in February 1942 that the invasion of Australia was a matter of hours away. Most of the community were dispersed to the bush, but military authorities demanded that thirteen "half-caste" girls from the dormitory and six infant boys, described as "comprising those who had no natural male protector", be immediately evacuated to the mainland. Here the older girls were contracted out as domestics and the remainder sent to Doomadgee,[17] a mission started in 1936 by the Plymouth Brethren initially on the Gulf, but soon moved one hundred kilometres to the south. In an intriguing corollary, several girls later married Doomadgee men, in-

spiring a minor religious spat after war's end as to which
mission "owned" the families.[18]

The panic on Mornington Island proved presumptuous,
but the threat to shipping movements and the comman-
deering by the army of all serviceable craft left the Gulf
missions in crisis. Frequent bombing raids disrupted con-
signments processed through the department's Thursday
Island depot. According to Presbyterian authorities, however, losses to bombing were nowhere near as devastating
as consistent and extensive pillaging on the wharves. "Shipping matters are so desperate that we are fortunate if we
can get our foodstuffs through with comparatively small
loss", wrote Rev Dan Brown, "and there seems to be no
redress, as all the shipping is in charge of the Military
Authorities".[19] Deprivation was compounded by the department's refusal to sanction ration coupons, thus preventing mission authorities from dealing directly with State
Stores.

Wartime correspondence reveals that the Gulf missions
were commonly deprived of food, clothes, tobacco and
medicines. With no tobacco, the major incentive exploited
by missions to elicit regular attendance, many of the men
from Edward River went bush or frequented the cattle
stations seeking supplies, causing "serious aggravation" to
mission authority. On Mornington Island, clothing was in
tatters and people stuffed holes with grass "to hide their
bodies ... Pants have been issued sparingly to the females,
made from all sorts of unpicked garments, sheeting etc". At
Mitchell River, superintendent MacLeod complained that
half the petrol ration had "gone astray" after dispatch from
Thursday Island. Without petrol the mission boat was useless and "we are back more or less to bush food". But the

petrol-driven wireless was a more critical loss: endemic sickness came hand in hand with poor diet, and the Normanton doctor could not be contacted. "It is rather hard to have to sit down and watch youngsters just pass out for the simple reason that you cannot get food supplies for them."[20]

On the more southerly Palm Island settlement evacuation was not a threat although air raid shelters were dug as a precaution. Even though all available men were sent to the mainland on manpower programs, admissions ceased in 1941 because of drastic underfunding and war shortages. A public service inspection for that year makes grim reading. Residents were forced to drink from creekholes where dogs and fowl paddled, sanitation was deplorable, children lacked milk, and no vegetables had been issued for four months.[21]

In an attempt to relieve the situation, Cherbourg and Woorabinda were pressured to take about fifty "healthy, good conduct men and women" — after all, admonished O'Leary, Palm Island had for many years accepted "practically all your refractory cases". To avoid trouble, superintendent Foote from Palm Island urged secrecy, but O'Leary was adamant any transfers should be voluntary. Skilled men from Palm Island were to be dispatched to build the necessary bark huts. When the carpenters refused to work without proper pay superintendent Foote ordered them south on *reduced* wages.[22]

The wartime exposure of Palm Island's population crisis prompted a change in policy: in mid-1942 it was decided to reduce numbers by 20 per cent. All families possible, except "incorrigible aboriginals" would be transferred to home missions and country reserves. This repatriation continued over several years. Half the patients on Fantome Island were also returned, and, with the subsequent breakthrough of penicillin treatment, the VD clinic closed down in 1945. Henceforth the policy was to operate Palm Island as a "corrective settlement" of no more than one thousand persons.[23]

Although all missions and settlements were severely disadvantaged by wartime shortages and military pressures, ultimately only one institution was evacuated. This was the Lutheran mission at Cape Bedford near Cooktown, hardly in the remote north or exposed in the Gulf of Carpentaria. Why was this so?

Death in the south

It was a press scandal (later proved false) over alleged treasonable activities of German missionaries in New Guinea which brought all those working in Australia under suspicion. The Presbyterians were called upon to vouch for the loyalty of Rev Braunholz, temporarily in command at Mornington Island. At the Lutheran mission at Cape Bedford, anti-German paranoia over Pastor Schwartz was compounded by an army security report relaying rumours of pro-Japanese sentiments among the Aboriginal population: "Aboriginals openly stated that the Japs told them that the country belonged to the blacks, had been stolen from them by the whites and that 'bye and bye' (the Japanese) would give it back to them".[24]

Military authorities demanded the mission be disbanded. While plans were finalised, Rev Schwartz was kept under armed guard and his belongings searched. The mission car was confiscated in April 1942 leaving no transport for medical emergencies. In May it was decided to send most of the 271 residents to Taroom, now renamed as Woorabinda. Because "they may not be able to stand the cold at Woorabinda",[25] elderly people and pregnant women were to go to Palm Island: subsequent evidence suggests this did not occur.

The relocation was appallingly bungled. Under military and police guard, people were refused time to gather clothing and belongings. Apart from a meal at Cooktown no food was available next morning, nor on the fourteen-hour boat trip to Cairns, nor on the overnight train until 5.30 am at Cardwell. Nothing was provided from that evening until Rockhampton was reached the following afternoon.

Woorabinda was nowhere near ready to accept them. The camp at the Blackboy site was not ready despite several months' notice. When finished, the single-layer bark walls and roofs let in wind and rain. Although in a known frost area, the northern arrivals were issued only one single blanket each and had to sleep on the ground. An epidemic of mumps was raging, the milk was contaminated, and on the week of their arrival the water once again tested unfit for human consumption. Almost immediately a spate of gastric problems confirmed the indigestibility of settlement rations for those accustomed to a diet rich in fish, fruit, game and maizemeal. Within six months seven women and thirteen young children were dead from gastroenteritis, influenza and pneumonia. Even in this crisis, according to the evidence, visiting medical officer Dr Blackburn attended the settlement for only one hour a week.

The terrible attrition escalated as an epidemic of measles swept the settlement in January 1943. Diagnosed at Coomera where men were harvesting arrowroot under the manpower scheme, carriers were not quarantined (as were the whites) but were returned to Woorabinda. Within a month 126 lay stricken, far more than the settlement clinic could accommodate. Records show Dr Blackburn still visited only once weekly. The death-rate among evacuees from Cape Bedford reached thirty-three — five adults, fourteen babies and fourteen children.

At this point Cilento stepped in, sending senior health officer Dr D. Johnson to investigate the deplorable mortality.[26] Johnson condemned both medical negligence and the lethal environment. Most adults and children were thin, weak and listless, he reported, describing their protruding abdomens as symptomatic of gross hookworm infestation. Most of the child deaths were directly attributable to hookworm debility: despite laboratory tests taken six months earlier which identified the disease, no action had been taken. "I can only conclude", reported Johnson, "that the Visiting Medical Officer was indifferent and that he did not realise the seriousness of hookworm disease".

Johnson's critique ranged from the clinical to the operational. He condemned substandard shelter, milk so scarce children got only 10 per cent of *minimum* needs, and people forced to use contaminated wells and creek water because the turbid, metallic-tasting tap water petered out midmorning. In a heated defence, superintendent Colledge denied starvation on the settlement, and placed blame for the "susceptibility to illness" of the newcomers on their "deplorable condition" on arrival, after a journey so traumatic that several women went into premature labour resulting in neo-natal deaths.[27] Someone was lying. A letter on file from Dr Blackburn declares that all evacuees arrived "in a healthy condition".

Colledge's attitude to his charges appalled Johnson, who described him as "an uncouth individual, fond of complaining". He bitterly resented the complications caused by the Cape Bedford arrivals, wrote Johnson, and "does not appear to have the interests of the aboriginal at heart at all times". Johnson described this mentality as all too typical of Aboriginal administrators: negligence and indifference to Aboriginal needs were a "national characteristic". "An impression has developed that a white person is entitled to better treatment than a black person, because the aboriginal is an inferior being. This feeling is obvious at Aboriginal Settlements, where the white officials live under much better conditions than do the aboriginals." Complaints dismissed as trivial, and habitual disinterest in Aboriginal needs, prevailed on every settlement he visited. Aboriginal patients did not receive "the same personal attention as would patients in a public hospital" at the poorly equipped and poorly staffed settlement substitutes.

O'Leary conceded that Dr Johnson's observations were "essentially true in the main" but declared that the department "consistently sets it face against such attitude". The principal difficulty, said O'Leary, "is the type of official appointed to an Aboriginal Settlement".[28] Blaming the officers was the easy option. What of the substandard hospitals? Inadequate staffing? Hovels for housing? Unsafe water and contaminated milk? It was much more than the poor calibre of superintendents which made life so precarious: these state-controlled institutions were impoverished communities of impoverished individuals.

It was during the war years that a federal government scheme was launched specifically to alleviate family deprivation and distress through the provision of personal financial subsidies. How did the state respond to this initiative? What were the outcomes for Queensland's Aboriginal families?

Social security

To facilitate the war effort, the Commonwealth government had assumed sole rights for the collection of income tax. As recompense for state revenue loss, a series of social security programs was initiated. Child endowment payments were introduced in 1941 for all mothers, including *de facto* and foster, with dependants under sixteen years of age. Only those Aboriginal mothers living nomadic lives were excluded from these benefits.

Aboriginal mothers with "a preponderance of white blood" had been eligible since 1912 for the Commonwealth maternity allowance. But records show that this cash bonus was routinely and unlawfully usurped since 1928 on missions and settlements, and used to cover clothing and medical expenses which were legally an institutional cost. Mothers of dormitory children received only 20 per cent of the allowance, and only 50 per cent was paid to mothers with children at home.[29]

Altered qualifications in 1942 enabled all "full blood" women to claim the maternity allowance, provided they were not living on state-controlled communities. In a vehement and protracted campaign Queensland's native affairs department sought to reverse such anomalies. No such exclusion clause prevails for "half blood" women, they protested, so why should some women be penalised on a purely "colour" criterion? And why, on the basis of residence on an Aboriginal community, should Aborigines also be excluded for old-age, invalid and widow's pensions?

There is a simple solution, replied the Commonwealth: release them from state controls and they will qualify.

This avid pursuit of pensions cannot be taken at face value. The department was profiting very nicely from the private pensions. With the introduction of child endowment all settlements promptly applied for recognition as state institutions, thus procuring a bulk monthly payment on the grounds that the mothers might not use the cash for the child's benefit. Only a fraction was paid to the parents.

Mission authorities, urged to take similar measures, were excited at the financial bonanza. With three hundred eligible children, the Presbyterians were soon flush with funds, the first quarterly payments netting £926 and £973, an annual equivalent of 40 per cent more than the *total* government grant. We will have to demonstrate we are using the money to the children's best advantage, Rev Dan Brown cautioned the missionaries, ticking off items such as new dormitories, schools and better qualified teachers, clothing, "probably some extra necessaries in the homes of some of the children at least", and perhaps 25 per cent should be set aside "on extra foodstuffs for the children".[30]

Their euphoria was short-lived. Savaged by evacuation costs for Cape Bedford and Hammond Island in the Torres Straits, the department slashed mission subsidies in 1942. "I cannot say that it was unexpected so far as I am concerned", wrote a disgusted Dan Brown. "I was sure when we received the Child Endowment, that the State would attempt something of this kind." "Blankets, clothing, and all other things are cut right out. They quite evidently think that the Child Endowment is going to cover their omissions", he informed MacKenzie. But government grants for rations and clothing now totalled only one-tenth of child endowment revenue, and this latter could by law only be spent on the children. Without the federal income "we should have been in desperate financial straits ... just what we are going to do for the older people, I do not know".[31] In fact, the state grant of £2,400 represented barely "one penny per head per day for all the people on our stations".[32]

At the Anglican missions, and in the Torres Straits, the child endowment quota was passed on in full. Parents on the Presbyterian missions successfully challenged mission authorities, who were forced to follow suit, excepting only those families with children in dormitory care.

At the level of individual families, the effects of the federal income were mixed. Even at the discounted rate, Semple reported improved living conditions for the majority of Cherbourg families: "Natives are better dressed and have furnished their cottages to their ability". But from Aurukun, where all the children were sent bush with their parents as a war precaution, MacKenzie feared that ready availability of cash would spell the end for traditional skills. "I would have all the bush people returning here", he told Dan Brown. "They would live on the store and lose their hunting craft and crowd into the Mission." From Mornington Island Rev Braunholz also extolled the benefits of bush living: the children have become fat, he wrote, clearly benefiting from the return "to their own accustomed life." [33] At Yarrabah, however, benefits of the new pension were starkly apparent: it was alleged that prior to child endowment payments every patient admitted to Cairns Base Hospital suffered from malnutrition.[34]

At Mapoon, with a large part-Aboriginal population, income was flowing in from a second source: the men on manpower work. Here full wages, even after deductions for department and mission funds, left many families with unanticipated bank balances. Several men had up to £100 for spending at the mission store, and profits lifted. "Do not show these figures to the DNA [director of native affairs] as he will want to confiscate the money that I am holding for some of them and they will rise up in arms about that", warned Frank Cane.[35] There were social, as well as financial, repercussions. Army service and manpower schemes presented unexpected opportunities for departmental "wards" to compare the strictures of institutional controls with life in the wider community. Mission authorities anticipated problems and discontent in "settling down" after the war. "Their contact with the world outside and the glamour of what to them must seem almost unlimited money to spend, must have an unsettling effect", reflected Rev David Galloway.[36]

The Presbyterian committee foresaw resistance far beyond their own domain. Observing that the department had "cleared out and left these people to all and sundry", Cane declared that the government had no right to take over Aboriginal income now. There would be trouble, he warned Dan Brown, when the war ended and Aborigines who had profited during the war had "to go back to where they were before". "The general opinion is that the Department have killed themselves up here for after the war", he reported, "when one considers the amount of money that is being played around with the natives in general". Brown also sensed the critical times: "I think sometimes it will mean the end of our Missions as they are constituted at present".[37]

Why, indeed, would men who had worked side by side with other Queenslanders in army service or on manpower

programs, sharing wages and social experiences, be willing
to accept meekly the appalling conditions on the Aboriginal institutions? At Yarrabah, for instance, where a high
percentage of inmates were committed because of youth or
sickness, dependency on government funding was acute.
With reductions in subsidies and under continual pressure
to reduce costs, officials protested that "the natives could
not possibly get any less than they are receiving now". For
five years the Cairns dentist who treated the community
railed against the criminal neglect which, he charged,
threatened the very survival of "full bloods" and so weak-
ened the "half-castes" they often could not work. The
dormitory diet consisted of bread and tea for breakfast and
dinner, and beef bone soup and bread for lunch. Fed up
with departmental inaction he notified Cilento, who made
a prompt inspection. Cilento found 750 people dependent
on water which regularly tested polluted, and identified
seventeen malaria cases. Sanitation procedures, he informed the archbishop of Brisbane, "in any other circumstances would lead to prosecution".[38]

The lethal link between bad sanitation and high morbidity was evident on all missions and settlements. With funding insufficient even to meet nutrition needs amenities
remained dangerous. The health inspector found gross
contamination from latrines at the Monamona mission and
ordered huts be moved immediately to higher ground.
Officials protested that there was no money to buy roofing
iron, pan-stands, or even soap. In these conditions clinical
tests revealed 26 of the 29 boys in the dormitory were
infested with hookworm *and* 33 other parasitic worms.
Nearly 70 per cent of mission population was infected to
some degree.

"Nauseating" was the word Commonwealth tuberculosis campaign officers used to describe Mapoon. Here there were only 45 huts for over 280 people. Health department head Dr Abraham Fryberg, who succeeded Dr Cilento in 1946, scorned protests by superintendent Allan that money was insufficient for repairs let alone for reconstruction: "You will just have to do something about it", he directed. At Doomadgee, after reports of malnutrition and scurvy, an inspector from the Aboriginal department described the diet as "adequate", but revealed most families still lived in gunyahs, and dormitory children ate their meals on the ground. There were no beds, nor desks or chairs in the school.[39]

At Palm Island fifty-eight people died in the first six months of 1943. Poor housing and lack of clothes proved the deadly combination: the elderly fell to chest disorders and the children to colds and diarrhoea. Pneumonia raged in cold weather when families huddled in huts for warmth. Contaminated well-water caused outbreaks of diarrhoea, and meat and butter routinely was rancid by the time they reached the store. Chronic malnutrition, lack of dietary fats, lack of bedding and a total absence of washing facilities underpinned persistent high child mortality and filthy and diseased skin in survivors.[40] In contrast to settlement health, Dr Power noted that returning manpower workers were in "splendid condition mentally and physically", a direct consequence, in his opinion, of healthy living conditions and work environments, and better food.

With a death rate of 7.7 per cent at Palm Island, and infant mortality fifteen times the Queensland average, the Health department's senior officer, Dr Johnson, was once again directed to investigate a government settlement.

Child diets, he reported, were grossly deficient in milk, vegetables and fruit. And hospital conditions were so pathological that infants routinely contracted septic sores during treatment. How could this be? The reports of Matron Rynne, sent from Cherbourg to assess hospital practices, leave little to the imagination. Children's cots and mattresses were found to be filthy and crawling with cockroaches; older patients slept on soiled and shabby mattresses; the labor ward was cramped and dirty; and food storage rooms were unventilated in the heat, and full of flies and uncovered slops.[41]

Given these appalling circumstances, most Palm Islander's refused to report illnesses and submit to official attention. Power's professional approach compounded avoidance: "He frequently boxes the ears of out-patients even if they attend within regular hours. Such treatment does not win the confidence of aboriginals", wrote Johnson in a breathtaking understatement. "Many of them apparently do not like to bring their children to hospital unless they are fatally ill." Johnson deplored Power's neglect of pneumonic, tubercular and hookworm patients. For this latter category, Matron Rynne found her only common ground with Dr Power, agreeing that mass purgatives for hookworm eradication could prove fatal in a population in such a weak state of health. She refused ever to work with Power again.

So disturbed were health bureaucrats that Dr Fryberg himself made an inspection. He looked to social, as well as hospital and medical, predispositions for morbidity. Five people were crammed in each small room of the pandanus-leafed huts in the various outcamps. Very few had kitchens; cooking was done in old tins out in the open. Drinking water was untreated and obtained from shallow wells, and water shortages precluded any bathing or laundry facilities. Meat came from Townsville by boat in full sun on the decks and was routinely spoiled by the time it was unloaded. With no refrigeration or meat safes, the issue to each family had to be cooked and eaten immediately otherwise "it will go bad or become fly-blown".[42]

Overcrowding, filth and unsafe practices were root causes of tuberculosis, a disease prevalent in the Aboriginal institutions. During the late 1940s and the 1950s, the national push to identify and eradicate tuberculosis took campaign director Dr F. Macken to Queensland's missions and settlements. She was horrified to find families forced to sleep on earthen floors in overcrowded and poorly ventilated huts. But her most bitter remarks were directed at conditions in the various dormitories, set up ostensibly to bypass parental neglect but in practice uniformly pathological structures. At Palm Island, for instance, congestion was so acute that women slept head to foot in beds. At Cherbourg nothing had changed since a visiting justice ten years previously had described the high-set girls' dormitory as structurally unsound. All access was boarded up except for gates which were locked at night. In this fire hazard eighty girls were impounded for ten hours in cramped unlit rooms.[43]

"Pernicious", offensive and counter-productive was how Dr Macken described the practice of incarcerating adolescent girls and young women as a strategy of sexual control. At Doomadgee, she wrote, where all able-bodied men were sent out to revenue-producing jobs, it was like a slave camp. Girls were locked up at night and confined to a compound for daytime labour at domestic chores in addition to cultivation of crops. "If these coloured women are to become properly adjusted to normal life", the dormitory system "must be broken down", she insisted. "It is completely futile and artificial and unnatural to enclose, or rather encage, women, and to expect any sort of normal psychological balance on their release."[44]

Order and cleanliness

With such a barrage of condemnatory reports from state and federal health professionals in hand, department staff had long been pondering the need to "eradicate harmful conditions and secure improved health" for Aboriginal wards. Although documents clearly expose gross under-funding as the root cause of defective living conditions, analysis of procedures introduced from the mid-1940s indicate an intensification of policing at the level of individual practices, in effect moving the blame from finan-cial deprivation to defective medical and hygiene behav-iours.

Detailed regulations, allowed for under the 1939 *Aborigi-nals Preservation and Protection Act* but not finalised until 1945, pick up on the medico/policing mentality. Discipli-nary powers of superintendents were increased, 32 hours (unpaid) work each week was made compulsory, and it became an offence to act in a manner "subversive of good order" on a reserve. Aboriginal police, appointed, pro-moted and dismissed by superintendents, now had powers of arrest and imprisonment on reserves according to rules and penalties set by superintendents. Aboriginal courts, under direction of the superintendent, were established to adjudicate minor breaches of regulations. Aboriginal coun-cils, part elected and part appointed, could confer with the superintendent over general welfare matters, but were excluded from commenting on police or external employment.

All these new agencies were co-opted, via an extensive range of offences and penalties, to increase personal supervision and to enforce the behavioural changes upon which Aboriginal health was said to depend. By-laws stated that every resident "shall observe habits of orderliness and cleanliness", and shall attend, and cause their children to attend, all medical examinations and treatments. It became a duty to keep a dwelling and surrounds neat and tidy "to the satisfaction" of the superintendent, and to report any disease or injury. It became an offence to neglect to report any case of sickness. Medical examinations on departure and return from employment became mandatory. Superintendents exhorted police and councillors to promote, monitor and prosecute these duties and offences, and the courts to process them vigilantly.

Hygiene inspectors were introduced on all communities. All camps were visited weekly "with a view to improving living conditions of the people"; medical and hospital attendance was policed, ex-patients were watched to ensure proper feeding and care, rubbish and waste-water disposal were closely regulated, and huts were checked for mosquito and bug infestation. Monthly reports went to superintendents listing the "dirty and untidy" families who needed closer surveillance, including surprise inspections. Gradually, wrote Dr Monz, visiting doctor at Cherbourg, Aboriginal families are beginning to realise "that maintenance of these standards is intended and is necessary to help protect them against the many diseases of infectious type, against which they have no inherited immunity".[45]

Nurses from the baby welfare centre, opened on Palm Island in 1946, acted as a further policing agency. Homes of children under five were liable for inspection and report on cleanliness and hygiene, bedding could be checked, and the state of cutlery, crockery, food storage and washing facilities was recorded. Women said to lack domestic skills had to attend weekly classes and mothers were supervised in health and baby care.[46] Superintendent George Sturges declared himself well satisfied: many lives had been saved because the children "are not now hopelessly sick and neglected".

Every now and then, over decades of health and hygiene reports, a glimpse is given of the context of community life. Dr Macken, for one, was keenly attuned to systemic, rather than merely individual, neglect. Behind the main road at Palm Island, she wrote in 1950, "one finds shacks and hovels consisting of minimal sheet-iron and earth floors, and no effort at building at all, where life becomes correspondingly primitive and unhealthy. Overcrowding of all houses is, as ever, a most serious problem".[47]

Dr Monz, visiting doctor at Cherbourg, was similarly blunt. Huts are filthy and overcrowded, kitchens dirt encrusted, toilets leaking and smelling, clothing and bedding unwashed, he reported. "Overcrowding is a marked feature and is to be condemned. It would seem that in some instances four or more people sleep in the one bed. How some of the babies survive the night must seem a miracle … It does seem amazing that the babies and toddlers manage to survive infancy and childhood, considering the menu … It appears to be mostly a case of damper and syrup for breakfast, dinner and tea." His recommendation? Regular house inspections and fines for negligence.[48] But a survey of housing conditions revealed a chronic absence of bedding, cooking and eating utensils, weatherproof shelter, toilets and water. The dormitory kitchen was filthy, no condensed milk was available, and neither milk nor fresh produce was available at the store.

Perhaps it was largely a matter of priorities: of weighing domestic squalor against overcrowding and lack of running water; of weighing poor feeding practices against inadequate rationing and non-existent fridges and stoves; of weighing empty store shelves against departmental policy which saw "surplus" produce from the Aboriginal settlements consigned to institutions at Dunwich and Wooloowin and distributed free to eleven local hospitals well into 1948. Certainly it was no new tactic to blame the victims. If this was life on the "protected" missions and settlements during the 1940s, what conditions prevailed for the estimated nine thousand people living in rural areas?

Country living

With Aboriginal labour at a premium during the war years this should have been a time of relative prosperity. Documentary evidence suggests, however, that workers continued to be penalised by flawed wage processing and rogue protectors. At the very first step, the payment of a "pocket money" portion during the work period, the system failed. By 1942 single workers were entitled to 25 per cent and married workers 50 per cent of wages for items such as tobacco and food and all employers were required to keep a book of each cash outlay. But it was common practice for station managers to get thumbprints on wages sheets against grossly inflated amounts; in fact, many claimed that the total wage had been outlayed for "sales" from station stores.

Many protectors reported that they were too busy to investigate complaints by Aboriginal workers; some simply transferred people to new positions rather than get involved in disputes over money owing. At Coen, the protector described the pocket money system as "farcical" and only benefiting white employers. He demanded that all pocket money be paid to him so workers could make their own choices in town. Even so, he lamented, some were quickly drawn into gambling schools and duped out of wages and even clothes.[49]

Feedback in 1943, after the pocket money component to cover living expenses was raised to between one-third and three-quarters depending on worker "maturity", reveals how erratically policy fitted with practice, particularly in remote areas. Several protectors opposed the rise on the grounds that employers would only filch the increase. A few station owners suggested that the increase should be greater, although internal checks showed several of these respondents had "poor records" in credible bookkeeping. At the Doomadgee mission, superintendent Read largely ignored the pocket money system. He demanded that full earnings be paid direct to the worker's credit in mission trust funds and only those with good savings balances were allowed cash during their work period. As late as 1965, head office admitted that some workers never received *any* of the cash component despite the fully thumbprinted books tendered at the end of contracted periods.[50]

Workers had to run the gauntlet of protectors even to access the portion of wages paid directly to their bank accounts. No withdrawals could be effected without permission, and frequently head office intervened to monitor transactions. One man's spending was restricted because he bought two pairs of trousers four months after a previous clothing purchase: "see that he is not allowed to become too extravagant in this clothing requirements", directed O'Leary. One couple, despite ample funds, were denied permission to visit the Brisbane Exhibition because "they really have not made much effort to curtail their withdrawals". Another woman's request to buy a sewing machine was made dependent upon whether she was "careful in looking after other household goods". An application by a man to buy a leather coat was granted because, in O'Leary's opinion, "this boy has had very little clothing within the last year … he is a very careful boy".[51]

Examination of departmental audit reports reveals many instances of police fraud on Aboriginal accounts. The Croydon protector, caught making false deductions for rations, objected bitterly when he was ordered to allow workers to make their own purchases: "I am very indignant to think that I cannot be trusted with a few paltry shillings belonging to unfortunate Aboriginals who do not know the difference between a shilling and a 2s piece". Ticked off for slothful record-keeping, this officer offered to work faster if he were paid 10s per day for his trouble![52] A later protector from the same station was found guilty of fraud on at least five Aboriginal accounts after an Aboriginal tracker reported he was forced to sign blank cheques, threatened with banishment and starved of food. "I have been given no fresh beef only old dry corn beef, tea but no milk or sugar and bread and dripping … my children are crying they are hungry all the time … Mr O'Leary is that fair or can you help me."[53]

Allegations of physical abuse by police were not uncommon, but routinely neutralised by internal police inquiries which often maligned the victim or the complainant and endorsed police integrity. In one case at Boulia it was stated that no action was warranted because the Aborigine was a known liar, the complainant a poor payer of wages, the assault not witnessed by others, and the constable had resigned. As late as 1943 the Coen protector was supplied with leg-irons and chains, as "handling gear, for the purpose of escorting and ensuring the safe custody" of Aborigines.

The security of those living in station camps was dependent on the disposition of the boss and the local protector, who could at any time invoke the law to facilitate "clearing" of families from properties. Vulnerability to deportation made complaint hazardous. Sexual assault on domestic workers or on the wives of station employees was widespread. The arrival of a mixed-race baby prompted one rural protector to question a station camp. He learned that for many years the manager assaulted women and girls when the men were sent out mustering, and several children acknowledged him as their father. In this case the families insisted they would remain "until they die" on the property, and informed the protector that abuse had ceased after threats to report the manager both to the police and to the department.

As with the Aboriginal tracker at Croydon, it frequently took direct action from the worker to redress malpractices. Knowledge was the most useful weapon against abuse: "M., like many other employers in this part of the state, have not got out of the way of thinking that 'anything is good enough for a nigger', they do not realise that the natives are gradually becoming more educated, and soon complain of any bad treatment ... due to the Missions, and the presence of intelligent half-castes, they are obtaining much better treatment".[54]

Country workers often followed seasonal jobs, finding temporary accommodation in rented houses or doubling up with friends. All too often, through lack of income or local ostracism, shanties on vacant Crown land were the only option. In rural areas camping, water, hospital or national park reserves all offered free space. Departmental responsibility only extended over Aboriginal reserves, and local council authority was only valid over town reserves. Anomalies in control were often exploited by authorities either to pressure Aboriginal groups into relocation or to evade costs of providing amenities. Frequently Aboriginal families were left in limbo.

At Ravenshoe, for instance, forty people were living in hessian and sheet-iron sheds in 1947 on a national parks reserve, carting water for over half a mile to the hill on which they camped. The local council sought to shift the problem to the Aboriginal department, offering a small parcel of land for an Aboriginal reserve. But the Aboriginal department ignored the offer, having no funds for essential shelters or amenities. Four years later no action had been taken. A missionary worker described the camp: "The present hovels are dank, musty and unhealthy and their living conditions unsanitary in every way ... The children are denied the right to education, being debarred from the local state school because of the disgraceful and unsavoury homes from which they come." [55]

Children at the Cooktown camp were also banned from the school. Here a critic called for children to be "sent out to work" rather than "run wild" in the town. An investigation revealed sixty people living in earthen-floored rusting tin sheds of "deplorable condition", not waterproof and unfit for human habitation. The local headmaster rejected the protector's attempts to enrol the children, because "parents of the white children would object" to their dirty condition. The Education department was willing to develop an Aboriginal school, but this was deferred over several years as the local council delayed allocation of land. Then the Aboriginal department opted to leave the problem to the Lutheran missionaries when they re-established after wartime evacuations. In despair, the school inspector declared that the local council was victimising Aborigines "whom they wanted hunted from pillar to post". The families were ignored by Brisbane bureaucrats who, he wrote, needed an "Automic Bomb" [sic] to move them to act for the children's best interests.[56]

Of the range of strategies which could be activated against rural Aboriginal groups by hostile local councils seeking their eviction, the health alert got the best response. But a brief glance at files on a few camps reveals that council allegations often did not go uncontested. At Talwood west of Goondiwindi the council health inspector said a local family should be removed to a settlement. The five adults and twenty children lived in earthen-floored tin sheds with boards as mattresses; their wretched conditions, he argued, "robbed the children of reasonable care and attention". Asked by the department for his report, the protector refuted the claims; the huts were clean and the children well cared for although somewhat undernourished. Local publicity on their plight resulted in rental

Brisbane 1863: Presentation of government blankets outside the Police Office in Queen Street (demolished in 1871 to build the General Post Office). *(Courtesy John Oxley Library)*

Cloncurry 1896: "House Gins" Lelavale Station. *(Courtesy John Oxley Library)*

Myora, Stradbroke Island 1891: Children outside mission huts. *(Courtesy John Oxley Library)*

Fraser Island mission c. 1900: "Married Aboriginal's Huts". *(Courtesy John Oxley Library)*

Aurukun c. 1905: First road through the bush. *(Courtesy John Oxley Library)*

Bellenden Ker 1904: Women bring botanical specimens to Archibald Meston's expedition camp on Tringilburra Creek. *(Courtesy John Oxley Library)*

Ipswich c. 1905: Aboriginal family in the Ipswich district. *(Courtesy John Oxley Library)*

Cloncurry c. 1906: Washing day on Granada Station. *(Courtesy John Oxley Library)*

Deebing Creek settlement 1907. *(Courtesy John Oxley Library)*

Yarrabah mission c. 1915. *(Courtesy John Oxley Library)*

Palm Island settlement 1919: "Serving Out the Soup". *(Courtesy John Oxley Library)*

Barambah settlement 1920/21: Photo taken during hookworm investigation. *(Courtesy John Oxley Library)*

Weipa mission 1933: "Old people's huts". *(Courtesy John Oxley Library)*

Mornington Island mission c. 1937: Mission girls on their daily chore as water carriers. *(Courtesy John Oxley Library)*

Patrick Killoran, (left) and Cornelius O'Leary discuss a project at Bamaga, 1952.

Doomadgee mission c. 1940: "Two-room cottage".
(Courtesy Queensland State Archives)

Palm Island settlement 1960:
Erecting the power house.
*(Queensland State Archives —
A/69579)*

housing offered in town. All structures on the reserve were promptly demolished.

An outbreak of gastroenteritis which killed three children at Texas led the council to blame the Aboriginal camp as a danger to the community. In this case, the local health inspector said the riverside camp, where several families lived in sheds and tents, drawing water from a well and from the river, was not the source: similar deaths had occurred in the sewered town of nearby Goondiwindi. On learning they could not evict the group who were not on a town camping reserve, the council resolved to pursue the matter through the State Children's department,[57] no doubt hoping allegations of child neglect would stir the camp to move on.

At Gympie it was a case of typhoid fever which led the council health inspector to lodge a damning report on the victim's home. Local police, sent by the native affairs department to pressure the householder to clean up, were told to mind their own business. They filed a recommendation for the family's removal to a settlement, because "living conditions are most unsuitable and [that] same will tend to create disease". Sent from Cherbourg, superintendent Semple overruled the police report, describing "a nice little cottage with water laid on … the yard was clean". No action was taken. But after a subsequent typhoid infection in the same family, and finding the family now camped with seven children on the miner's reserve, a removal order to Cherbourg was effected, despite reports that the bark humpy was clean and swept.[58]

Although the majority of families living in country areas were exempt from departmental control, this in no way lessened official surveillance. Families were at all times at risk of being declared "in need of care and protection" and thereby losing their freedom. Overcrowded huts at Beaudesert, one sheltering a mother and ten children, another four adults and eight children, prompted the council to propose a housing program for "coloured people" in a "specified area" in the town. At the department's request the local protector provided an inventory of "their breed and if possible the breed of their parents". It was soon established that several men were employed, the women were receiving endowment, and all were exempt. The department, under severe financial privation, was quick to disclaim any obligation: "These people are self maintaining and enjoy the same citizenship rights as other members of the community". Revoking such rights, the letter continued, can only be done by a magistrate, and good grounds were needed for "transferring them to a Government Settlement where they would become a charge on the tax payer".[59] In contrast to the rhetoric on "rights", information from separate sources revealed that the department refused to let relatives return to Beaudesert because they might "place a burden on other Aboriginal families" if they failed to find work.[60]

The Beaudesert council was one of several to approach the department for support in providing housing and facilities. The government was well aware that endemic poverty of Aboriginal families across Queensland put home ownership or even rental property beyond their means: "In Charters Towers as in many other towns of the State, proper accommodation for the aboriginals is sadly lacking".[61] At the same time, the department routinely disclaimed any obligation, insisting that families who were not government wards were on their own. In fact, the state had resolved to pin responsibility for welfare housing on the federal government. Until it could extract supplementary federal funds, the state refused any duty of support for more than half its Aboriginal population. As the next section will show, entrenched Aboriginal poverty was ultimately exploited to bring development resources into Queensland.

"Special needs"

Notwithstanding the imprecise methods and means of counting those of mixed-race parentage, the accumulation of census information provided both the impetus and the justification for the states to demand funding concessions. Under the Commonwealth Grants Commission, established in 1933, states could claim "special needs", and Bleakley used dialogue preceding the 1937 Welfare Conference to argue, unsuccessfully, for Commonwealth input towards capital expenditure on Aboriginal institutions.[62] In 1943 it was mooted that a Commonwealth Powers' Bill might grant federal control over all Aboriginal policy. A referendum on constitutional changes, including a five-year program for centralised Aboriginal administration, was defeated two years later, a rejection of intrusive federal powers rather than of Aboriginal need.

At the 1946 premier's conference, both Queensland and Western Australia activated the "northern invasion" threat to demand federal funding for improvements on remote Aboriginal communities. It was essential for defence, they argued, that Aboriginal communities in the empty north be strengthened. In a flurry of speeches, Edward Hanlon, now premier of Queensland, linked the development and populating of the north with the survival of white civilisation in Australia.[63] It was the federal government's responsibility to eradicate diseases endemic in Aboriginal populations across state lines, Hanlon argued at the 1947 premiers' conference, and he called for mobile medical units and Commonwealth bursaries for primary education.

The demand for federal financial commitment to Aboriginal needs was equally matched by the denial of federal influence in administration. O'Leary was keen for a full survey and medical care for sufferers of venereal disease, leprosy and tuberculosis, citing a "considerable increase" in the latter after chronic wartime malnutrition. But the minister's adviser urged caution: "Any suggestion to the Commonwealth Government for hospital and medical assistance infers lack of provision by the State Government". Much safer, he suggested, to get funding for facilities and personnel.[64]

With much national fanfare the North Australia Development League was founded in 1948 to promote resource and land development, population expansion, and to "advance the welfare of native inhabitants". It attracted many demands for grants but had no authority to disburse funds: nothing eventuated for Aboriginal welfare and the committee soon lapsed. With only £1 per person per year allocated for Aborigines in the Northern Territory by federal Labor governments in power between 1941 and 1949, federal intent to improve Aboriginal conditions is suspect. Prime minister Chifley's own attitude can be gauged by his dismissive comment on state demands: "You are trying to leave a problem child on my hands".[65]

During the late 1940s and early 1950s, as the states continued to demand a greater share of federal funds, Hanlon emerged as the ringleader in dismissing any potential interference in state autonomy and rights. The election of Robert Menzies' Liberal government in 1949 offered new strategies: a committed anti-communist, Hanlon now linked retarded development with incipient subversion fomented by trade union infiltration. Year after year O'Leary tapped into the "threat" to national security to validate state claims: "Subversive elements are slowly but surely influencing the Torres Strait Islanders and aboriginals of the northern portion of the State to the detriment of the existent control ... In the event of an outbreak of hostilities, the Commonwealth Government will have to depend on the Torres Strait Islanders as it did in the last war ... The whole solution of this problem is financial assistance". Furthermore, he argued, since Queensland's fine record "materially assists" the Commonwealth to counter international criticisms of its treatment of Aborigines, then the Commonwealth "is morally bound" to advance £500,000 or more per year towards costs.[66]

In tandem with this pursuit of federal funds at a state level, Queensland continued to exploit "racist" anomalies in pension entitlements. All Aboriginal workers earning more than £3 per week had paid income tax since 1943, and all were covered by Workers' Compensation insurance. Therefore, O'Leary argued, exclusion of reserve residents from national pension schemes penalised tax-paying workers and the many retirees who had given a lifetime contribution to primary and pastoral industries.

O'Leary insisted that residence on missions and settlements did not necessary denote state institutionalisation, since many had "sufficient standard of intelligence" to qualify for exemptions but preferred to live with family and friends. But the prime minister's department was adamant: it was illogical, they contended, to confine people on reserves on the basis that their "level of intelligence" was insufficient for full citizenship rights while at the same time stating that they should fully qualify for benefits. There was also an aversion against the state, as definers of social capacity, to both adjudicate and dispense federal monies.[67] The ruling remained: no exemption, no pension.

The native affairs department was not averse to some creative labelling in its determination to access federal funds. In 1949 it exempted sixty-five Hansen's disease patients on Fantome Island from the strictures of the *Aboriginal Preservation and Protection Act*, but reactivated controls through detention provisions of the *Health Act*, renaming Aboriginal police as "health orderlies". Now, wrote O'Leary, we will apply for the invalid pensions to be paid through the Palm Island office.[68] But after four years' deliberation, perhaps suspecting a ruse, the federal government exercised its prerogative to refuse the pensions.

O'Leary moved his headquarters from Brisbane to Thursday Island in 1948 to enable "a greater measure of control, direction and management" of the 15,000 Aborigines living north of Townsville. At a conference of superintendents he stated that the backwardness of mission inmates was a consequence of equating Aboriginality with incompetence and laziness. From now on, said O'Leary, all able-bodied residents on missions and settlements would be expected to earn their keep and support their families.[69] This was a harsh judgement: church records confirm Presbyterian running costs for 1946 were over £20,000; the state's contribution to *all* missions totalled only £9,123.[70]

Queensland had been assured of a federal grant of £50,000 for Aboriginal needs, O'Leary told a meeting of missionaries in 1948, and Cabinet had allocated an initial sum of £20,000 for the Presbyterian missions. He now called for a program of intense development. No longer would "coloured people" be trained as "poor whites", he announced in his *Annual Report* for 1951. From now on Queensland's Aborigines were "on the road to self-determination". In a strategy to bypass what he termed the inefficiencies and poor management of the Brisbane mission committee, O'Leary set up a special Presbyterian Advisory Council, with himself as chair. Enthusiastically the missionaries listed their priorities: safe water supplies, power plants for lighting and coldrooms, upgraded hospitals, rebuilding of houses and dormitories, and trade schools and equipment.

It was not until after the 1957 election in Queensland of a coalition government that the state treasurer advised the premier, Frank G. Nicklin, that "the barometer for Federal Aid to this State has swung sharply towards 'Fair' ".[71] Two years later the federal government committed £1,000,000 for Aboriginal pensions "as evidence of the Commonwealth Government's intention to give them equality with other Australians in the field of social services".[72] Again nomads were excluded, but O'Leary confidently predicted Queensland would get £300,000 per annum: "Owing to the enlightened and vigorous Native Affairs Policy of the Queensland Government, all the coloured people of this State have passed beyond nomadic or primitive states". He added proudly, "We know the name, family history, and living conditions of every aboriginal in the State".[73]

* * *

This brief overview indicates how federal priorities during the 1940s impacted on Queensland's Aboriginal population. Federal health professionals continued to expose conditions on state communities to disrepute; federal electoral officers revealed anomalies in voting entitlement; federal war programs and army service increased community stress and disruption but also allowed some individual wealth and relative freedom of movement and association; any softening of family privation through federal pension schemes was obstructed by institutional default and intensified personal surveillance.

Postwar demands for a greater slice of federal revenue were most stridently voiced by Queensland and Western Australia. Both states claimed a "right" to extra funds on the basis of large, impoverished, and homeless indigenous populations. Both states linked neglect on Aboriginal communities with national security and an imperative to develop the "empty" north. But how did these communities fare when development enterprises coincided with their location?

7

Besieged

International military aggression during the early 1940s put the Aboriginal communities across northern Australia under threat of dispersal and evacuation as the nation prepared to defend its territory. The capitulation of Japan ended the external threat of occupation. But from the 1950s records show the Cape York communities again menaced by occupation and territorial excision. This time, however, the fight was against offensives by international venture capital. And these adversaries were aided and abetted by an *internal* agency, namely the will of the state.

Under greatest threat were the Presbyterian missions, which faced attack from mining companies and the government both conjointly and separately. The mobilisation of mining interests ignited a smouldering and increasingly acrimonious standoff between church and state. It will be suggested that as both these authorities sought leverage to assert their interests, they invoked the derelict conditions of the stagnating communities.

Missions run by other religious denominations were similarly characterised by ill-health and dilapidation. And by the mid-1960s most of the northern missions, across several denominations, had been transferred to government control. What is the background to this dramatic collapse of religious management?

Missions in crisis

The inflow of federal funds through child endowment and state grants had, paradoxically, increased rather than decreased the pressure on the northern missions by the early 1950s. The department pushed for investment in facilities such as lighting and refrigeration plants, and demanded upgraded nursing and teaching standards. But recruits could not be found. Short-staffed missionaries fell ill from overwork as leave was continually deferred.

The postwar trebling of food prices devoured revenue. An operating credit of £18,000 accumulated by the Presbyterian mission committee during war shortages decayed to a deficit of £10,000 by 1952. Repeated and desperate requests to the department for supplies and materials were refused. As essential boat transport became unreliable, near-starvation was added to chronic water shortages and primitive and congested housing. Flour and the curing salt essential for meat preservation were frequently unavailable for several months at a time, and the government rice quota was far too low to fill the need.

It was not until superintendent MacKenzie warned in 1951 that Aurukun children would be reduced to eating the cash crop of coconuts that O'Leary was moved to act. The department would come up with half the cost of a new boat engine, he informed MacKenzie, and the mission committee could extract the remaining amount from the mission trust accounts. These accounts comprised the compulsory levies on workers' wages for maintenance and support of non-employed residents, and were under joint church/government control. Documents show that Mapoon and Aurukun missions held cash reserves totalling £754 and £703 respectively.[1] But the department ear-marked this for development, not for essentials.

Community suffering continued while access to this vital nest-egg was effectively frozen. At Mapoon, superintendent George Holmes and his wife were solely responsible for the population of 685. Here, food shortages and unsafe water were also the norm. Overcrowded huts were so decrepit they were officially condemned; no funds were made avail-able for their replacement. Holmes wrote despairingly of being unwilling to risk poisoning a patient by using the one pair of rusting tweezers, and of a preventible death attrib-uted to the non-delivery of hypodermic needles and peni-cillin ordered two months previously. "One wonders what we are achieving at Mapoon", he reflected.[2]

Not for the first time, nor for the last, it was health professionals who blew the cover on the scandalous condi-tions endured by departmental wards. After a fatal epi-demic of gastroenteritis erupted on Mornington Island in 1952, disgusted medical workers went public. Newspaper accounts portrayed scorched foodcrops, long dried up wells, and people scattered around the island in small groups foraging for survival. Furious at the exposure, O'Leary delivered an ultimatum: if the committee did not act immediately to remedy the crisis or to remove the mission to the mainland, the department would take over.

Already deeply in debt, the committee bowed to the inevitable. O'Leary launched plans to move the people to Weipa and organised timber for emergency housing. Morn-ington Islanders were not consulted. Councillors were ada-mant that they would not move without a firm commitment of immediate return when the drought broke. Ultimately, superintendent Bert McCarthy backed his men, informing O'Leary that the community was determined "to battle out the hardships and to retain their native land ... Each family has well defined territory and their attachment to that land is marked. Even temporary evacuation is not acceptable to them at this stage".[3] Loathe to use force, the mission committee took the softer option and organised emergency deliveries by ship of food and water. O'Leary was furious. He claimed that funds had already been expended at Weipa for refugee housing, and described the committee as gutless for reneging on their agreement. McCarthy was temporarily suspended by the committee for rejecting orders to evacuate.[4]

Mapoon was also at flashpoint. Here the greater proportion of mixed-race men and women had long experience of off-mission employment, and many had played active roles in the war effort. Shortage of work, stalled improvements and a succession of untrained and disorganised officers fomented bitterness and unrest. This was exacerbated by the autocratic regime of Holmes, a man O'Leary described as "temperamentally unsuited to control the half-caste population at the Mission". Unable to curb escalating tensions, Holmes proposed to his committee that Mapoon be broken up. Some families should be exempted from departmental controls, some sent to "Palm Island or similar", and the remainder absorbed among the other missions.

He was not alone in this line of thinking. "I have been told that the D.N.A. [Department of Native Affairs] were wanting Mapoon half-castes for Bamaga", Holmes wrote, "I would have taken no notice of this except that the people of Mapoon have also heard this ... I wondered what was in it?"[5] Overstretched and underfinanced, the church hierarchy was not unreceptive to the possibility of such radical restructuring: "Do we continue to work in four Stations, or abandon one or all of them to the Government, or some other Church community?"[6] Holmes may well have been sceptical about rumours to develop an Aboriginal community at Bamaga, a reserve at the tip of Cape York gazetted under departmental control in 1948, but MacKenzie was obviously implicated in the speculation. A letter from him expresses amazement that the people were aware of the highly confidential discussions.

The people of Mapoon were incensed over the relocation rumours and sent twelve delegates to Thursday Island to lobby O'Leary, complaining also of stagnation at the mission and Holmes' overbearing discipline. If the mission were to be moved, insisted the councillors, it should be to the original site, still operating as an outstation, where all families had been allocated land by Rev Hey in the 1890s. So precarious was Holmes' command that he requested that O'Leary visit Mapoon to make a show of authority and restore order. This O'Leary did, accompanied by Bill MacKenzie from Aurukun. And in a scathing report for undersecretary Keith McCormack, he declared Mapoon was understaffed, lacked industrial policy, was ineptly controlled and should be closed down. Perhaps aware that the government would not finance massive relocations, O'Leary suggested that all "half-castes" should be sent to Weipa, and the one hundred "full-bloods" to Aurukun.[7]

But Aurukun was also in turmoil. O'Leary was later to lament that tight discipline had been lost forever during 1950, when long-term superintendent Rev MacKenzie had taken a year's leave of absence to fulfil his appointment as moderator of the Presbyterian church in Queensland, and Bert McCarthy filled the gap. Now, with MacKenzie helping quell hostilities at Mapoon, a popular revolt erupted at Aurukun against token payment for compulsory work. Again the committee requested a show of force from O'Leary. He was given a hostile reception. His response was to order the removal of seven "agitators" to Palm Island, invoking the 1945 regulations to charge the men with having "attempted to disorganise the mission by disobeying the rules of conduct and hygiene". The *Sunday Mail*, keen not to let the facts diminish a good story, wrote a sensational account of "an uprising of 700 Aborigines" terrorising staff. The committee reference was perhaps more accurate and not a little prophetic: some "unrest" due to the " 'pink' ideas of one or two young bloods who had association with stockmen in hinterland cattle stations".[8]

The committee's competence to manage and develop its communities was now severely compromised. They insisted the solution lay with the government. Grants did not cover even the basic needs of the mission communities: there was insufficient money for food, no money for building and maintenance, and none to cover employment on essential work. The department, however, took the opposite line: there would be no crisis funds or even increases in basic grants until there was effective management and a definite developmental program.[9]

With the church unable, and the government unwilling, to provide essential funds, the crisis deepened into 1954. Still smarting from the earlier reversal on Mornington Island's relocation, O'Leary brandished fresh condemnatory health reports to argue that the Island mission was imperilled. And he suggested that public exposure would discredit the church's reputation irreparably.[10] This appears to be a statement of coercion rather than concern. The undersecretary, bemoaning further unwelcome exposure from the medical profession following a series of deaths in the community, grumbled: "The Doctor comes along and says you are guilty of murder if you don't do something about it ... Sometimes I think Doctors are alright in their place".[11]

In fact, the pivotal focus of the government was economical and political: keep expenditure to a minimum and avoid damaging publicity. To this end a series of conferences was arranged during 1954 between church and government personnel. Minister William Moore opened by conveying Cabinet's alarm at the escalating costs of Aboriginal administration. All missions would have to be redirected to revenue production; funding would not be increased unless it served a "useful purpose". Moore proposed that the problem missions of Mapoon and Mornington Island should be closed, with the former absorbed at Weipa and the latter at Aurukun. O'Leary agreed. The position at Mapoon, he said, was hopeless. But would the Mornington Islanders be "happy in their minds" being shifted to the mainland? pondered the mission board's chairman of finance. "The mind of the Native is formulated by his leaders", retorted O'Leary in exasperation.[12]

A month later the mission committee agreed, subject to ratification by the General Assembly, that "Mapoon Mission should be closed as a separate entity and the people, over a period, should be transferred to Weipa Mission".[13] Weipa was to be redeveloped as an education training centre similar to Cherbourg and act as the main base for cattle operations on all remaining missions. The committee obviously felt a trade-off was due, and at the second conference they went on the financial attack. They argued that inflation had dramatically increased state revenue and this should have been translated into increased grants. But government subsidies had dropped nearly 20 per cent from £58,212 in the 1951–52 year to £46,900 in the 1952–53 year, an outlay of only £2 4s 6d per head per year and well below subsistence level. As a direct result, the committee was now £19,000 in debt and the church board was threatened with bankruptcy.

The undersecretary was unmoved. Residents should take more "responsibility" for their own needs, he contended. Did he realise, responded Rev Coombes with quiet fury, that workers on the average stockman's wage of £7 per week already forfeited 5 per cent for single men and 10 per cent for married men to the department? That the missions took a further £1 to £1 10s which "usually goes to the wife"? That mothers were levied £1 a week from their child endowment for rations and a further 4s a week for amenities? That at Mapoon and Weipa men built their own houses, cutting the timber and paying for fittings, an overall outlay of about £97? Their protests fell on deaf ears. Declaring himself "a bit sceptical" McCormack reflected, "Are we spoiling our Natives, doing too much for them, not making them carry their full responsibility — not making them as good characters as they ought to be?"[14]

If anything, the government had hardened its stance. Desperately needed funding increases were now made conditional on an active development program and a schedule for the Mapoon/Weipa and Mornington Island/Aurukun mergers. The committee was irate. Why had the government linked provision of rations for the indigent with evacuations of Mornington Island and Mapoon? The church had the right to consider mission closures "without pressure" and "without coercion". How can we finance capital development when we cannot even cover ration costs? protested Rev Sweet. If the government insisted that more than 10s per week should be spent on rations for each child, then the government would have to make that money available.[15]

In desperation, the committee now called the government's bluff: either subsidies were provided to cover feeding and care of mission inmates, or the church would forfeit its trusteeship: "Cabinet must decide whether the responsibility of the feeding and clothing of needy aborigines in particular, together with their physical care and education, rests with the Governments of our nation".[16] This hit home. O'Leary's figuring had revealed it would take an additional £21,000 per annum if the government supported the Presbyterian missions on a par with expenditure at Woorabinda. Since present outlays were £39,500 for the total mission population of 1340 compared with £61,075 for Woorabinda's population of 810, it was obviously in the government's interest to shore up church costs rather than take over.[17] £22,000 was allocated to clear mission debts, but vital subsidy increases were still withheld.

For the Mornington Islanders, at least, the pressure had eased. Underground water had been tapped by new drilling, and relocation was costed as prohibitive. But in a revealing exchange, Sweet bluntly challenged O'Leary on Mapoon: Are you wavering from your previous position "that neither yourself as the Director, nor the Committee would wish to use force in the implementation of the move from Mapoon to Weipa?"[18] In fact, from the first official discussions on the merger councillor Jackson Mamoose had clearly stated the people's unanimous rejection of any move. At that time O'Leary was confident that if the leaders were swayed the people would follow. Rev Sweet had also gauged the resistance as "token" and easily overcome by tact and subtlety. By late 1955, however, although Sweet had explained the church's inability and the government's refusal to continue funding at the present site, the people insisted they had "only one policy at present and that is to remain at Mapoon".

Faced with this unified defiance, Sweet informed O'Leary that the committee would not "try and argue the Mapoon people into a move to Weipa", but would rely on changing attitudes as Weipa development progressed. O'Leary was furious, sensing a repeat of the aborted backdown at Mornington Island. The church had promised early action but now said the people had no intention of leaving, he wrote in frustration. Buildings were dilapidated, improvements halted, and there was no teacher. The church *must* convince the people to leave, he declared, otherwise "the onus will fall on someone to forcibly remove them, and that onus will not be accepted by the Department of Native Affairs".[19] But despite the committee's declared lack of capital, at no time did the department extend finances for the Mapoon/Weipa merger, apart from a promise of timber from the Bamaga sawmill.

It was at this point that the struggle between church and state to bring Mapoon to submission was thrown into turmoil. New players in the field irrevocably changed the status of the Cape York missions from remote insignificance to unprecedented potential.

Bauxite bonanza

Huge deposits of iron ore had been identified on the Weipa/Mapoon Aboriginal reserves as early as 1902. In fact James Winn, superintendent at Weipa since 1938, had sent bauxite samples to Brisbane in 1940,[20] in response to requests from the government geologist. By 1956 British-based mining giant Consolidated Zinc Pty Ltd had applied for a 100-year lease over most of the Mapoon and Weipa reserves. Rather naively, the church anticipated that the mining bonanza "will flow into the billabong of all our Missions". "It has always been tacitly agreed", conceded the moderator in his General Assembly address, "that should discoveries of extensive mineral wealth be found" national importance would require policy decisions "on high Government level". But all parties — church, government and mining company subsidiary Commonwealth Aluminium Corporation Pty Ltd (Comalco) — were "emphatic", he continued, that mining development should consider "the interests of both white and black Australians".[21]

There is no doubt that the church saw the vast mining project as a ticket out of poverty and dependency. For years the Cape York communities had been caught in a double bind: refused vital revenue without industrial enterprise, and unable to initiate development because of abject destitution. "Changed circumstances" flowing from the mining operations, the committee informed the minister in September 1956, meant the merger date for Mapoon with Weipa could not be finalised. In relaying this information to Patrick Killoran, his deputy at Thursday Island, O'Leary advised that no improvements would be undertaken at Mapoon, nor should any departmental assistance be provided.[22] Mapoon was officially placed in limbo.

The official version, oft repeated in government correspondence, has been that the merger was aborted *prior* to
mining initiatives and because of church impotence. This
is untrue in several respects: no merger had been finalised
or funded by 1956; and the department was well aware by
that time that Weipa mission was itself under threat. Although a start had been made there for the expected
Mapoon arrivals, this site was now projected as a white
mining town and port. Documents show that the church,
state and Comalco agreed as early as February 1957 that the
Weipa mission would have to be relocated.[23]

With the terms and specifications of the multi-million
pound development still in flux, the church pursued an
aggressive line in negotiations, seeking to maximise benefits for the two communities. A list of basic principles was
compiled to underpin a "claim for a capital compensation
grant" from Comalco as well as "the guarantee of recurring
maintenance expenses". These, declared the moderator,
"will be the basis of future negotiations with the Government and the Mining Company".[24] A commitment was won
from Comalco to provide assistance "to lift the standards of
living of all Mission Stations" in keeping with the "model
township" planned for white mineworkers at Weipa.

Once again, however, fate was to intervene. There is little
doubt that the election of a coalition government in
Queensland in August 1957 destabilised the church's negotiating status. Comalco immediately expressed "dismay"
with presumptions of financial obligations for Aboriginal
welfare. "We will meet the cost of transport for the physical
move from Weipa to Aurukun", wrote Comalco executive
Maurice Mawby. "But we do not accept that our financial
responsibilities extend as far as the Committee seeks to

establish". Mawby conceded that some "protective measures other than immediate removal" could also be negotiated for Mapoon,[25] now doubly in jeopardy with a Canadian
aluminium company, Alcan, prospecting in the hinterland
behind the mission.

O'Leary was quick to get new minister Dr Henry Noble
on side. Mapoon was a "pretty sorry story", he said. Since
1953 a merger had been arranged, and "the Government
was to find the money", but the church had prevaricated in
the face of the people's reluctance. O'Leary made no
mention of the church's stated inability to fund the merger,
nor the government's failure to do so. While he lamented
the mission's continuing "deterioration", he conveniently
omitted reference to his own directive to freeze development expenditure. "The Department can no longer close
its eyes to the Mapoon situation", advised O'Leary, characterised as it was by continuing mismanagement and malnutrition. "The Church has too long postponed any positive
action", he informed Noble, and "the time is now oppor-
tune for a firm decision by the Government".[26] Move them
all to Bamaga, he wrote, where they would be directly under
departmental control.

Negotiations between the committee and Comalco to
relocate Weipa residents to Aurukun, 30 miles (48 kilometres) distant, were denounced by O'Leary as unworkable
and disruptive. Aboriginal mineworkers, already numbering 70, should be assimilated in the mining town at Comalco's expense, he told Noble, with cavalier disregard for
the committee's attempts to maintain some integrity for the
Weipa community.

It was from this point that the board of missions found
itself excluded from negotiations. The premier and chief

secretary's department took over the consultation process, a process allowing no forum for Aboriginal interests. Church protests were rebuffed with the assertion that no safeguards for Aboriginal rights needed to be written into the impending legislation "because these rights could be secured just as effectively by Orders in Council following Letters of Undertaking being submitted by the mining company". So covetous was the government, that in their haste to pass the Commonwealth Aluminium Corporation Pty Limited Agreement Bill both missions were swallowed by the mining lease, contrary to statements to parliament by the minister for Mines. The government subsequently had to renegotiate with Comalco to surrender small portions for mission operation, initially 75 acres (30 hectares) for Weipa and 500 acres (200 hectares) for Mapoon.[27] As from January 1958 Comalco was granted an 84-year lease on over 2,270 square miles (5800 square kilometres), or 93 per cent of land which had been officially reserved since the nineteenth century for the Aborigines of Mapoon, Aurukun and Weipa.

Faced with this *fait accompli*, Sweet wrote angrily: "Such action does not engender confidence or good relationships between the Committee and your Government". With no concessions secured even for pastoral rights on the land, the moderator described dealings with the government as "highly unsuccessful and very frustrating". And to rub salt into the wounds, despite its outright rejection of three detailed submissions by the church, the government had given the impression in parliamentary debates, "by inference if not in actual statement", that the church had raised no objections regarding the Bill and its implications for Aborigines on the peninsula. This was patently untrue.

"Strenuous representations" to have the interests of the Aborigines "acknowledged and safeguarded" had been "to no avail". "Before the enactment of the Comalco Bill", declared the moderator in his annual address, "the interests of the Mapoon, Weipa and Aurukun Mission Stations and the natives thereof were not fully safeguarded by agreements entered into by Government and Company".[28] The Comalco Bill, Rev James Stuckey later remarked bitterly to the press, was "a faulty piece of legislation".[29]

Although the government had trampled Aboriginal welfare in its eagerness to get the mining venture under way, the committee continued to fight for flow-on benefits for the communities. They lobbied the government in an attempt to bolster Mapoon's earning potential and thereby its very survival. Sweet argued that Mapoon was hopeful of gaining employment with Alcan as well as developing a cattle industry on the unused portion of the reserve. If it was government policy to tie the future of the Weipa people to Comalco's development, he continued, "would not the interests of the Mapoon folk be linked with the only two productive sources of income and dignified self-support in their own area?"[30]

Comalco also was subjected to a determined, and equally fruitless, campaign. The committee insisted that since the government had made no formal undertaking to relocate the mission prior to passage of the Comalco Bill, then Comalco was "legally responsible to do the same thing for the natives at Mapoon as it has undertaken to do for Weipa".[31] The company had conceded that mining on the Mapoon reserve was not imminent, and the committee pressed strongly that the mission remain undisturbed and that the vast unused portion be made available for the continuation of Mapoon's grazing project.

When agreement was reached between Comalco and the government on the final boundaries for the plundered Aboriginal reserves, Mapoon was left with only 480 acres (194 hectares), excluding the deepwater anchorage at Cullen Point. Significantly, this grossly truncated area was contracted to revert to Comalco "if in the future the land is vacated by the Mission".[32] Weipa reserve was ultimately set at 500 acres (200 hectares), with Comalco again holding first option should the land "become available for mining in the future". Comalco had already reserved the right to move the mission south of the Embley estuary if the "presence of the native reserve ... interferes with the Company's operations".[33] The government was only too happy to agree. After all, the total bonanza to the state was estimated by minister Henry Noble at around £250,000,000.[34]

In the face of the public outcry over the excision and occupation of Aboriginal reserves, and over the glaring absence of any concessions to Aboriginal interests, either territorial or monetary, O'Leary could only make generalisations. The company had accepted "its responsibilities to the aboriginals" and the government had insisted that Aboriginal mineworkers would receive full award wages. This meant, he declared egregiously, that Aborigines were "placed in a more advantageous economic position than ever previously".[35]

Central to the government's strategy to reclaim the high moral ground, and as a direct retaliation against damaging evidence from the church over botched negotiations, the coalition and the Native Affairs bureaucrats unleashed a campaign of public condemnation over deplorable mission conditions. Newspaper revelations of atrocious housing and amenities on the stagnating northern missions were augmented by "concerned comment" as to the virtues of pro-development interventions. The Presbyterians and Anglicans were united in their insistence that progress was irrevocably linked to some form of legal tenure.[36] With no security over land tenancy, they pointed out, there was no access to development funds, and as wards, Aboriginal residents were also precluded from bank loans. Rev Sweet went further, arguing that mineral leases and mining rights should be vested in Aboriginal trustees so that essential revenue could be generated for community independence.

But O'Leary claimed the push for land rights, by lease or otherwise, was only an outcome of agitation from the Anglican mission at Lockhart River, where an Aboriginal co-operative worked a small commercial goldfield. Indeed the Anglican mission board was critically attuned to the perils of mineral exploration, and followed closely the abortive Presbyterian–Comalco negotiations. In counterposing land tenure to mining rights, O'Leary invoked a powerful, and enduring, principle. Large deposits of valuable minerals which might exist on Aboriginal reserves "cannot be held by the Mission against development in the interests of the State", he wrote, blithely conjuring an opposition of interests where none had been mooted. Departmental policy "will never permit locking up of extensive mineral deposits so urgently needed in the interests of the State and National economy". "It is immaterial to which source royalties obtained from mining ventures in Queensland are paid", he declared fulsomely, because his department was "generously treated" by the state government.[37]

The path of progress

The tide of mineral enterprise, the end of postwar austerity, and the vigour of a pro-development government in Queensland, brought the winds of change to the previously insular church missions in the early 1960s. Records show that the Presbyterian committee warned their Anglican counterparts as early as 1957 that the government would readily evict the missions at both Lockhart River and Yarrabah to expedite mineral development. In fact the Anglicans were already considering resiting the Lockhart River mission, which was crammed on an inaccessible coastal strip at Lloyd Bay. By 1961 they had identified a more fertile and approachable area adjacent to the reserve and within the nearby Claudie gold and mineral field. With the publicity disaster of the Comalco/Weipa expropriation fresh in mind, O'Leary helpfully suggested that the mission board apply to occupy the region at a token rental as a special lease, rather than as an Aboriginal reserve.[38] This would, by no coincidence, preempt any claims of Aboriginal "rights" to land or benefits should the areas be later resumed for mining.

But the Anglican board of missions could not finance reconstruction. Despite full knowledge that the department intended relocating the community to Laradeenya pastoral holdings near Bamaga, and regazetting the old reserve as public lands, they struck a deal with the department to hand over control of the Lockhart River mission. It is evident that both the Anglicans and the department were apprehensive of a potential press furore. In 1963 a plan was hatched to sell the scheme to the public on the basis that the church had requested the takeover and relocation as essential for greatly enhanced health, education and employment prospects.[39] Despite propaganda from the department to the contrary, in 1965 the Bishop of Carpentaria, S. J. Matthews, conceded the "unanimous desire" of the Lockhart River community to remain at the old site. Bombarded with angry letters protesting yet another "stealing" of Aboriginal lands, unwilling to court further opprobrium, and with finances again overtaxed, the government quietly put the plans on the back burner.

Available records suggest that the Anglican board of missions was exceedingly sensitive to adverse publicity. In contrast to the remote Presbyterian mission, the primary Anglican mission at Yarrabah was easily observed by nearby Cairns. Home to perhaps the most vocal and socially experienced community, Yarrabah had been a hotbed of dissent and defiance throughout the 1950s. And with good reason. Internal departmental reports chronicle dilapidated shacks housing over eight people, lacking bathrooms or ceilings, with leaking roofs and open, overflowing drains. Files show that workers and pensioners were unpaid except through coupons usable only at the mission store; not until 1959 did mothers receive any cash from their child endowments. All doors and windows at the schoolhouse had to be closed in wet weather making the rooms too dark for teaching. Seating and desks were second-hand and adult-sized, contributing directly to the prevalence of posture problems in Yarrabah children. And the Cairns Council, which zealously pursued dispersal of the community and resumption of the prime site for public use, was always eager to publicise the stream of adverse reports generated by their health inspector.[40]

Disciplinarian tactics of Yarrabah's superintendent, ex-army captain James Wilcox, included physical assaults on residents as well as the routine punishment of gaoling on bread and water, and greatly intensified bitterness. Under his regime nearly two hundred people left the mission, many expelled as "troublemakers", handed £10 per family and told to fend for themselves. This they did, with most setting up camp on crown land at nearby Bessie Point. Their experiences typify the beleaguered status of Aboriginal family groups in the general community. The Cairns council immediately agitated against their presence citing appalling and unhealthy living conditions, while at the same time rejecting calls to provide water or sanitation because it would only encourage occupancy. Council claims were refuted by the department's inspector who reported a clean site with children in good health and attending school, and most of the men in regular work, some with their own boats and others leasing land.

Although the council had failed to have the camp expelled on unsubstantiated health grounds, and the department acknowledged it had no legal right to force relocation of Aborigines who were exempted from the Aboriginal Acts and were not living on an Aboriginal reserve, agitation to disperse the Bessie Point group continued. Files disclose a proposal in 1959 to transport them to crown land near Gordonvale. This provoked immediate and "incensed" agitation from local cane farmers, who lobbied member for Mulgrave Charles Wordsworth that the ex-Yarrabah inmates would be a "menace to the health of people who operate valuable properties" in the district.[41] The proposal lapsed.

Ultimately it was not the steady leakage of people to Bessie Point but a wide-ranging protest letter to Thomas Gilmore, Country Party minister for the Tablelands, which triggered a full-blown crisis at Yarrabah. Penned by ordained minister Margaret Willey, this letter was part of her campaign of support for present and past Yarrabah residents, and detailed grievances against Wilcox's brutal supervision. Forced to respond, the department sent superintendent Bartlam from Palm Island, who confirmed most of the accusations were sufficiently truthful "to be dangerous to the uninformed", and observed that Wilcox "seems to have a special flair for antagonising people".[42]

With premier Frank Nicklin himself lobbied by disgusted church workers who were forbidden access to the mission, the government demanded that O'Leary furnish a personal report. At a meeting of over 400 residents the depth of hostility was palpable. Following a homily on the need to assist administrators who were working "for their benefit", Wilcox challenged the people to state publicly any complaints. "There then commenced a tirade of abuse of the Superintendent and his administration", O'Leary related, which attained "such a crescendo of shouting" that continuation of the meeting was downright "dangerous". He detailed abuses: women, some of them pregnant, confined to their yards for months for petty breaches of discipline; people threatened for requesting sheet-iron or timber for house repairs; one man, acknowledged by O'Leary as having given long service to the mission, was refused permission to live in his own house and banished to work on one of the outstations. Men and women were routinely threatened with eviction to other missions or to Palm Island. The woman whose discussions with white friends in Cairns had provoked the initial protest letter to Gilmore had been subjected to interrogation by Wilcox and subsequently restricted to the mission for twelve months.[43]

The Anglicans, weary of the constant battle against poor

funding and unsuitable staff, conceded they would "give the Mission back to the Government with grateful hearts if they would accept it". "The Church at Yarrabah is no longer running a mission", lamented Ian Shevill, Bishop of North Queensland, "but a large Social Service project" beyond the manpower and the resources of the church. A recent offer by the state to take over the mission and, as minister Henry Noble had said, perhaps "shift it and create something like Cherbourg"[44], was too good to resist. With mounting Aboriginal dissension and amid a barrage of adverse publicity, the Yarrabah mission committee handed control to the government in July 1960. In contrast to the protracted and pernicious financial attrition endured by the mission committee, more than £150,000 was now earmarked for an immediate expansion program in housing and amenities.

For the Seventh Day Adventists, who ran the small community of Monamona near Kuranda, 1960 also spelled a watershed in mission management. On a cramped and unsuitable site agriculture was impossible, housing decrepit, sanitation noxious, and hookworm and malnutrition endemic. Denied increased government grants because of lack of "self-sufficiency", by 1950 the mission had developed a small timber industry supplying railway sleepers. Forced to unionise their labour force, superintendent Zanotti had engineered a successful transition from ration handouts to wages. Productivity dramatically increased, and in 1957 Zanotti's successor Pastor Ferris reported that families enjoyed a much higher standard of living.

But this experiment in private enterprise was too limited to lift the whole mission to financial independence. And as a pile of damning medical reports hit head office — from hookworm, tuberculosis and leprosy specialists — O'Leary hit out at the "extravagant" leakage of funds to wages for the 83 mill workers. The government never agreed to a system of wages rather than rations, he wrote angrily. If you did not indulge the workers there would be ample funds to cover rations for all. According to the department's inspector, families could not survive on the standard weekly pay of 15s; meat was available only once a fortnight, and no one had seen fruit or vegetables for several months. But president W. Richards of the Seventh Day Adventists insisted that the meagre wages in fact reduced dependence on the government grant, which did not even cover rations for remaining families. While the impasse dragged on, in November 1957 the mill burned down. O'Leary admitted that the Welfare Fund, whose holdings should readily have been available for rebuilding, was cleaned out after poor investments in agricultural projects, remittances for departmental costs, and provision for relocations of Mapoon and Lockhart River.

Ultimately it was a massive hydroelectric scheme, mooted to start within two years and destined to flood the mission site, which precipitated a request for the state to take over the Monamona mission from January 1962. The people refused categorically the department's proposal to disperse them among the Palm Island and Yarrabah communities. If they could not remain on the outskirts of the Monamona reserve they demanded to settle as a group on tribal land near Mareeba.[45] The church maintained command until December, and was "generously" granted ownership of all "native cottages" on the condition that the department had no obligation to cover removal and re-erection expenses. From the files it appears that most people moved into the Kuranda area, with several families renting properties purchased by the department and leased back through the church.[46] Although the dam scheme soon lapsed, there is evidence that all attempts by ex-residents to lease or purchase at the former site were blocked by the department.

Schemes for takeovers or relocations of missions at Lockhart River, Yarrabah and Monamona were relatively straightforward when compared with ongoing dilemmas at Mapoon and Weipa, muddied as they were by outspoken church resolve and the diplomacy of winning concessions from Comalco. In 1958 Comalco had signed a formal agreement to commit nearly £100,000 for a new "Aboriginal village" on the truncated Weipa reserve. Plans included a trade school and a dormitory for single workers from other missions also working on the Comalco development project, but suggestions that an extra fifteen houses be built at the Weipa village for an "experimental number" of relocated Mapoon residents were rejected.[47]

Comalco soon rethought the proximity of the Weipa mission, and lobbied vigorously that both "the interests of the natives" and "the overall assimilation consistent with Government policy" would be better served if the Weipa people were "further removed" from contact with the new white township. Their preferred site, across the estuary at Hey Point on the south bank of the Embley river, failed to convince either O'Leary or his minister.

Comalco executives were not deterred, and changed tack to take a political, rather than a policy, approach. After touring the area with the federal Minister for Supply, Comalco's director wrote a confidential letter to Noble. Rebuilding of the Weipa mission at the present Jessica Point site would cause "great dissatisfaction" to those remaining in decrepit huts at Aurukun and Mapoon. And such a discrepancy in living standards, insisted Mr Byrne, would be an embarrassment to both the government and the church. Since Rev Sweet was also worried about the proximity of the mission to the mining township, Byrne now proposed that Weipa be relocated near the Aurukun mission, described by MacKenzie as a "hunters paradise". Byrne played his trump card last: if Weipa were rebuilt at the present site, it would be the government and the church who would bear responsibility for the "inevitable impact which these primitive people must suffer" in the culture clash with the white labour force.[48] He struck a raw nerve. In May 1961 Cabinet decided that the Weipa people would indeed move to Hey Point.

Within a few months plans were well in hand for the move across the estuary. A new reserve was to be gazetted for the mission and a larger area earmarked for hunting access. The existing Jessica Point area would revert to Comalco. The church now pushed for more than the 45 houses originally agreed to, and for equitable compensation for the homes relinquished at the old site. Once again, all parties bargained without due regard for the tenacity of the people. It was well known that any proposals to merge the Weipa community with Aurukun had been "turned down flat", Rev Stuckey acknowledged in mid-1962. But now, he informed O'Leary, "they retracted the agreement to move to Hey Point, too ... with Parliamentarians talking of citizen rights, broadcasts on the AAL [Aborigines Advancement League] conference at Adelaide and some pretty unwise remarks by Company reps., the people were in no mood really to consider it". Their main concern? That in relocation away from Jessica Point they would miss out on work opportunities.[49]

What was the context of such forceful opposition? Why the public uproar from parliamentarians and Aboriginal pressure groups? What had exposed the shrouded cosy dealings between church, government and mining company to such heightened attention? To appreciate the situation we must pick up the threads at Mapoon, a community under siege by state and church at the time Stuckey wrote of Weipa's unyielding stand. A community soon to be shattered.

A *process of attrition*

It would appear from departmental documents that the fate of Mapoon was sealed as early as December 1957. Claiming that several families had requested to move from Mapoon to Bamaga, and with cavalier disregard for overwhelming resistance, deputy director Patrick Killoran argued for mass relocation. And in his budget estimates for the 1957–58 year, Noble informed fellow ministers he was "reasonably certain" Mapoon would be transferred by the end of the year. It would, after all, be the easy option for a government eager to smooth the path to mineral wealth.

But the church was actively pursuing both Comalco and the government to secure some spin-off for Mapoon from the mining bonanza. And while the trail remained warm, Rev Sweet told O'Leary he adamantly opposed any coercive evacuation "irrespective of the arguments adduced in favour". Infuriated, O'Leary considered making Sweet himself the scapegoat for the mission crisis. "It may be necessary", he advised his superior, "if Mr Sweet continues with his critical attitude of a determined Government policy, to publicise many matters with respect to Mission administration".[50]

With all structural work frozen at Mapoon, the department now manipulated its financial options in order to smash opposition and expedite the "determined Government policy". Cabinet documents of the time reveal that annual subsidies were twice as much per head for government settlements than for church missions. While the people suffered, the department maintained its hard line against any increases in grants. "No one can logically argue that £26 per person per annum is an adequate subsidy even if Child Endowment payments are added with respect to the children", protested Sweet in April 1958.[51] Indeed a telegram intercepted by Killoran in May revealed that Mapoon had been "short or out of rations for two weeks"; this was passed on to O'Leary with the malicious observation that the information "may be of use at some later date" as evidence of church dereliction.[52] And in July the department callously tightened the screws further to demand "greater measures of economy" from the Presbyterian missions. The government subsidy had now dropped to only 8s per week for the 760 residents. For the first time the church buckled, and pondered handing "temporal responsibility" of the missions to the government.

The department now utilised the media to hijack public opinion and undermine Presbyterian credibility. Minister Henry Noble orchestrated a tour late in 1958 and expressed dismay that conditions on the missions compared badly with government settlements. "Concerned" parliamentarians hit the press: conditions were "deplorable ... Mission Stations have failed miserably". There were calls for an official inquiry and a government takeover because "Gulf missions were not doing anything for the money the Government granted them". Six months later further funding cuts had reduced the food allowance to five pence per day, insufficient even to meet the official basic ration scale.[53] Irate, Anglican board of missions chairman Rev F. Coaldrake told the press it was the Queensland government which had failed Aborigines in the north.

As the stand-off continued, a new site of dispute was opened up to exacerbate public and financial attrition. Misinformation unsettled the resolve of the Mapoon community, now unsure who they could trust. After a visit in July 1959 Sweet reported that people "have lost confidence in the white man. They are suspicious of anything that the white man tells them". A distinct pattern of resistance against the superintendent had emerged. Sweet demanded the department resolve the impasse but again told O'Leary that "The known attitude of the Mapoon people is very definitely antagonistic towards a move to any other site than one close to the present Mission".

Unrest at Mapoon, retaliated O'Leary, could be blamed on an indecisive committee and on rebellious "cross-breed" individuals, who had a "totally different outlook" after working with whites in the war years, and were consequently susceptible to "influences not always beneficial to them".[54] While O'Leary stalled, his deputy Patrick Killoran was launching a strategy to break the community. At a hostile and highly volatile meeting at Mapoon he urged that six men, any six men, should visit Bamaga, report back, and sign a commitment for the whole community. As added ammunition Killoran had taken with him Dr Fryberg, head of Queensland health, whose inevitably damning report on living conditions was accompanied by an exhortation that "action should be taken as quickly as possible".[55] Killoran phoned head office stating that the people "are looking to the Government for guidance and assistance in the future".

Rev Sweet, who arrived the following day, was ropable. Residents distrusted the government just as much as the missionaries, he reported, and he ridiculed the claim that a few individuals could sign commitments for the whole community on the strength of a visit to Bamaga. Ultimately only three men made the trip, reporting that hunting might be difficult, sea access was limited, and it was up to the people to plan Mapoon's fate "wherever it may be". It was hardly a ringing endorsement.

Killoran's next ploy was to buy submission with a package of inducements. Accompanied by Sweet, he offered accelerated exemptions from departmental control, pockets of farming land near Bamaga "of sufficient fertility and area to guarantee a reasonable living standard" for exempted families, and a two-thirds priority for ex-Mapoon residents for secure-tenure cattle holdings on the sub-divided vacated reserve.[56] His propositions met with "unanimous negation". Ominously, Killoran reported that most would reach a "willing decision" to leave after the benefits were explained to them by nine chosen delegates, five of whom were community police, and he busied himself with plans "to achieve the dispersal of the population".

Killoran chose Hidden Valley near Bamaga as the site for "new Mapoon", estimating costs for bridging the Jardine river, thirty houses, water reticulation, a school and an aid post at £28,000. But the government, perhaps hard-pressed after its £8,000,000 outlay on harbour and facilities at Weipa, slashed the requisition from £20,000 to £12,000. Desperate to make a start, Killoran found £3,000 within his department's budget and garnisheed £2,764 from the

Mapoon mission trust fund. Suddenly it was possible to plan two completed homes a month for the beleaguered Mapoon residents.

Opposition against the move hardened at Mapoon. Superintendent Garth Filmer applied to forcibly expel "one or two families", and obtained authorisation to "peruse but not censor" all private mail to counter "contentious and possibly subversive" material flowing from Aboriginal support groups.[57] Early in 1962 Killoran advised Sweet that removal orders would be issued "to transfer some of the organisers of the opposition".[58] Of great significance at this time was Killoran's decision to bypass Rev Sweet's Queensland committee to deal directly with Rev James Stuckey, general secretary of the board of missions in Sydney. This stimulated a flurry of "Dear Pat, from Jim" letters which attest to a more single-minded approach. Stuckey outlined a "programme of removal" which would see the mission cleared by June 1963, after six months winding down including closure of the store and school and demolition of buildings and transport.

Church and state were now united in their resolve to emasculate rebellion and dissolve the community. Filmer routinely refused to allow the return of those leaving for medical or work needs, and houses were demolished to prevent reoccupation. By the end of 1962 the authorities were in damage control as a wave of protests from Aboriginal organisations and trade unions erupted over the beleaguered Weipa and Mapoon missions. Rev Sweet himself was called in defence. "It is not true to talk about coercion", insisted Sweet, labelling Aboriginal activism as "political agitation". "We, who are opposed to communism, are not guilty of communist tactics."[59]

At Mapoon the resolve was obviously unsettling the authorities. The Aboriginal Advancement League in Cairns acted as a conduit for support and supplies. O'Leary deflected ministerial disquiet with the claim that it "is a political and disruptive organisation with no record of any practical helpful action in the interests of coloured people".[60] Several men had found work with Alcan, on nearby stations, and in trading crocodile skins. Stuckey wrote anxiously to Killoran that the people might sit out the siege despite increasing hardships.[61]

By May 1963 the people were suffering severe deprivation. Store goods were run down and the school closed. To compound the squeeze, Killoran had also implemented a suggestion Stuckey had floated twelve months earlier that all "Social Service benefits and personal finances" be redirected through the department "as the people remove from Mapoon".[62] Not only did this check the cash flow but, as Stuckey had callously commented, "I warned them if there was neglect of their children, the law would operate and coercion could take place".[63]

Killoran was keen to legitimate his actions in the public sphere. Endorsing Stuckey's approach, namely that any neglect of the children would mean a "removal order would be legitimate and enforced", he sent stipendiary magistrate B. Scanlan to make a report shortly after the government took control in June. This confirmed dilapidated shanties, lack of food, the women's concern for their children, and the men's frustration with official inaction. Killoran's conniving is clear. Stuckey quotes him as saying that the magistrate's visit was "the greatest thing we had in our favour".[64]

Noting hypocritically that "neither he [Stuckey] nor I could face the public if we allowed the people to starve", and acknowledging "possible political repercussions", Killoran sought ministerial approval to remove the "troublemakers" who had used the magistrate's visit to lodge complaints over their deplorable plight. But abhorrence at the siege of Mapoon had spilled into national and international forums and the minister declined to take action. Prime Minister Robert Menzies had been lobbied by the Federal Council of Aboriginal Advancement (FCAA) to terminate the "long persecution of the Mapoon people", and was demanding explanations at the highest level. FCAA had also petitioned the United Nations over exclusion and expulsion of Aborigines from Cape York reserves. The state line was parroted: the move was gradual and voluntary; the process pre-dated the bauxite enterprise.

Premier G. F. Nicklin assured Menzies the matter would receive his attention. And so it did. Under cover of a November federal election campaign, Killoran struck. On the basis of what manager Charles Turner described as a peaceful meeting, Killoran issued removal orders for eleven men and women and their families, plus any others Turner might "desire ... also to accompany the party." Aboriginal organisations suggest forty-two people were deported. Accompanying the armed police contingent from Thursday Island was a "work party ... to commence demolition of the vacated shanties on the Reserve". The boat arrived at night, families were marched into a mission hut with what they could carry and confined under armed guard until deportation at dawn. Houses were demolished and burned, furniture and household goods destroyed. The deportees were off-loaded at Bamaga, as Constance Cooktown later recounted, "like a mob of cattle with nowhere to go".[65]

The government, through a compliant press, spread the message of the two hundred people who had "gone quite happily to New Mapoon" during the previous eighteen months, of the danger of starvation for the remainder who "were incapable of supporting themselves", of the absence of force — "only a show of uniforms had been needed". At Bamaga, so the story continued, there was good hunting and fishing, new houses and a hospital, and areas for agricultural development. In fact the department's building program was so chaotic, with forced relocations at Monamona and Lockhart River, that Killoran had admitted six months' previously that Mapoon's transfer would be difficult to justify. New Mapoon, a windswept and waterlogged site with few homes, rampant unemployment and poor hunting and fishing, was quickly dubbed a "hungry place".[66]

Comalco, meanwhile, must have watched aghast at this deplorable perversion of public relations. Late in 1962, after several years of wrangling over the number of houses required, they suggested that the church should take charge of the £150,000 program to rebuild Weipa. The committee was pushing for "simpler but adequate" houses, allowing a residue to cover costs of a ferry service to the mining town. And Comalco, "having a regard to their own public image" sought to disengage itself from any lowering of standards. Aware that the committee might be "open to probable criticism that they are seeking to get their hands on the money for their own purpose ... a ludicrous suggestion but one which appears to cause embarrassment to your Department",[67] Stuckey suggested that the department should handle the building of houses similar to those at Bamaga. The department declined.

Building finally commenced in 1965. Although Comalco ultimately positioned its mining town fourteen miles (22 kilometres) away from Jessica Point, the new mission was commenced three miles (five kilometres) back from the old beach-front homes. And by this time relations between church and state had lost the cavalier camaraderie of the Mapoon campaign. Having replaced O'Leary as director of the department, it appears that Killoran intended the "model village" at Weipa to expunge criticism of his handling of Mapoon. The church hierarchy, on the other hand, was looking at total community needs, including a viable cattle industry to replace jobs lost as construction work at Comalco neared completion.

But the £150,000 of 1959 was decimated by the harsh realities of inflation. Despite a rumoured $10 million in state and federal aid to Comalco, approaches for additional backing for Aboriginal housing brought outright refusal from a government still seething with resentment. In a formal and bitter letter to Killoran, Stuckey vented his frustration that the department held the church to a total building program, including water supply, toilets, laundries and even upgraded housing specifications, at the same time as it avoided the implications of an inadequate funding pool. This "utterly irresponsible delay", Stuckey told Killoran, "could disastrously and permanently injure the image of Mission and Government with the people".[68]

Neither the mission committee nor the department intended the new homes to be allocated free of charge to Weipa residents. The board of missions was keen for purchase of freehold tenure which would promote pride of ownership and allow families to qualify for the £250 commonwealth housing grant. "Whilst in the ultimate this is the desirable title", countered Killoran, it would "render null and void any rights of control" over the properties by either the board or the department.[69] His suggestion of purchase through a housing fund which would allow a "form of ownership" was greeted with great suspicion by the people. Their old homes had been wilfully destroyed behind them: why would they pay for a new house if there was no security of title?

In September 1965, as building neared completion, the board of missions was secretly negotiating to hand control to the government on a "walk in/walk out" basis. Government documents contrast projected running costs of $22,500 for the four months period from the February 1966 takeover to the end of June with the total of $9,000 per year paid to the board. "In the light of experience in both Mapoon and Lockhart River Missions", Killoran advised his minister, the change should be effected expeditiously to avoid a "feeling of frustration or apprehension" by the Weipa people. He urged that all negotiations be kept secret until after the official opening of the village in November 1965, after which two "reliable" community leaders might be shown over the upgraded Yarrabah settlement "preparatory to informing the residents".[70]

In his celebratory speech at the village opening, minister Jack Pizzey linked "the aboriginal's feeling of inferiority" with the substandard housing "to which, in many cases, he has been condemned by his European neighbours".[71] It was a convenient deflection of culpability. In fact the 56 three-bedroom and six two-bedroom houses lacked electricity, they were unpainted, without sinks or handbasins, and communal laundries were not provided for a further three years. Small wonder that the costs of $4,600 and $3,226

respectively for three- and two-bedroom houses compared
so economically with the price of $28,000 for Comalco's
mining accommodation.

The systemic discrimination of rehousing was matched
by a more subtlely introduced bias by Comalco. While
claiming an open school policy in the white township,
Comalco insisted on "grade for age" in the classrooms,
effectively barring most "mission" children. And rather
than blow out the mining hospital budget by $57,000 to
provide sufficient facilities for "mission" patients, the government took the cheaper option of allocating funds for an
extra room, if it proved necessary.[72]

By mid-1967 the mythical bonanza of unlimited employment had dwindled to a paltry fourteen positions for
Aboriginal employees. Although public rhetoric reinforced
the "recognition" that Aboriginal workers were unreliable
and racially unsuited to steady work, Comalco's statistics
show a turnover in the *white* workforce exceeding 100 per
cent.[73] Killoran was later to admit that the "degree of
adverse notoriety" accorded both Comalco and his department in part derived from the gratuitous excision of reserve
lands which had been vital for the "significant" hunting
activities of the remote communities. Vital not because of
customary practices, but because the paltry $7 to $12 per
week paid to mission workers was insufficient to sustain
family life.[74]

*   *   *

By the mid-1960s most of Queensland's missions had un-
dergone radical change. Mapoon and Monamona had
been eliminated from the localities which had been home
to their people since time immemorial. Lockhart River was

threatened with the same fate. Weipa and Yarrabah had not been uprooted but had nonetheless been detached from the church stewardship that had shaped the parameters of social life for around seventy years. Official rhetoric predicated on church "neglect" promised a new dawning under government management, a promise soon to be challenged.

The political terrain of Aboriginal affairs in Queensland was also irrevocably recast. Where the succession of departmental heads had operated in comparative obscurity and political disinterest, the pursuit of wealth now brought to bear the unwelcome gaze of a critical public on the operations and ideology of the department itself. And the "needs" of the state fostered interventions by ministers and premiers who imperiously tailored departmental directions to maximise other agendas.

8

Double standards

According to conventional wisdom, the mid-1960s mark the point when Queensland was finally forced to liberalise its restrictive management of the Aboriginal population. Bowing to a groundswell of national antipathy, the government finally renounced the reserve mentality which had seen so many families subjected to involuntary removal to missions and settlements.

Civil rights were reluctantly recognised as the national referendum of 1967 overwhelmingly approved full citizenship for Australia's indigenous inhabitants. And the Commonwealth arbitration commission enshrined in law the edict of equal pay: no longer would Aboriginal workers be underpaid on the basis of race. Federal funds poured into the states to finance a remarkable program to bring Aboriginal housing and health into line with standards enjoyed by other Australians.

It is certainly a wonderful scenario. Unfortunately, experience over the last three decades belies these expectations. Housing, health and employment deficits have not been reversed, despite outlays of millions of dollars. Was the liberalisation sabotaged by recalcitrant states? Or is the notion of "liberalisation" itself a mirage?

Labour as commodity

In June 1957, according to reports in the *Brisbane Telegraph*, one thousand Palm Islanders rose in rebellion, and twenty police were despatched in an RAAF crash boat to restore order: a massive overreaction by police and press. There had been no violence and no property damage: merely a noisy demonstration against the pitiful pay of £2 per week, a threat to strike, and the release of a fellow protester from the Island jail.

The native affairs' chief had no patience for "these half-castes" who threatened "good order and discipline" by demanding a fair wage. Prior to any inquiry, on O'Leary's orders, seven men and their families were arrested at 3 am the next morning and shipped off *in leg irons* — three to Cherbourg, three to Woorabinda, and one to Bamaga.[1] This peremptory authoritarianism was typical of life on the Island. "You could be jailed for little — or nothing", recalled Neville (later Senator) Bonner. "If you were late for work, you could be punished. If you weren't in your own house when the 10 pm curfew bell rang, you could be arrested."[2]

Conditions on Palm Island were dreadful. Hardship and discontent were aggravated by overcrowding and the escalating influx of rebellious men removed from other settlements for "disciplinary purposes". But the root cause of friction was the wage. Most of the able-bodied Palm Islanders worked at cane cutting on the mainland, where, according to the 1945 Aboriginal regulations, all employees except those in the pastoral industry were paid full award rates.

Under those same regulations, however, every able-bodied settlement resident was compelled to work at least 32 hours per week without pay. By the 1950s a token "training allowance" had been introduced as incentive in some positions. Evidence from 1959 reveals that the Presbyterians were paying only £2 per week plus rations to men who could earn £14 per week in seasonal rural work.[3] Workers were well aware of the inequity of this practice, made more unpalatable by discrepancies between the settlements themselves.

It is clear from the files that many men and women with the qualifications to earn good money were unwillingly detained on the settlements providing essential skilled labour for a pittance, a point made by the Building Workers Industrial Union (BWIU). Challenging the euphemistic "training allowance" on its own terms, they reproached the minister, citing a complete lack of evidence of any trade instruction. "It seems to us therefore that a large percentage of such so called training is in reality employment of Aborigines to carry out essential work for your Department at rates and conditions well below those prescribed by the Building Trades Award — State".[4] Incredibly, the "distribution" of a set wage pool among as many workers as possible, to maximise industry and minimise idleness, remained departmental policy as late as 1986.

The Townsville branch of the Trades and Labour Council (TLC), as chief lobby group, was denied its own inquiry into the Palm Island "uprising". Their interest in Aboriginal matters was "to the detriment of the peace and contentment of the aboriginals", according to O'Leary, who urgently assured his superiors that dissension was limited to only a few troublemakers "subject to outside influences [who] have been illicitly preaching a doctrine contrary to good order and discipline on the Reserve".[5]

But such was the clamour of trade union agitation

against victimisation, especially of those who sought to withhold labour, that the new minister for Native Affairs, Dr Henry Noble, found it prudent to take a party of parliamentarians to Palm Island to placate political unease. Describing the complainants as "not very dependable sources of information", he declared that the institution was efficiently run "in the interests of its native residents".

In defence of his policy, O'Leary publicly maintained that the value of rations and housing gave a monetary return well in excess of award rates. But minutes of a 1960 conference contain his admission that payment of award wages where due would throw the institutions into "a state of chaos". He conceded it would necessitate a 75 per cent cut to the workforce, threaten operations and control, expose settlements to union disruption, and complicate the ejection of such workers from the settlements.[6]

O'Leary's private unease over the legality of his stance is revealed when challenges by the Amalgamated Engineering Union drove him to seek an official opinion from the solicitor general. He was advised that Queensland's industrial court had the power to make specific exemptions from awards, as was the case in the pastoral industry. Importantly, no such variations had been, or ever were, sought or granted. Killoran betrayed no misgivings. In 1963 he threatened to have anyone dismissed who pursued award rates on the settlements, prompting the TLC to request that Noble have his officers refrain from victimising or disadvantaging workers who sought the legal rate of pay.[7]

If organised labour was branded as "harmful" to Aboriginal interests, the peak employer body was seen as positively commendable. The pastoral industry soaked up rural labour, collaborated in departmental controls, taught skills

on the job, and provided the main private revenue source
for the department. It worked both ways. Since 1919 pastoralists had profited from a wage advantage of 33 per cent
for Aboriginal stockworkers, who formed the backbone of
their industry. Even this level was not secure, being subject
to negotiation with the United Graziers' Association
(UGA). Records show that as late as 1950, when the white
rate was £7 6s 6d per week plus allowances, Aboriginal
station hands received only 66 per cent of the *1938* rate of
£2 15s; and pay rises to £4 17s 6d in 1950 and £7 in 1952
were still well under the 66 per cent parity.[8]

When the department lifted the rate to £10 in 1957 the
UGA baulked at the "arbitrary" wage increase, trotting out
the myths of the irresponsible Aboriginal worker and the
brood of costly dependants: they do not "compare with
experienced white stockmen", argued UGA representatives, and pastoralists were forced to carry "half the
tribe" of stockworkers. After a tour of the Gulf country in
1956, deputy director P. J. Richards dismissed such allegations out of hand. Noting "the marked and growing reluctance of white stockmen to accept employment in the
remote areas of the State", he declared, "it is becoming
increasingly apparent that the continuance of pastoral pursuits depends on aboriginal stockmen". Unfortunately, it
was equally apparent to Richards that graziers were "more
concerned with obtaining aboriginal labour as cheaply as
possible than with paying wages in terms of the real worth
of the native stockmen".[9]

And employers profited from, rather than patronised,
workers' dependants. Regulations decreed wives could be
worked *unpaid* for twelve hours a week. And despite a legal
minimum of 14 years, exploitation of child labour was

entrenched, as the manager of the Stock Breeders' Association conceded. O'Leary was well aware of abuses: "There has been a fair amount, and probably still is ... utilisation of child labour. Some of them have been brought into the towns for medical attention, broken arms, legs ... " He cautioned against putting "undersized and weedy" children to hard labour, remarking with breathtaking condescension: "We try to look on these people as human beings ... Nobody is going to put his own child out too young and we have to think of that with these people".[10] Noting that no employers claimed the available allowance for dependant's rations, O'Leary commented acidly: "Possibly it is cheaper to feed the dependants than pay wages for the work they perform".

In fact the UGA argued strongly for official apprenticing from as early as twelve years, "when they were more interested, and also grew up in the right surroundings". Missionary reluctance to release youths until seventeen or eighteen was said to "ruin" children who were then "too old to be taught anything". But protests by the Edward River superintendent against the forced return of several "absconders" from Strathburn station shows the other side to this equation. Living quarters comprised a shed of galvanised iron walls and roof, no windows, one opening but no door, antbed floor, no bunks, blankets or light at night, a bark lean-to for eating with no walls and no table; pocket money consisted only of 2oz tobacco and two packets of matches.[11]

Such blatant contraventions of regulated conditions were rarely challenged. Few police protectors had the time or the inclination to check outlying cattle stations, and in 1956 the department arranged that industrial inspectors of white accommodation should also check that "fair treatment" obtained for Aboriginal workers. Little changed. The files abound with reports of appalling abuses including sexual assaults, wet living quarters, rough handling, brutality with chains, poor rations, lack of clean water and cooking sheds, and widespread hookworm and ill health, especially among children. Workers who walked off bad jobs were pursued by police and forcibly returned. Many protectors ignored Aboriginal complaints, labelling them as untrue, unsubstantiated or merely vindictive.[12]

Having successfully driven the 1957 £10 wage down to £8 10s by strategic lobbying, the UGA allowed it to be reintroduced unopposed in 1961. But on discovering that allowances had also been increased, they bypassed O'Leary to target minister Henry Noble direct. The government once again buckled. In a face-saving exercise it retained the notional base rate, but *reduced* hourly rates for all Aboriginal work. Employers simply took the cheaper hourly option: Aboriginal station workers remained, as the TLC observed, "shockingly exploited", often working twelve hours a day, seven days a week for less pay than before, and the grazing industry profited to the tune of an estimated £2,000,000.[13]

Adjusted allowances and manipulated rateage were only two of a range of artful dodges separating Aboriginal labour from the standard wage. Categories such as "active/non-active" enabled wages of men over forty-five to be cut from £10 12s 6d to £5 7s 6d; youths in the 16-18 and 18-21 years group received only 59 per cent and 46 per cent of the white wage respectively; and cooks and domestics were paid only 55 per cent and 42 per cent. In the face of TLC denunciations that the wage discounts were "scandalous" and "inconsistent with public utterances", Killoran feigned impotence. Aboriginal penalties, he alleged, were "determined by the

Industrial Court" and were not "an Arbitrary decision by a Government or a Department".[14]

It was the tag of "slow worker" which provided the easiest of economies for pastoral wage bills. Activated with Australian Workers' Union (AWU) consent, this only required a protector to prevail upon a worker to "agree" his capacity for work was diminished and sign his contract accordingly, and cheap labour was assured. Claiming that "practically all aboriginals" came under this category, "not so much from a lack of ability to acquire skills as a lack of mental capacity to cope with certain situations", the UGA blocked submissions by the TLC that an industrial magistrate be empowered to judge Aboriginal ability. Streaming Aboriginal station hands onto normal pay would cause major complications logging overtime, sick leave, etc., argued the graziers; not to mention difficulties under the *Workers' Accommodation Act* which stipulated that "white workers should not have to live in the same sleeping accommodation or eat in the same dining room as coloured workers".[15]

In a climate of escalating pressures over the repudiation of Aboriginal civil rights (discussed below), Queensland once again found itself uncomfortably in the spotlight. "In view of the world-wide attention focused on racial discrimination", Pizzey admitted in 1964, opposition to the push for equal wages "is not considered prudent". Killoran also conceded that the principle of non-discrimination, now also pursued in the federal industrial commission by the AWU, "could not reasonably be opposed". Even allowing for an industrial magistrate to arbitrate lower rates "where necessary", Killoran calculated it would be possible to retain access to employment which the full wage might jeopardise. After all, he intoned, "the Aborigines' interests warrant intervention".[16]

Contrary to "equality" rhetoric in the national arena, new regulations gazetted in Queensland in April 1966 continued to defer to the UGA in the underpayment of Aboriginal station hands. They were not alone in this. Prime Minister Robert Menzies had confidentially assured Queensland's premier, Frank Nicklin, a year previously that while the Commonwealth publicly supported the AWU push for equal wages, this would only apply for former "wards". The "slow worker" clause will remain, he confided, and for workers from missions and settlements, deemed "trainees", full wages would be phased in "over time".[17] In March 1966 the Commonwealth arbitration commission handed down its judgement requiring "equal pay" to be in place from December 1968.

"Civil rights" as social strategy

When the Menzies' government committed £1,000,000 towards Aboriginal welfare "as evidence of the commonwealth Government's intention to extend equality with other Australians in the field of social services",[18] the promised age, invalid and widows' pensions were eagerly awaited in Queensland. Even before the private benefits became available, O'Leary had determined that they could legally be "diverted to revenue": as in white institutions, authorities could pocket 66 per cent of the pensions of mission and settlement residents, with the residue distributed at the discretion of superintendents.

Documents reveal that O'Leary contemplated confiscating the whole windfall by simply reducing operational grants by an equivalent amount.[19] This got round the thorny problem of withholding the pensions on missions, whose "continuous appeal for funds" was public knowledge. In 1960, however, Commonwealth officers visited the Presbyterian missions and offered direct pension allocation, infuriating O'Leary who claimed this was inconsistent with white institutions.

Even the cash component to individuals, set at 33s out of the 95s per week pension, was not secure. Superintendents claimed it would disrupt work programs because it exceeded the "training allowance", and would only be wasted on the pensioners. All missions apart from Yarrabah initially passed on only 10s to 15s per week from the pension benefit of 95s, but at Mapoon and Weipa people refused this token amount, forcing the committee to reinstate the 33s payout. Pensioners demanded to know why their funds should be docked at all, when their wages had been levied during their working lives. Why, demanded a Cherbourg man of premier Frank Nicklin, should pensioners have to pay "all over again"? why was an elderly man reduced to 10s per week when he got the full pension "outside"? why did an exempt lady living on the reserve but drawing her pension from Murgon retain the full amount?[20] Why, as a subsequent petition demanded, can we not even see our own pension books to check official transactions?

In 1959 the push for Aboriginal "civil rights" was again news, and formed part of a raft of constitutional changes which Dr Herbert Evatt urged should go to national referendum. Queensland opposed the motion as "impetuous". Apart from the 19,300 part-Aborigines already enjoying full citizenship rights, O'Leary claimed Queensland's Aboriginal population "are incapable of accepting the responsibilities of citizenship and do not desire them".[21] Minister Henry

Noble went further: the granting of citizenship, he said, "would serve no purpose other than virtually condemning them to a state of degradation".[22] Convinced of its superior approach, Queensland, according to O'Leary, "could never agree" to a federal takeover of the "care, control, and management of its aboriginal people". The optimum policy was one of gradualism, which centred on the "training" of Aboriginal families towards assimilation.

Internal documents reveal the punitive, as well as the educative, component of "assimilation" in Queensland. Portrayed as a policy to "lessen the indigency of our native people", Cabinet decided to clear "eligible people" into the white community. This would be engineered by reducing support for settlement families to "encourage independence", and by promoting the adoption from the settlements of as many "light skinned" children as possible. Warning of opposition to this last measure, O'Leary informed his officers, "You have to educate coloured people to make the sacrifice to have their children adopted and so give them the chance to enjoy the privileges of the white community".[23]

The underlying impetus in the push to "assimilate" mission and settlement residents into the general community was, as always, economic. O'Leary had revealed to a meeting of settlement superintendents in October 1960 that both he and his minister were under pressure from the treasury "to say how many people are being put off the Settlements. The demand came that the Minister shall show how the population on the Settlement will be reduced saying the cost of maintenance of these people should be cut".[24] And the artifice that part-Aboriginal children should be relinquished to enjoy "white" privileges was also unmasked: "The Government is not going to allow white and near white children whether their parents are black or white to remain on the Settlements at the cost of the tax payer". From the files it is clear that neither the parents concerned nor the state children's department (which declared the matter the province of native affairs) were persuaded to participate in this scheme, despite avid promotion over many years.

While the question of Aboriginal rights was defeated at the 1959 referendum, a federal policy statement two years later did assert the right of Aborigines to "attain the same manner of living" as other Australians. Once again Queensland's repressive controls were exposed to unwelcome scrutiny. The national media circulated reports of unpaid compulsory labour, of discriminatory wages and managed savings accounts, of forced detention on reserves, of censored mail, of controlled marriages, and of schools without trained teachers. These criticisms were dismissed as exaggerations.

With damaging international attention focused on the plight of Australia's indigenous population, a "correct" version of national policy was circulated confidentially to all overseas embassies in an attempt to keep the "Aboriginal question" off the United Nation's agenda. In part this alleged that the communist party was behind the human rights push in what was described as a politically motivated campaign.[25] Taking advantage of international sympathy, the Bishop of Carpentaria used a visit to London to test his chances of accessing support through the Freedom from Hunger Campaign, stating that entrenched malnutrition on Queensland's Anglican missions derived from underfunding by state and federal governments.[26] Acutely embar-

rassing for the Australian government, a major contributor
to the fund, this gambit was aborted after a flurry of letters,
on the grounds that aid programs were available only to
underdeveloped countries.

To defuse international opprobrium, in 1962 the
Menzies' government granted Aboriginal Australians full
voting rights in federal elections, neatly reversing rhetoric
which had previously predicated "civil rights" upon a "capacity" to exercise them. During parliamentary debate on
the Bill, Queensland's policies were singled out as "probably the most restrictive on any Australian statute-book ...
Every person who has the specified degree of aboriginal
ancestry may have his rights and his freedom taken from
him at a stroke of the director's pen". In the midst of the
siege of Mapoon, Killoran was targeted for bitter personal
criticism; Liberal MLA John Howson called him "the un-
crowned king of Thursday Island" and "a wicked man",
whose policy "adopted for many years now is entirely
wrong".[27]

When under pressure, appoint a committee. Queensland's Nicklin government did just this, sending a special
committee of justice, health, education and university personnel around the state "to investigate every aspect of
aboriginal welfare".[28] In fact the rhetoric of assimilation,
while philosophically "progressive", also accorded neatly
with Queensland's economic imperatives. The main policy
objective, O'Leary informed committee members, was to
get people out of the institutional environments despite
acknowledged resistance. Native affairs' bureaucrats went
so far as to consider setting age or ability limits as mechanisms to clear the settlements of the many inmates rejecting
"assimilation", who, as O'Leary observed, "think they own

the place and they don't want to leave".[29] Only the briefest reference was made to the consequences of such de-institutionalisation, when O'Leary conceded the existence of the "line of demarcation between coloured and white people" in "every Queensland town",[30] which operated to exclude Aboriginal families from rural housing.

The special committee's final report was not tabled in parliament until November 1964, by which time Patrick Killoran had taken the reins from O'Leary as Director of Native Affairs. A public servant since 1913, and associated with Aboriginal affairs since 1922, O'Leary's retirement capped a career in which, according to the *Annual Report* of 1963, "A humanitarian outlook in all phases of administration has been the practice". Killoran became only the third man to control Aboriginal affairs since Bleakley took the position in 1914.

The Act to Promote the Well-being and Progressive Development of the Aboriginal Inhabitants of the State and of the Torres Strait Islanders certainly had the right ring of humanitarianism. Based on the special committee's report, but deliberately crafted to replace "outmoded" laws with legislation "general in nature" so as not to attract specific criticisms, the 1965 *Aboriginal Affairs Act* gave the appearance of reversing the rhetoric of control by creating a category of "assisted" Aborigines. This category encompassed any person with a "strain of Aboriginal blood" living on a reserve, their children, or any person deemed by a magistrate to be in need of "assistance" under the Act. This "reversal" of control was, in Killoran's estimation, a diplomatic triumph. Henceforth each Queensland Aborigine would be "born a free citizen" — albeit commonly deemed in need of "assistance" — and this "would create a much more favourable psychological image within the aboriginal communities", he exalted.[31]

"Image" was certainly an appropriate expression for the new "freedoms". Under the renamed Department of Aboriginal and Islander Affairs it now became necessary to hold a "certificate of entitlement" to reside on a mission or settlement, revokable at any time by the director, who maintained his power of enforced transfer between reserves. It was no coincidence that this reversal of tenancy rights also neatly removed impediments to reducing settlement populations and evicting dissenters. It also legitimated the longstanding practice of excluding exempted families from return to their home communities: "There are plenty of people who want to go back to the settlements ... but you must stand on them and keep them away for a few years".[32]

Aboriginal property and accounts could still be taken possession of, retained or sold at the director's discretion, although appeal could now be made in a magistrate's court against such seizure; and alcohol consumption, although still prohibited on missions and settlements, was no longer illegal in the general community. The duty of "protection" was transferred from rural police to clerks of courts. Was this latter a dramatic reform? A transferral of Aboriginal management from the police to the secular? Hardly. In many rural towns the positions were combined. And as Killoran privately advised: "it would still be very necessary for the Police Force to actively co-operate in the administration of such legislation".[33]

Aboriginal electoral rights in Queensland underwent a similar cosmetic "liberalisation". Previously, all "Aboriginal natives" and "half-castes" under departmental control and supervision were excluded from voting in state elections. Shortly after passage of the 1965 *Aborigines Affairs Act*, amendments to the *Elections Acts* enabled, but did not compel, all Aborigines and Islanders to vote. The qualification was purely political: Cabinet was acutely sensitive to the effect bulk Aboriginal votes might have in marginal seats. Rural councils embracing large Aboriginal communities had lobbied aggressively that inclusion of the new "citizens" might jeopardise established authority. They might "take over the Shire Council", screamed the Burke shire council, with reference to both Doomadgee and Mornington Island constituents.[34] Councils for the Cook and Carpentaria shires, province of Hopevale and the Mitchell and Edward River missions respectively, also sent hostile letters to the premier. It was decided to maintain white "security" by simply disqualifying reserve residents from local government electoral rolls.

Implicit in the granting of citizenship "rights" was a further danger to official controls, namely the potential for political electioneering to broach departmental doctrine. "It is not desirable for political canvassers to be allowed unrestricted access to Reserves", cautioned Killoran, "particularly representatives of some of the more radical political persuasions whose activities engender unrest and would create major administrative problems".[35] Cabinet agreed heartily. Aboriginal reserves were declared off-limits.

In July 1967 Mr J. Bjelke-Petersen, Acting Minister for Education, used the platform of the national Aboriginal welfare conference to advertise the "liberalisation" of Queensland's reforms. "The Act which we proclaimed in 1965", he told state and federal ministers, "removed most of the restrictive measures we had, but it still retains certain protective measures". His sanguine evaluation was not shared by peak Aboriginal associations who declared: "The 'freedom' expected, particularly by people on reserves, varies widely from the 'freedom', the 'handing over of responsibility', visualised by most D.N.A. officials."[36]

The intensification of surveillance became appallingly apparent to reserve residents with the gazettal of new regulations in April 1966. With the judicious and deliberately loose terminology at their disposal, superintendents, now renamed managers or district officers, could exercise almost limitless constraints over personal behaviours. A whole range of conducts now became punishable offences: failure to conform to a reasonable standard of good conduct; exhibiting behaviour detrimental to the well-being of other persons; committing acts subversive of good order or discipline on reserves. It was an offence to be idle, careless or negligent at work, to refuse work or to behave in an offensive, threatening, insolent, insulting or disorderly manner. Dormitories were redefined as places of detention for any boy or girl who committed an offence against discipline, who departed or attempted to escape from a community, who was guilty of "immoral conduct", or who failed to obey instructions in hygiene, sanitation or infant welfare.

"Democratisation" of communities was ostensibly underpinned by the formal constitution of Aboriginal councils, Aboriginal courts, Aboriginal police. Touted as analogues of local government, councils were instructed to "oversee the good rule and government of the reserve or community". But half the members were appointed by the director who could sack those who displeased him; and managers were empowered to reject nominations for positions, thus excluding outspoken or "inappropriate" candidates. Managers could also rescind indefinitely any council orders, and, contrary to public statements, a uniform set of by-laws devised at head office was imposed on all communities. As Fred Clay commented of the Palm Island council, "we on the council were just rubber stamps."[37]

And the much-vaunted Aboriginal courts and police? Community courts had to comprise a majority of council members. They were limited to the adjudication of imposed by-laws, breach of which could bring fines or arrests by the community police. Police were appointed by the manager "to assist in the maintenance of good order and discipline on and supervision of a reserve or community". Rules for police were set by the manager who was empowered to "promote, disrate, suspend, or dismiss any policeman on the reserve". Not surprisingly, police, courts and councils were perceived as operating as expressions of official, rather than Aboriginal, will.

A *living wage*

As a strategy to "provide an incentive for residents to advance in grading and status",[38] the ration system which had formed the crux of government assistance for nearly seventy years was finally jettisoned in 1968 in favour of a cash economy. But no funds were made available for the transition, making a mockery of recommendations from Tom Murphy at Yarrabah that workers should receive the state's basic wage of £16 4s 6d a week. Ron Bartlam from Palm Island was closer with a suggested wage of £6 10s, further reduced by a levy of £4 to cover rent, electricity, water and cleansing charges.[39]

Ultimately Killoran set the wage at £12 10s. Cash in hand,

however, was a fraction of this amount — £3 plus a 15 per cent "margin for encouragement"; £7 was withheld for services.[40] Even this pittance proved totally beyond the department's budget. The Palm Island workforce alone comprised 244 men and 97 women, but Killoran allowed for only half the required $240,000 wages bill, and ordered half the workers to be sacked. What is the use of adding a further 122 people to the unemployment benefits' waiting list of 250 Palm Islanders? queried Bartlam. Already all work gangs were pared to a minimum, and with 10 per cent of the population lacking both work and money, further cuts would only increase "lawlessness". "The possibility of having 105 young people at a loose end is one that gives rise to grave concern", he cautioned.[41] Killoran was unmoved.

The paltry payments, even with "incentive" for skill, brazenly ignored the many community tradesmen who qualified for award wages and were so paid on the mainland. Comparisons reveal the level of exploitation: the police sergeant was paid $16.50 when the award rate was $45; mechanics got $16 rather than $40; carpenters $12 rather than $40; engine drivers $16 rather than $42. The TLC campaigned aggressively against these illegal rates, describing the system as "virtually robbery". Killoran's unconvincing assertion that the difference was more than compensated for by the value of clothing and accommodation was described as a "spurious allegation".[42] Given Killoran's own valuation of £7 ($14) for such services, this was an accurate appraisal.

Killoran's brutal approach to the waged workforce wreaked havoc on the communities. He informed Yarrabah's new manager, Rob Yarrow, that no pensioner was to be given work, and that "those persons who cannot secure jobs within Yarrabah establishment will, of necessity, be required to seek employment elsewhere". From Palm Island Bartlam opposed such deportation of "surplus labour". Seasonal cane work had been decimated by mechanisation, no work was available in Townsville, or indeed throughout rural Queensland, and where would youngsters stay if they were sent to the mainland away from their families?[43]

As cash goods replaced rations, pensioners complained to visiting justices that they could not survive on the fraction, commonly around $10, which they received per fortnight. At Yarrabah meat sales dropped to $12^1/_2$ per cent of the previous ration allocations. Killoran demanded price increases to cover the butchery's operating losses, and overrode Yarrow's objection that this would further depress sales. "Prices must be adjusted forthwith to sell at our cost", ordered Killoran, adding that staff "must encourage use of funds for meat purchases or include an order as part of wage if budgeting difficulties".[44]

Even those who spent their money wisely were, according to Yarrow, severely disadvantaged under the new system. There was "considerable unrest and criticism", he reported, and public denunciations by the council and by respected families were "becoming a source of embarrassment". The department's "stock answers" — that the government never guaranteed full wages, that mission wages were even lower, that people weren't compelled to stay on reserves — cut no ice with the people, said Yarrow. The majority "regard Yarrabah as their home and are reluctant to move out". Lack of food or cash for lunches had sent school absenteeism soaring. "I would appreciate advice as to what action could be taken to assist the family man", wrote Yarrow. Make a slight increase, said Killoran, but cut the labour pool to cover it. How can I? responded Yarrow. The building program depends on a larger, not a reduced, workforce.[45]

In 1971 the National Tribal Council demanded Killoran's resignation, asserting that wages were so low children went without food. A protest meeting by 200 Palm Island residents confirmed the deprivation: families could not survive the low wages and high cost of living, they petitioned the minister. Huts were severely overcrowded with ten or twelve people, but the $5 rent for the new community housing was beyond the reach of those in greatest need. Contrary to ministerial statements to parliament two years earlier that wages ranged between $33 and $63 per week, departmental figures in response to the petition show an average wage of only $23.80, compared with the (white) basic wage of $41.65. Opposition senator Jim Keeffe demanded that the federal government intervene: "Does the Government agree that these are inadequate weekly wages for aborigines, and, if so, when will the Commonwealth Government avail itself of the new powers granted by referendum in respect of aborigines to ensure that all receive the minimum adult wage?"

By the early 1970s the matter of Aboriginal community wages was exciting attention in the federal sphere, and would provoke a bitter struggle between state and federal governments into the 1980s, as will be discussed in later chapters. It was the 1967 referendum, according the Commonwealth power to intervene directly in Aboriginal affairs, which irrevocably changed the balance of power between the two spheres of government. The next sections will investigate just how this redefinition of powers impacted on the lives of Aboriginal Queenslanders.

Bargaining on poverty

Acknowledging the "new and unexpected responsibility for Aborigines"[46] ensuing from the 1967 referendum, Harold Holt's coalition government formed a small Office of Aboriginal Affairs (OAA) and set aside $10 million in the 1968–69 budget for distribution among the states. Half of this sum bankrolled a capital fund "for Aboriginal corporate or individual ventures with economic potential". The remainder was split for housing, education and health programs, of which Queensland's first allocation amounted to $800,000, $325,000 and $325,000 respectively.

Queensland politicians and bureaucrats remained highly suspicious of Commonwealth intent. Killoran maintained it was "problematical whether the proposals will achieve any material benefit for the Aborigines of Queensland", and the premier echoed his conviction that the new powers might facilitate "a further whittling of State Sovereign rights".[47] The federal Aboriginal Affairs minister, Bill Wentworth, hastened to reassure his state counterpart, Vic Sullivan: "Under no circumstances would we approve an advance without prior consultation".[48]

The injection of housing funds was crucial in Queensland where the Aboriginal affairs' department consistently absolved itself of responsibility for the plight of "nonwards". In more than one country town "adverse criticism" over appalling living conditions was appeased simply by extracting the considerable funds required for reserve amenities from the private bank accounts of local Aboriginal families. In one case, thousands of dollars were stripped from the child endowments of Palm Island mothers to finance a hostel at Aitkenvale near Townsville in the 1950s.

Publicly, and against appalling evidence of utter destitution, the state defended its policy that "coloured people not subject to the Acts were not the concern of Native Affairs Department" by passing the buck. "If necessary", such problems were said to be "the concern of citizens and Church Organisations".[49] In contrast to this public disavowal, the state had been playing the poverty card for a decade in attempts to extract federal funding to finance housing. Since 1960 Killoran had petitioned for funds on the grounds that the 20,000 fringe dwellers "can fairly be regarded as the responsibility of the State to assist in their housing problems".[50]

In 1961 Nicklin threatened to dump the whole problem on the Commonwealth unless funding parity was adjusted: "I would be prepared to support any constitutional amendments which handed over the care of our coloured people to your Government ... [or] to make our entire administrative machinery or any part of it available to you".[51] Arguing that the Commonwealth had no constitutional responsibility for Aboriginal welfare, Menzies pointed out that Queensland already enjoyed "a 'betterment factor' " in its state grants, "designed to assist the States to improve the standard and range of their services".[52]

Late in 1961 the Coloured Welfare Council of Ipswich invited the governor, Sir Henry Abel Smith, on a media tour of Aboriginal shanties on the local reserve. Every hut, the governor admonished the premier, was condemned as unfit for habitation: how could assimilation possibly proceed under such privation? O'Leary conceded more than one hundred near-Brisbane families, some with considerable incomes, lacked housing, and suggested that his minister use this deprivation as leverage in the push for federal funds.

Because they would operate outside departmental controls, the government was highly suspicious of "state-wide propaganda" for community welfare councils to respond to Aboriginal needs. When Ipswich business and church leaders formed the One People of Australia League (OPAL) to tackle the "coloured" housing problem, O'Leary was sent to monitor proceedings at the inaugural meeting, and reported with approval that "no Union representatives were present".[53]

The government quickly endorsed OPAL branches as rivals to Aboriginal organisations such as the Cairns-based Aboriginal Advancement League, described as being "under Communist domination".[54] Endorsement also gave the appearance of active commitment: "By working through OPAL", the 1968–1973 president, Neville Bonner, later acknowledged, "the Queensland government could stave off growing criticism that it wasn't doing enough for Aborigines".[55] Gordon Bryant, federal Aboriginal Affairs minister in the Whitlam government made a similar point, describing state interest in OPAL as "pure tokenism".

The department was not averse to blaming shortages on the state housing commission. Noting that poverty put the £250 deposit beyond most Aboriginal families, Killoran argued unsuccessfully that it should be restructured as part of the buying price. Approaches by O'Leary that cheaper homes be constructed for "coloured persons" were rejected out of hand by the commissioner, who angrily refused to lower standards on the basis of colour.[56] O'Leary even contemplated lifting £3000 from the Welfare Fund as a housing pool, but was cautioned that such expenditure on "unassisted" families would be "unwise". This refusal triggered a variation, also rebuffed, whereby a lump sum would be taken from loan funds and reimbursed by rejigging legitimate Welfare Fund allocations.[57]

The department was, of course, sitting on vast sums of trust monies — from the bulk of Aboriginal savings accounts, and from compulsory trust levies. Could not these be utilised to relieve Aboriginal destitution? Unfortunately not. For decades they had been fully committed to various government utilities, with interest factored in to departmental revenue. And since 1956, courtesy of adjusted legislation, the files catalogue vast sums derived from Aboriginal earnings which were *offered* to several hospital boards for expansion projects. By 1963, of around £987,000 of trust monies diverted to revenue production, more than £510,000 was on loan to white provincial hospitals.[58]

Although local councils had been encouraged to access Loan funds to finance housing for "coloureds" around Queensland, it was not until federal funds flowed through after 1968 that a concerted program got under way. The funds were specified as *in addition to* current spending, and each state was directed to operate a separate State Aboriginal Housing Trust (SAHT) account for their dispersal on low-cost housing for rental and purchase. Not more than 20 per cent could be invested in "transitional" or inferior homes, and apart from a 20 per cent administration component, rental would accrue to the fund.

It is apparent from the files that Queensland exploited the SAHT scheme to entrench assimilation aims. Blatantly disregarding need, houses were scattered "in various areas in the various towns". Family groups were further alienated by Killoran's practice of allocating homes only where there was secure employment. Despite the heavy reliance of many rural towns on the spending power of their Aboriginal residents, prejudiced vendors routinely refused to sell or rent to Aboriginal families or even through the department. In Cairns the Aboriginal and Islander Legal Service advised prospective buyers to pretend to be white.

It is clear that Killoran rejected those whose plight was most desperate — namely, families living on Aboriginal reserves, whether rural reserves or missions and settlements. The Commonwealth certainly made no distinction as to locality of home ownership other than on a basis of need, but the Queensland government had no intention of allowing the acquisition of homes on departmentally controlled land, conscious of the profound implications for state proprietorship. Extreme dissatisfaction with the engineered insecurity of the rent-only policy was well known to the department, and families demanded the right to purchase rather than merely rent SAHT homes: "We want something of our own, on our own land", was the demand from Aurukun. From Mornington Island, Rev Belcher relayed the conviction that "ownership, once achieved, relieves the person of further payments". But, as he was well aware, it also implied land tenure rights. "In my opinion", he declared in 1968 with considerable foresight, "the hot potato is the question of title to the land".[59] Residents declared their intention to "wait for our own homes" rather than pay the higher rent on new houses, even after it was explained that it might take years "to change the mind of the Government".

A proposal floated by the Presbyterian board of missions that a home building program could provide training, employment, *and* the mission wages which could be ploughed into purchase of the finished products was rudely dismissed by Killoran, who impugned the capacity of

Aboriginal people even to understand the implications of financial commitment and responsibility.[60] Although an offer by federal minister Bill Wentworth to give the Presbyterian committee direct funding for Aboriginal enterprise projects appears stillborn, in 1970 he responded to their appeals and directed that $80,000 from the SAHT funds be allocated to build forty homes at Aurukun and Mornington Island. Furthermore, he decreed that Aboriginal labour be used to the maximum extent in all SAHT construction.[61]

In fact, Queensland's perverse conduct of SAHT programs was bitterly resented in Canberra. In April 1969 Queensland was severely reprimanded for streaming SAHT funds through the department's operational standing account, in direct breach of Commonwealth instructions that a separate fund be established. By September 1970 168 homes had been constructed in rural towns and 82 on country reserves, but when federal Aboriginal Affairs' secretary Barrie Dexter made his own tour of inspection he was furious to find most "non-assisted" people had been ignored, while $257,000 remained unexpended from the previous financial year. And why, he demanded of Killoran, were the houses incomplete? Despite directives that SAHT houses "should be of a standard usually required by a Local Authority", he discovered to his disgust that Queensland routinely dispensed with essentials — most homes were not ceiled or lined, and lacked power, toilets, showers or laundries.

Under SAHT conditions, rent was to be set according to family income, but Killoran had long utilised rents as a means of inducing economic "responsibility", and directed his officers to set SAHT rents at a minimum of 15 per cent of wages.[62] Aboriginal families in Townsville took advantage of Dexter's visit to complain that they could not afford food and clothes as well as the rent. This provoked another angry letter from Dexter. "As you know, our aim is to assist you to get Aborigines and Islanders properly housed as rapidly as possible", he thundered, barely disguising his contempt. "It has never been our desire that (rents) should be collected at a level which would impose a heavy burden on the occupants of the houses."[63] Killoran retorted that "paternalism" only served to discourage acceptance of "normal responsibilities": the state, he declared, could not afford to subsidise rentals for impoverished Aboriginal families.

This brief glimpse of housing strategies during the 1960s indicates discrepancies between state and federal approaches. The Commonwealth clearly decreed that the massive post-referendum funds should be separate from, and in addition to, state projects, providing affordable rental and freehold homes according to need. Queensland, as we have seen, utilised this financial bonanza to further its own objectives, both in the merged accounting practices and in the placement of "cheap" housing. Surely the health dollars could not be so overtly compromised?

Health as discipline

Until 1967 Aboriginal housing had been solely a departmental affair: criticisms were deflected by assertions of non-accountability, impugning of political motives, or claims of lack of funds. In matters of Aboriginal health, by contrast, decades of clinical inquiry and condemnation were not so easily dismissed. As federal health professionals had traversed northern Queensland in campaigns to combat tropical diseases, their reports had, since the 1920s,

presented a consistent exposure of departmental malpractices, an exposure bitterly resented by Aboriginal Affairs'
politicians and bureaucrats alike.

Recurrent health crises on Aboriginal communities attest to the minimal reforms. Filthy homes and sickening
food-handling habits appalled the health inspector investigating a fatal outbreak of gastroenteritis at Woorabinda in
1960. More dangerous still, he remonstrated, was the hospital effluent discharging into the local creek 150 yards
above the settlement's water intake, the fly swarms in dormitory and hospital kitchens breeding on uncovered food,
and the rusting plates and pots used in 90 per cent of the
homes.[64]

In the early 1960s the filthy state of the hospital and
grounds at Palm Island was directly blamed for the fly
plague which increased the parasitic contamination of
child patients.[65] When twelve children died from amoebic
dysentery in the summer of 1963, cross-infection from the
hospital was again seen as the culprit, along with unsafe
domestic food-handling and hygiene practices. At that time
homes had only one cold water tap, and the settlement
lacked sufficient wood-burning coppers to wash even contaminated clothes.

The continuous flood of child illnesses, clinical malnutrition and ear and parasitic infections on Palm Island had
frustrated a succession of doctors. "Do we just treat blindly",
lamented the superintendent of the Townsville Hospital,
"or do we attempt to help and advise the Local Administration in matters pertaining to public health?"[66] A 1964
survey into chronic dysentery revealed parasitic infection
rates of 48 per cent in infants under 3 years, 45 per cent in
the 4 to 7 age-group, 48 per cent in the 8 to 14 group, and

29 per cent in those between 15 and 21 years. The following year yet another survey exposed an infection rate of 37 per cent among hostel and dormitory inmates, provoking a long-running argument with the Health department as to who should foot the £1,600 bill for essential treatment.

The intensified clinical attention on Aboriginal communities was focused primarily through the Queensland Institute of Medical Research (QIMR) which had taken up the mantle in 1945 of the long-defunct Institute of Tropical Medicine. As a federally funded body, QIMR research projects delivered medical assessment virtually free of charge to the state. In 1967 QIMR decided to make Aboriginal ill-health a specific field of research and appointed paediatrician Dr David Jose to coordinate surveys and outline remedial strategies. The result was an explosion of morbidity and mortality statistics.

A major project was launched to assess infant mortality rates on ten Aboriginal communities under departmental control between 1967 and 1969. Data revealed a stillbirth rate 4.2 times the general rate, premature baby deaths 3.9 times higher, neonatal deaths (under one month) 3.8, infant deaths (under one year) 6.3, and toddlers (one to four years) 13.4.[67] Half the deaths of neonates, and 47 per cent of all child deaths between 1 and 16 years, resulted from gastroenteritis and/or pneumonia.

And malnutrition was identified as the key factor in the deaths of 85 per cent of infants under 4 and 50 per cent of all children between six months and 3 years. Malnutrition, stated Dr Jose, underlay chronic ear and chest infections, diminished antibody response, and impaired school and employment performances. So sensitive was this issue that Jose's report was vetted prior to media release. Locations were censored and a statement was deleted which revealed that infant mortality on Aboriginal communities was six times higher than the Queensland average.[68]

With an eye to Queensland's post-1967 referendum health bonanza, initially set at $325,000 per annum and prioritised for preventive programs in nutrition and sanitation, health bureaucrats called on the Aboriginal department to establish a network of health professionals. There was a desperate need, they argued, for a full-time specialist in paediatrics and Aboriginal health to oversee a network of trained health inspectors, trained nutritionists, trained maternal and child welfare sisters, regular dental visits, and full-time parasite control teams. Health education programs and antenatal clinics were also essential.[69]

The educative aspects of suggested health disciplines primarily targeted Aboriginal women, due to the attribution of failure to women who, it was said, did not achieve safe levels of health, nutrition and child feeding. The post-weaning period was identified as critical: extreme growth retardation and anaemia in the second year of life was characterised by the chronic diarrhoea symptomatic of high loads of bowel parasites, and commonly led to terminal gastroenteritis or pneumonia. From Yarrabah, following several infant deaths from malnutrition, the visiting justice observed, "I found that usually the mother had no knowledge of what she should do and no means of feeding young children properly".[70] In fact, as one Palm Island nurse reported, the mothers themselves were at risk from malnutrition.

All too rarely, however, do official criticisms go beyond the personal. The same Palm Island nurse clearly linked ineffective mothering to poverty, noting that for many families income was at best irregular and at worst non-existent. "There are now some mal-nourished mothers — this has surely contributed towards deaths of children before three months of age and the lower number of mothers able to breast feed their babies".[71] The systemic deprivation characteristic of all Aboriginal communities was also rarely recorded by officials, but this 1972 description of Palm Island is typical of conditions: the majority of homes lacked refrigerators, and the only store routinely had no milk or fresh foods and kept irregular hours, placing a tremendous strain on housewives.

As QIMR's Aboriginal health specialist, Dr Jose insisted that a mass feeding program was the only way to bypass the spiral of starvation and parasitic contagion. Doomadgee already required the daily attendance at the clinic of all pre-school children for a prepared and supervised midday meal. More desirable again, in Jose's estimation, was Aurukun's scheme where a trusted and experienced nursing sister assisted families with a history of malnourished children. This was not only the cheapest response, he noted, but involved "no disruption of family life or responsibility. It is the natural method favoured by most Aboriginal people".

But as federal health funding streamed in, the department did not avail itself of the "natural method favoured by most Aboriginal people", choosing instead to initiate a mass supplementary feeding scheme (SFS) to provide one meal a day on all communities for the 1,445 children between 3 and 6 years of age. Officially, and in line with federal "assistance", there was no compulsion for mothers to take part; unofficially non-attenders were continually pressured, even to the extent of soliciting action from community councils and police. On Palm Island, however, the SFS was resisted by management for several years, described as "a 'backward step' considering rationing had just ceased and Cash Economy started".[72]

QIMR personnel continually stressed the link between increasing fatalities and defective social indices: "All new housing should be planned with due regard to the health measures being taught. Essential requirements include no over-crowding, more complete water reticulation to all living quarters to provide separate kitchen, bathroom and toilet facilities".[73] And in 1969 the QIMR extended its attack on the "massive infection loads resulting from substandard living conditions" to argue that Aboriginal communities were grossly underserviced by qualified medical personnel, berating the "lack of effective action by infant welfare, medical and community services".

The director of maternal and child welfare services, Dr Jean McFarlane, made the same point after her tour of northern peninsula communities and Woorabinda: poor child health was linked to inadequate medical attention. Once again Killoran's first response was attack. He accused her of "overlooking" the practical difficulties of servicing the communities and showing "lack of appreciation" for departmental appointees who, "though academically may have some shortcomings, at least practically meet some of the needs of the field of Aboriginal Welfare".[74]

In fact, delivery of health care on the northern missions had dramatically worsened after the government takeover — no longer were nursing needs filled by underpaid and overworked missionary wives. After coming under secular control, missions at both Edward River and Lockhart River operated for months without any qualified health personnel. On most communities, records reveal that apart from brief and infrequent visits from doctors, most medical attention was dispensed by "female welfare officers" for which position nursing experience was listed as a "desirable" prerequisite — as was competence to inspect children, instruct mothers in the best use of rations, and visit camp homes to assist women in "improved home management and hygiene methods".[75] Although federal grants would finance new amenities — hospitals, dental clinics — on some communities, the department did not always apportion funds for the highly qualified personnel upon which their success depended. "Native nurses" and visiting medicos were the norm well into the 1980s.

Rather than financing a network of medical staff, Killoran built a network of social police. According to the instruction manual, "Health, hygiene, infant welfare, maternal and child health, are the concern of the Liaison Officer", the first strata of social monitors appointed courtesy of federal health funding. "It does seem that closer oversight by liaison officers in homes will help in the development of children",[76] declared Killoran, who designated "parental incompetence" as a major factor in poor responses to feeding and illness, and thereby the endemic growth retardation which successive medical surveys identified.

There is no doubt that "closer oversight" encompassed much more than the "preventive health" envisaged in federal health guidelines. Liaison officers were directed to visit and inspect homes, police school absenteeism, mediate between teachers and parents in cases of behavioural or educational problems, intercede with police or children's services department staff in cases of child neglect or crime, help organise formal and informal community meetings, and assist in employment or social security problems.[77] In urban and rural areas officers also assisted in procuring rental houses, pursuing rent arrears, and monitoring "domestic management", particularly where overcrowding led to unacceptable living standards.

But social liaison was only one facet of operations. A reading of the liaison officer's manual betrays the surveillance mentality. Officers were required to "acquire a knowledge of all the individual residents", transmitting to head office "their names, where they live, how they care for their families, standard of housekeeping, work record, personal problems and difficulties, particular abilities and any other material that may be of value".[78] This intensified attention to private practices was bitterly resented, mothers on Palm Island rebuffing official intrusion in 1973 because "the Dept. is interfering with their family life".

Partly to circumvent resistance, and also to bypass vacancies arising from the high turnover of liaison officers and the policy exclusion of married women from the position, a second tier of supervisory administrators was introduced late in 1973. Women from within the communities were recruited to the new strata of "domestic advisers" in an effort to generate "appropriate" habits and attitudes.

As well as liaising with hospitals, schools and maternal and child welfare centres, domestic advisers were instructed to encourage mothers to utilise medical amenities, to "stimulate interest in all health and educational matters", to assist and advise in cooking and sewing skills, to "stimulate families' interest in home beautification including general home care", and, not least, to provide information for the attention of community managers and liaison officers.[79]

Killoran lobbied persistently but unsuccessfully for the Commonwealth to fund these "service personnel", necessary, he claimed, to monitor the adjustment of Aboriginal families as the housing program "reaches into the more depressed social levels".[80] In effect, the provision of SAHT-funded houses for select Aboriginal families had triggered an intensification of social surveillance.

While attention remained focused on domestic incompetence, home visits also exposed abject destitution. "An important factor has been revealed by home visits", reported Woorabinda's acting manager in 1973. "Empty cupboards, wood stoves that are never lit, no electrical appliances, in fact no real sign of food preparation for a basic meal. Bread and syrup appear the base of major meals." And why such poor nutrition? As he observed, "budgetting for say a wife and 4 children, rent, electricity, fire wood, soaps/detergents, clothes, food and some luxuries appears beyond most householders on community wages."[81]

Liaison officers appointed to communities and country towns, and domestic advisers delegated from within Aboriginal communities, effectively acted as agents to advance the implementation of the state's assimilation policy at an individual level. Perversely, the more "advanced" or "suitable" families were given access to the new housing and the more impoverished and destitute were passed over. In Queensland, those whose lifestyle was inconsistent with assimilationist policy remained on the outer.

*   *   *

Analysis of documentary evidence for the late 1960s and early 1970s does not suggest a "liberalisation" during this period. Massive federal funding allocations did not bring a "release" of Aboriginal families from decades of institutionally induced poverty, from grossly substandard housing or from pathological levels of health "care". Nor did reformulated Aboriginal and electoral laws bestow upon Queensland Aborigines "civil rights" commensurable with those available in the general community.

Rather, the altered parameters of housing, health, wages and voting entitlement, although generating new possibilities for Aboriginal interests and activism, at the same time enabled intensified state strategies in assimilationist dispersal and personal policing. Although the abstracted concepts — equal pay, "civil rights", housing and health parity — might embody an assumption of "liberalisation", at the level of individual experience the legislative and administrative changes merely varied the contested domain of Aboriginal affairs.

9

A state of paranoia

It is generally held that successive federal Liberal governments failed to assert their 1967 mandate to force state governments to reform discriminatory policies and practices in Aboriginal affairs; that a cosy coalition *laissez-faire* was fractured — briefly — by the Whitlam Labor government between 1972 and 1975; that when it came to tactics, Whitlam was outmanoeuvred by the sharp cunning of premier Joh Bjelke-Petersen, and the subsequent Fraser government was ineffectively weak-willed. Does documentary evidence support these hypotheses? What can be learned from internal correspondences about the reshaping of race relations during the 1970s?

Non-cooperation

In 1966 Australia had signed the International Convention on Civil and Political Rights. Ratification depended on the elimination of all racial discrimination in federal and state legislation. With its involuntary designation of "assisted" persons, restriction of movement, detention on reserves, and official controls on personal savings, Queensland's "progressive" Aboriginal legislation was stigmatised as grossly inequitable.

The discreetest of pressures from the federal government of John Gorton threw Killoran onto the attack. In an aggressive response drafted for his minister, Killoran fumed that handing back the savings accounts would effectively increase government welfare costs by the $4 million currently flowing out in private withdrawals for "the maintenance and support of the bread-winner and his family". He argued that the Commonwealth should be threatened with all extra costs if they used their legislative powers to force the issue.[1] In fact the combined holdings of the 10,450 savings accounts were a valuable revenue source for Queensland: of the total credit of $1.8 million, $1.435 million was invested in Commonwealth bonds and hospital building programs, with the state capitalising on the interest.

All federal offers of negotiated reforms were brushed aside by Queensland, and a tour of the state by the federal Aboriginal Affairs Council to gauge Aboriginal opinions was privately ridiculed as "political grandstanding without responsibility". Early in 1971 Bjelke-Petersen echoed Pizzey's threat to Menzies that if duress continued the state would opt out of Aboriginal affairs and leave the Commonwealth to pick up the $12 million bill.

But "publicity and notoriety alleging discrimination", as Queensland's Minister for Aboriginal Affairs, Neville Hewitt, termed the continuing uproar, was not easily silenced. The government directed police special branch to investigate local "radicals" who were supported to some extent, according to Bjelke-Petersen, by Commonwealth agencies. Emerging Aboriginal spokespersons were disparaged as a professional elite, or "pseudo Aborigines who were disassociated from the mainstream of Aboriginal society".[2] Academic support for Aboriginal activism was described as "sabotaging the democratic processes of life".

In a lame attempt at damage control, Hewitt explained that the state's "favourable discrimination" was in place only to ensure Aborigines could "participate as fellow Queenslanders", and that requests to live on communities were an endorsement of departmental management. But in an internal document, Killoran maintained that although the term "assisted" might need replacing, it was vital to maintain power to restrict access to reserves as a means of minimising state liabilities.

Following a cursory survey, conducted by a briefly constituted Aboriginal advisory committee comprising chairmen of community councils, the government brought down the *Aborigines Act* of 1971. Under this new "non-discriminatory" legislation, the "assisted" category was exchanged for a permit system covering visitors and residents on reserves — permits which the director was empowered to grant and cancel. Mining leases over reserve land could not now be granted without consent of the trustees: Killoran now assumed this position over all reserves, displacing church personnel on the northern missions. The cash "training allowance" was formalised, but expressly excluded from any provisions of industrial awards. Councils could now set conditions for beer canteens on reserves; and state police were authorised to operate on communities where necessary. Only now could departmental "wards" manage their own property and accounts, unless a magistrate upheld an objection from the director as to their capacity to do so.

The Aboriginal Advisory Council (AAC) was perpetuated to "consider and advise" the minister on those matters of progress and well-being which were referred to it by the director or the minister. Contrary to official assertions, this was in no way a representative forum of Aboriginal interests since it comprised only the community chairmen, who had no jurisdiction over issues elsewhere. The needs and interests of the majority of Aboriginal Queenslanders were thus peremptorily excluded. Nevertheless, the AAC was touted as the legitimate voice, as opposed to the politically tainted "radical" bodies such as the AAL and FCAATSI. A motion passed by the first AAC conference "accepting" the new legislation was proclaimed to the media. In undisclosed private dialogue with Office of Aboriginal Affairs (OAA) federal secretary Barrie Dexter, however, members expressed a unanimous conviction that the Act should be repealed.[3]

The high level of tension between state and federal coalition governments intensified as a range of subtle sanctions were applied, out of the public spotlight, and at that most critical point — treasury. Indeed there had for several years been a steady decline in state grants and increased leakage directly to Aboriginal organisations outside department control, leading Hewitt to object bitterly in 1971 to a "progressive erosion" of funding. Conditional clauses directly confronted Queensland's assimilationist policy and supervisory controls: community hospitals, schools and welfare centres were funded but not white staff; special grants went to local councils for public works *provided* they employed available Aboriginal labour. By mid-1972 so vehement was federal resolve that the McMahon government blocked further housing funds for state communities until Aboriginal societies were set up to receive and manage the investment.[4]

The election of the Whitlam Labor government late in

1972 brought a dramatic increase in federal funds for Aboriginal needs, and an expressed intent to deal directly with Aboriginal organisations where possible. The Office of Aboriginal Affairs was upgraded to full departmental status, with all state administrations *except Queensland* as branch offices. Queensland's rural housing policy was now also challenged: federal Aboriginal Affairs Minister Jim Cavanagh, demanded a "revised progam" which would have "greater impact on the housing situation in places where it is clearly more pressing". Houses, he directed, "should be built or purchased in those areas where the needs of the people are known to be extensive", rather than the present custom of scattering "a single house or two" through rural towns.[5]

This was a direct rebuff to Killoran's vigorous campaign to "phase out reserves" in country areas. Ignoring both individual preference and abject poverty, Killoran systematically dislodged from country reserves families lacking interest in or access to housing. Where he succeeded, prompt degazettal of the reserves as Aboriginal areas then precluded re-occupation. His obsession with preventing "Aboriginal enclaves" on such reserves, many of which had *always* been "blacks' camps", meant families lived under constant threat of eviction, often on the grounds of health risk. Provision of water, sanitation and shelter on departmental reserves was, of course, the responsibility of the department. Even so, there were several occasions when rural councils were so concerned with Aboriginal destitution that they sought permission to upgrade facilities on local reserves, only to meet with rejection because it would "encourage permanency". Documents for the Mt Isa reserve, for instance, show that Killoran refused the proffered full amenities and good shelter in the mid-1970s. Instead he organised a few temporary toilets and an imposed camping fee, thus condemning the 176 occupants to a continuation of sickening conditions.

At Redlynch the story was similar. When the Cairns Progress Association protested against the appalling plight of families on the Aboriginal reserve who lacked cooking, washing or sleeping facilities, Killoran justified inaction by claiming the occupants were "transients" and "squatters". He directed police to evict them, ordering "the entire 'fringe' community to be cleared up" and families relocated in town. Like many others, this group refused to move, citing "a tribal affiliation for this area", a connection confirmed by the federal DAA officer who declared that the community had long occupied the area, maintaining tribal and sacred links. Similar processes of attrition covering several decades are well documented on official files for communities at Normanton, Croydon and Birdsville, to name just a few. The consequent destitution and disease are an indictment on official obduracy.

In an aggressive campaign to dismember rural enclaves, Killoran missed few opportunities to exert pressure. A Seventh Day Adventist worker assisting local Aboriginal families at Kuranda was informed that "a condition of payment of further subsidy" was his agreement to inculcate "right assimilation attitudes". You must "conform to departmental policies of assimilation", he was told, and "encourage movement of former Mona Mona mission residents now in the Kuranda area to those centres where work opportunity presents".[6] Although direct federal housing funds were available for local Aboriginal communities who formed the prerequisite co-operatives, this information was not passed on by state departmental officials keen to disperse groups to available employment. Killoran also rebuffed those councils and welfare associations seeking to assist local groups in this process.

Neither would the state sanction long-term leases on reserved land, thus precluding Aboriginal access to the federal Aboriginal Enterprises Capital Fund set up to boost vocational or commercial projects. Reserved lands, declared Killoran, were held "generally" for the benefit of all Aborigines and would not be allocated to specific-purpose groups. Where file evidence exists on the granting of a few special leases, these were stipulated as only short term, "thereby ensuring that areas are not 'tied up' by lease unduly long whilst perhaps remaining undeveloped".

Increasingly targeted for suspicion, given their strong pro-Aboriginal stance, was the Presbyterian mission hierarchy. Records from the early 1960s reveal Killoran's misgivings over existing joint church/state trusteeship of reserves. The formal espousal of Aboriginal land rights by the Presbyterian church in 1969 had raised the spectre that the board of missions might enlist federal support to frustrate further mining developments — a possibility aborted by vesting sole trusteeship in Killoran under the 1971 *Aborigines Act.*

In order to enforce ideological uniformity on the church communities, and despite obvious impoverishment, the Queensland government manipulated desperately needed funding. Killoran's crafting of a ministerial dispatch to Cabinet urging the application of funding constraints exemplifies this penchant for subsuming welfare to politics: "A 'civil rights' attitude is developing at Aurukun and Mornington Island, apparently condoned by Mission Staff, who are obviously not impressing that with 'rights' also are 'responsibilities', and the probable progression of this attitude occasions concern, particularly as Missionaries' attitudes do not appear to be favourable to governments and this appears to be, to some extent, communicated to the Aboriginal residents".[7]

The department's ideological determinism distorted even the state's own health programs. Despite repeated overtures over several years from Queensland's health bureaucrats that available federal health funding be taken up, it was not until 1970 that Killoran condescended to the appointment of a medical specialist to oversee Aboriginal health.

Dr Ian Musgrave immediately made an extensive tour of all communities, vowing that his Aboriginal Health Program (AHP) would redirect services from the curative to the preventive. By attacking the "underlying causes", he informed Commonwealth health department head Dr Patrick, eventually there could be "the elimination of the field of Aboriginal health as a separate public health problem".[8] For Musgrave, the key to bridging the health deficit lay in Aboriginal involvement. It was his opinion that " 'White Man's advice' does not influence Aboriginals often". Communication barriers of language, social reticence and hostility to Europeans combined with "an acceptance of inferior health standards as being a natural part of the Aboriginal heritage".

A team of qualified nursing sisters under health department authority was essential. But these professionals should be buttressed by "special health scouts of Aboriginal descent", appointed to seek out and counsel sick persons and health problems. But the Aboriginal empowerment envisaged by Musgrave in no way accorded with Killoran's notions of authoritarian instruction.

Killoran was inherently suspicious of this maverick health team, which, although funded through his department, was answerable to state Health. Killoran's forebodings were confirmed when, in September 1973, Musgrave's public health nurses publicised the deadly levels of malnutrition and sickness on Palm Island. Their inquiries revealed that 75 per cent of child outpatients were underweight — not surprising in conditions where vegetables, fruit, milk and bread were delivered only twice a week and sold out, unwrapped, within hours, with many families left empty-handed. Indeed, malnutrition on the Island was so severe that Townsville Hospital's medical superintendent described many children as looking like "starved Biafrans". At this time gastroenteritis swept the settlement killing one child; a further fifty-five were hospitalised, with ten critically ill children sent to Townsville.

Offers of federal health assistance during this protracted and fatal epidemic were rejected by the Queensland government on the grounds that it would be "too difficult" to incorporate federal specialists in the Palm Island health team. Furious with the highly public exposure and suspicious of federal motives, the proffered assistance was rudely rebuffed as an "intrusion" into state matters. Killoran's draft for his minister's reply read: "Cannot agree you assume from health department responsibility and/or supervision health activities which in my understanding are being adequately administered".[9] Calls by the Palm Island community chairman Fred Clay for the Queensland government to declare a state of emergency were ignored. Also in vain was Clay's flight to Canberra seeking federal funding to rectify living conditions on the Island, and the residents' petition to the prime minister, Gough Whitlam, that he invoke federal powers and take control of the island.

In an attempt to retrieve his reputation, Killoran tried to shift the blame, telegramming federal health authorities that the epidemic arose as a direct result of "lack [of] acceptance [of] responsibilities [by] local parents and Council". Musgrave disagreed. He pointed to the high incidence of salmonella and ascaris (threadworm) infestations, noting that a campaign against the latter had been cancelled in 1972 because of lack of staff.

In fact, the state health department had lobbied unsuccessfully to take over all Aboriginal medical and health programs. Killoran, however, refused to yield control even over maternal and child welfare centres, arguing obversely that it would "isolate Aboriginal people from access to the conventional services … and retard rather than stimulate development".[10] For years the Palm Island community of over 1500 people continued to be serviced by medical trainees seconded from Townsville Hospital on nine-week rosters, with barely time to acquaint themselves with patient histories before being withdrawn.

Internal documents suggest that both Killoran and his close adviser John Burless spurned Musgrave's Aboriginal health program, apprehensive of the cannon loose in their sphere of action. As Burless remarked in mid-1975: "I have been inclined to oppose the establishment and expansion of Dr Musgrave's Division since its inception".[11] For his part, Killoran assiduously subverted potential government confidence in the expanding AHP, planting through Hewitt the spectre of an arbitrary withdrawal of federal support which would leave the state responsible, he said, for more than two hundred health personnel.[12]

In their efforts to influence the ideological agenda, both state and federal governments loaded the health dollar with political valency. Federal health funds were streamed directly to the AHP but excluded white state-appointed community nurses; funds were available for Aboriginal hygiene workers but not for white state-appointed inspectors. Ultimately, of course, it was the communities which paid the price for internecine hostilities. Federally funded hospitals at Aurukun and Mornington Island were crippled by Killoran's refusal to cover operating and maintenance costs estimated at over $33,000 annually and way beyond church capacity. Try the health department, said Killoran hypocritically, having for years resisted proposals by that department to take control of all community hospitals.[13]

As Bjelke-Petersen proclaimed in 1974, the 1967 referendum may have granted the federal government powers to make laws for the nation's Aboriginal population, but it had no power over state lands or administrations. Or had it?

Raising the stakes

Amid intense speculation on Aboriginal "land rights" in the federal sphere, and despite the findings by Mr Justice Blackburn in the 1971 case of *Milirrpum and Others v. Nabalco Pty Ltd and the Commonwealth of Australia* that Aborigines held no recognisable title to land, the Queensland government was desperately concerned about federal acquisition of land for Aboriginal groups. Early in 1971 federal minister Bill Wentworth had recommended a capital fund be established for this purpose, and in 1972 the

McMahon government pledged $5 million, although it appears the OAA's parent body, the department of Environment, Aborigines and the Arts, deleted this from the supplementary estimates leaving only $600,000 for the 1972–73 year.[14]

Apart from outright rejection of federal funds available for farming and pastoral enterprises, routinely castigated as facilitating "apartheid", Queensland fretted over the possibility of clandestine manoeuvres under existing common law. A ministerial warning to colleagues, almost certainly originating from Killoran, reveals the depth of distrust: "There is a real concern", declared Hewitt in 1972, "that the Commonwealth could acquire large areas of Queensland by purchasing freehold and leasehold properties under the 'Land Acquisition Act 1955–1966', identifying these tracts with Aborigines only, thus isolating them racially from the mainstream of population".[15]

Killoran increased paranoia a further notch when he floated the possibility, subsequently confirmed by the solicitor-general, that the Commonwealth might assert its rights over all reserves as "public purpose" land. In a rather hysterical outburst drafted by Killoran, Hewitt alerted fellow ministers that this could lead to economic ruin with land claims for "total ownership of Australian land areas" and demands for compensation "probably from 1788 with interest to current date".[16]

By mid-1973 the Bjelke-Petersen government was at loggerheads with the Whitlam Labor government on several fronts, including proposals to alter the nation's northern boundary, ceding several islands to Papua New Guinea. This was vigorously opposed by the premier, who declared that he acted in respect of wishes of the Torres Strait

Islanders who pleaded to remain "loyal Queenslanders". In fact, Bjelke-Petersen suspected that Whitlam might use Torres Strait Islander emancipation as a lever to destabilise the state's hold over the Aboriginal population.[17]

It appears that his parliamentary colleagues did not share Bjelke-Petersen's enthusiasm for state control of Aboriginal affairs. During his absence in London, where he challenged Whitlam's right to abolish appeals to the Privy Council, Queensland's cabinet signalled its intention to vote 13–1 in favour of a federal takeover of Aboriginal affairs. The lone dissenter was the premier himself: when the vote was taken on his return, the proposal was rejected outright.

The Whitlam government now directly confronted Queensland on the matter of discriminatory regulations, threatening to introduce a Racial Discrimination Bill ratifying the 1965 Convention on Civil and Political Rights, thereby rendering contradictory state legislation invalid. In a move to discredit this gambit, Hewitt invoked AAC "support" to declare that the 1971 *Aborigines Act* had been formulated with "full consultation and [with] the sanction of elected representatives of the Aboriginal and Islander people". He added the bizarre claim that "The Queensland Government has developed, over many years, a firm bond of trust and mutual respect ... We have undertaken to respect their wishes." [18]

By January 1974 Killoran was convinced that this "bond of trust and mutual respect" was being sabotaged by the federal DAA. Experience had shown, he now alleged, that past statements by this agency were either a "political decoy" or subject to dramatic revision; present assurances, therefore, should be treated as "either intentionally misleading or only valid for a limited period." Again Killoran stressed the danger inherent in accessing DAA options on funding through leasehold and community tenure, warning that this would enable the Commonwealth to "create an environment of great confusion" — a "confusion" which would be "most amenable to manipulation by Commonwealth Officers" who would then encourage claims for sacred sites over most reserve land. Killoran was convinced this hidden agenda was actively abetted by the Australian Institute of Aboriginal Studies, set up, he said, to prepare "an elaborate rationale for future 'Land Right' policies", and funded by the government "to provide the evidence that they require".[19]

Against Whitlam's threat to bring forward Racial Discrimination legislation to release communities from state restrictions, the Queensland government retorted it could redefine all Aboriginal reserves, including Palm Island and the Torres Strait Islands, as local government areas. Queensland politicians and bureaucrats were well pleased with this counter-threat, based as it was on opinion solicited from Sir Arnold Bennett QC, leader of the Queensland Bar. It was Bennett's contention that federal acquisition could also be blocked by regazetting the reserves as recreational or national parks, although such a tactic would remove them from Killoran's control. Bennett also raised the significant point that although the Commonwealth had the legal capacity to compulsorily acquire reserves in the name of Aboriginal councils, it would thereby be liable for compensation — including for mineral wealth — to the state.[20]

To counter damaging publicity, Bjelke-Petersen intimated that Whitlam had been taken in by a few "radicals". The AAC, claimed the premier, had recorded its preference for Queensland's guardianship. This claim was ostensibly substantiated by the twenty-three identical telegrams received by federal minister Jim Cavanagh, all post-marked from the department's Thursday Island office, purporting to come from individual community chairmen expressing "concern for their future well-being" if Commonwealth legislation was enacted to override Queensland procedures.[21]

Although the public clash over policy and power centred on the management and status of Aboriginal reserves, a second and more bitter battle front had opened up on the periphery of media attention, over the matter of community wages. Late in 1974 the Palm Island council requested through Labor senator Jim Keeffe that officials of the Federated Engine Drivers and Firemen's Association (FEDFA) investigate underpayment of qualified operators.[22] Of the more than 1,200 workers on the Island, reported FEDFA, only one person was paid an award wage; senior plant operators were underpaid by $81, receiving only $45 a week and yet living costs were higher than on the mainland. The council was subsequently sacked on the dubious legal pretext of a "petition" taken twelve months previously and later challenged by many "signatories".

The state Industrial and Arbitration Commission called a compulsory conference between FEDFA and the department. Here Killoran argued that the pay was a "training allowance" not a wage, that the Commission had no jurisdiction over Aboriginal wages under section 68 of regulations under the 1971 *Aborigines Act*, and that social concessions such as cheap housing took remuneration to more than the award amount. Taking his lead from the Aboriginal regulations, commissioner Ponting declared he was powerless to act on the matter of wages. From Cherbourg came a letter disputing Killoran's sanguine assessment: one man wrote that he could barely support his family of eight on the department's pay of $30 after deductions for rates, rent and electricity. Many children, he said, were so hungry they stole spoiled food put aside for the piggery.

Queensland jealously guarded its right to grossly underpay workers on Aboriginal communities. It has been said that the state profited nicely from a $575,000 project to upgrade the Palm Island water supply because workers received less than half the federally costed award wage rates.[23] And disputed wage rates were behind Killoran's refusal to allocate the funds necessary to operate the new hospitals at Aurukun and Mornington Island. Having directed the Presbyterians to approach the health department, he forewarned the latter : "BOEMAR is seeking to obtain moneys which will enable them to pay full award wages to the hospitals' staff at Aurukun and Mornington Island" and this would have serious repercussions in the flow-on to other community hospitals.[24]

Although it had set the rules for its own benefit, Queensland was not immune to external pressure on wages. From the federal sphere, minister Jim Cavanagh stipulated that all federally funded housing projects should employ Aboriginal labour wherever possible, adding: "naturally Aboriginals employed on such projects should receive at least the guaranteed minimum wage payable in your State".[25]

Hewitt hit out furiously at the expanding range of economic sanctions, labelling these tactics "financial and political coercion", evidence of a deliberate plan to embarrass the state government and take control not only of its "in-digenous citizens" but also of "much of the Northern sea-board of the State" by pushing land rights.[26] In retaliation the DAA lobbed a new directive onto Hewitt's desk, de-manding that the guaranteed minimum wage be paid on *all* federal projects. Records show that the state department was incensed at the inevitable friction that would occur as workers realised the financial disparity between state- and federal-funded housing jobs, and also when workers on federal projects were stood down on completion and re-verted to the "training" wage. Internal assessments reveal that underpayment was saving the state government around *$1.588 million annually* compared with just the *minimum* wage.

With Queensland maintaining its refusal to establish Aboriginal-controlled housing cooperatives to coordinate community housing on reserves, funding to reserve pro-grams was halted and $3.19 million diverted to rural Aboriginal corporations. Disregarding his own govern-ment's obstructionism, Hewitt protested that community residents were being penalised "for the support that they have given to the State Government". For years Queensland maintained it had been cheated of this sum, bitter that it had been left exposed to commitments of $1.98 million for the 1974–75 year. In an attempt to thwart the consistent lag by the state in its application of available housing funds, in August 1974 Cavanagh introduced quarterly returns to enable closer federal scrutiny of state activities.

The financial screws were turned a further notch in 1975 when *all* federal Aboriginal funding was channelled di-rectly to individual state departments. More than $11 mil-lion went to health, education, welfare services and forestry,

with a further $5 million to Aboriginal housing corpora-
tions — all distributed as per budget estimates. Aboriginal
department requisitions, in contrast, were severely cur-
tailed with only $2 million made available for housing.[27]
Several large projects were made entirely conditional on
Aboriginal title and control: Queensland abruptly shelved
the proposed hostel on Thursday Island and the upgrading
of the Bamaga sawmill rather than accept these conditions.
In a diatribe almost certainly emanating from his senior
bureaucrat, new minister Claude Wharton castigated these
revisions as deliberate strategies "to bypass the authority
and to erode the status of this Department" and "fragment
Queensland's State activities on aboriginal advancement
projects presumably with the ultimate intention of total
control". Beleaguered, Queensland set up a state coordi-
nating committee under Killoran's authority to control and
supervise the policies and spending of all departments on
Aboriginal projects.

By the mid-1970s Bjelke-Petersen was articulating his
policies so aggressively against what he saw as an all-con-
suming centralist and socialist juggernaut that the state
treasurer warned of an economic backlash against the state.
And antagonism and paranoia did not diminish after the
change of federal government late in 1975. Queensland's
politicians and bureaucrats were soon disabused of any
reversal under the coalition government of Malcolm Fraser.
"Black magically became white", wrote Charles Porter, state
minister for Aboriginal Affairs between 1977 and 1979,
"and the electorate was treated to the unedifying spectacle
of Liberal and Labor lying down together in the same bed:
the agreed objective, of course, was more power for Canberra".[28] Killoran expressed similar rancour after two years

under the Fraser government: "Labor attitudes were bad, Liberal in recent two years have been worse".[29]

This acrimonious impasse between state and federal coalition governments would reach a critical point in 1978, played out through a series of confrontations over the Aurukun and Mornington Island communities. To tease out the relevant strategies, it is first necessary to update the struggle between church and state.

Brute force

Premier Joh Bjelke-Petersen was nothing if not consistent in his vitriolic slanders of those who attacked his government. The World Council of Churches, which released two scathing reports after investigating the northern missions, was disparaged as "a sinister, communist-led organization engaged in subversive activities". Amnesty International, winners of the 1977 Nobel Peace Prize, were similarly condemned as "an arm of communist propaganda" after having the temerity to criticise the state's legislation as "repressive and anti-human rights".[30]

Bjelke-Petersen's extreme sensitivity to criticism was well founded. Internal documents present a detailed, and appalling, picture of conditions in the 1970s on the Presbyterian communities, a picture more keenly abhorrent given Killoran's deployment of funding to engineer the church's submission to government policy. For the Mornington Island population of 650, there were 91 old huts with no partitions, no windows, no cupboards, stoves or sinks; plus five new homes lacking water, power or toilets. Slaughtered cattle arrived by open truck from the bush to a butcher with no cold room. Water shortages were typical, there was no hot water at the hospital, sewage was dumped directly into the sea, and hookworm ran at 77 per cent.

Aurukun was no better. Official reports described the huts as small and so derelict they should be burned. Only one water tap serviced each ten dwellings. The 650 people had access to only six showers and one laundry, and the main well was often contaminated with bauxite sediment. In the tiny hospital maternity patients shared general ward space and suffered cross-infections; the school was pronounced dilapidated and dangerous and unbearable in summer. Although the state finally buckled late in 1975 to permit the formation of Aboriginal cooperatives on reserves for access to federal housing funds, reports reveal that the building program was so disorganised that materials were often defective by the time they were used.

It was against this background that the international organisations made their condemnatory reports. In his rebuttal, Killoran ignored the systemic deprivations on the communities to blame "the significant degree of sickness" on the church's tendency to encourage "idealism untouched by the sense of responsibility". It was all a matter of discipline: "Much current social theory tends to emphasise the satisfaction of apparent needs" while subsuming "the usual prerogative of authority" to the "will of individual groups", lectured Killoran. "It is consequently unsatisfactory to regard all forms of insistence as a variety of paternalism or an attempt by Governments to repress Aboriginal individuality".[31] A visiting member of parliament concurred, attributing the apathy of the people to the church's preoccupation with self-determination.

The "idealism" of the church and the "current social theory" of self-determination were inextricably woven on

Aurukun with the management and exploitation of mineral wealth. Since the mid-1960s the Tipperary Land Corporation had been prospecting in the Aurukun reserve. Etched in BOEMAR's mind was the recent punitive debacle which had deprived the Weipa and Mapoon communities of land, livelihood and compensation. In negotiations with Tipperary into the 1970s BOEMAR insisted that the people should "share in the success" of any mining ventures through employment training, equity with white personnel and safeguards to monitor availability of alcohol. They demanded direct consultation with the people, Tipperary's solicitors agreed in principle, and the department gave assurances that full consultation would precede any formal contract.

Killoran also was keen to write a new script, albeit with different stars. His department had, after all, borne the brunt of the notoriety over the plundering of Mapoon and Weipa, but had received no direct financial gain. Wilfully disregarding current church negotiations he now claimed a 3 per cent "profit participation" for his department which he anticipated would bring about $150,000 per year through the Welfare Fund. Antagonistic mines' department bureaucrats denied his authority to negotiate and cried foul at this "double royalty" for Tipperary. But Killoran had prepared his ground well. Over several months he had, through his drafting of ministerial submissions, planted in the minds of the Cabinet the possibility of direct federal retaliation if the Aurukun people were cut completely from the profits. There could be covert counterstrikes as well, he warned. "Aborigines individually or as corporate groups" might "acquire a capital percentage in any company formed to develop mineral resources within

Aboriginal Reserves", through the federal enterprise fund.[32]

In an attempt to paper over Aboriginal protests that their interests had once again been abused by government appointees, Killoran crudely engineered a media event in 1971, flying the Aurukun chairman to Brisbane and proclaiming his willing endorsement of the mines policy and "profit sharing" — a claim the chairman later denied. Over subsequent years BOEMAR maintained that the enrichment of departmental coffers was no guarantee of benefit for Aboriginal interests. The 3 per cent buy-out, they argued, had in fact denied the Aurukun people the resources to determine their own futures.

Federal anti-discrimination legislation of mid-1975, namely the *Racial Discrimination Act* and the *Aboriginal and Torres Strait Islander (Queensland Discriminatory Laws) Act*, was formulated to override contrary provisions in state law, and gave apparent support to BOEMAR's "self-determination" stance. But the Queensland government had resolved to crush what they described as BOEMAR's "apparent intent ... to develop the communities under a philosophy inconsistent with Queensland's established policies". The budget for Aurukun and Mornington Island was slashed from $186,000 to a scant $51,942, while at the same time Killoran blamed deteriorating sanitation standards on BOEMAR's "seditious" administration. It has come to our notice, warned Killoran, that you are considering transferring community management to corporations, thereby seeking "exemption from certain State laws".

BOEMAR would not be bullied. In a long diatribe, Rev John Brown ridiculed Killoran's logic: all Aboriginal enterprise companies were incorporated under Queensland law;

and the ultimate assumption of local government status for the communities was also consistent with state policy. Furthermore, wrote Brown, BOEMAR's stance on the underpayment of Aboriginal wages, which Brown correctly attributed to departmental doctrine rather than alleged shortage of funds, would not waver.

Brown now threw down the gauntlet on land rights, declaring that there would be no retreat from the principle that Aboriginal land should be held secure for Aboriginal management: "We do not and cannot accept the present situation in the State of Queensland where Aboriginal people on the reserves have no firm land tenure at all and can at any time lose the land on which they at present reside and on which their forebears have lived in some cases for centuries". Brown urged Killoran to advise his minister to secure the people's right to land, including "very clear stipulation about mineral rights" and "the rights of the Aborigines concerned to negotiate with the companies". We are committed "to press for change in your Government's policies in relation to Aboriginal people", declared Brown, in order to achieve "a flexible policy that is more responsive to Aboriginal needs and aspirations".[33]

It would appear that this uncompromising articulation of principles brought matters to a head. Within three months, in December 1975, Queensland pounced. With Brown briefly out of Australia, and without informing other BOEMAR executives, legislation was rammed through parliament in three days, validating Tipperary's rights to mine at Aurukun. In the ensuing uproar Bjelke-Petersen claimed that the Bill had been held in abeyance since 1971 for ongoing negotiations with the church, a claim discounted by his own contemporary remark that the legislation was aborted because of an impending state election, and by mining minister Ron Camm's admission that no Bill had even been framed for passage at that time.[34] The degree of subterfuge is perhaps best exemplified by a legal representative for Tipperary who described the situation after BOEMAR's exclusion as "a very delicate issue ... negotiations must be kept secret until the first reading of the Bill".[35]

In the context of this web of deceit and double-dealing, the government demonstrated its arrogance by proclaiming the *Aurukun Associates Agreement Act* as a triumph of Aboriginal participation in consultation and benefits. In fact only two brief discussions had occurred between Killoran and the Aurukun council — hardly confirming Camm's allegation that both BOEMAR and the council had agreed to the terms. And the Bill was passed within days of the minister's visit to Aurukun to "consult" with the people. Perhaps BOEMAR and the Aurukun people were not the only dupes. Interestingly, neither Killoran nor Wharton were shown the Bill before it was debated — it appears that both advocates were effectively rolled by mining interests headed by Bjelke-Petersen and mining minister Ron Camm on the $1,000 million project.

In a pathetic attempt to extricate his reputation from the botched consultations, Wharton professed that the legislation was "only partly his responsibility". Killoran also dissembled. Unfortunately, he told BOEMAR, he was "placed in a most invidious position" because "as trustee of the reserve" he was "answerable to his Minister" and was therefore precluded from discussing the context of the legislation.[36]

The Aurukun people were not conned by this abnegation of responsibility. Killoran found himself served with a writ alleging breach of fiduciary trust, issued in the names of Aurukun chairman Donald Peinkinna and four councillors, objecting to his assent to a mining agreement outside the terms sought by the Aurukun community. Furious at this act of "disloyalty", and alleging that Peinkinna had been "persuaded" to the action by federal interests, Killoran entered a demurrer claiming that the councillors had no case at law. In March 1976 a petition signed by 320 Aurukun residents was delivered to state parliament. The petitioners urged that the *Aurukun Associates Agreement Act* be amended to acknowledge their own right to be party to negotiations with Tipperary. With absolutely no intention of acceding to Aboriginal interests the Bjelke-Petersen government opened up a two-pronged attack to defuse mounting public hostility. It deflected BOEMAR's complaints to the state's ombudsman, but then rejected his finding that a renegotiation of the Agreement was probably warranted. And it launched a media campaign blaming "misguided" Aboriginal protest on a "plague" of radicals, activists and militants.

When the Supreme Court upheld Aurukun's claim of abuse of trust in October, Bjelke-Petersen promptly put the case to the Privy Council in London, no doubt well pleased to have blocked moves by Labor prime minister Gough Whitlam in 1973 to abolish this avenue of appeal. In its decision, handed down in January 1978, the Privy Council declared that in his capacity as trustee of the reserve Killoran had been entitled to negotiate with the Tipperary consortium; it did not find, however, that Killoran stood as trustee to the residents. In 1977 Aurukun resident John Koowarta initiated action against the state government under provisions of the 1975 *Racial Discrimination Act*, alleging discrimination in its refusal to ratify transfer of a lease on a pastoral property on the Archer River which he had acquired through the federal Land Fund commission.

Killoran was furious that these highly public attacks by his departmental "wards" on his authority and integrity should be given legitimate status in the legal system. He saw BOEMAR's hand behind both the fighting mentality and the deployment of legal procedures. Warning Wharton that the "philosophies promoted by the Rev. John Brown" were "particularly ... hostile to State Government policies and programmes", he urged him to secure government support for an enforced state takeover of Aurukun. Despite the financial penalties of such a takeover, internal correspondence reveals that this option had been considered as early as February 1977, and only rejected then because of adverse publicity so close to the Tipperary agreement, and a fear of flouting the Privy Council appeal process.[37]

While the accelerating conflict with the church over Aurukun no doubt exercised Killoran's mind in favour of state control, it was a flare-up in spiteful intergovernmental relations which brought such action to the fore at that time. The catalyst was a disastrous cyclone in December 1976 which demolished the Mornington Island mission and caused major damage to the mainland town of Burketown. Not only did rebuilding programs throw unwelcome spotlight on the Island community's destitution, but in qualifying disaster fund allocations the Fraser government took direct aim at Queensland's Aboriginal housing programs. Of the $1 million allocated for rebuilding at Mornington Island the federal government demanded 30 per cent (as opposed to the state's proposed 15 per cent) be used on "upgraded" rather than merely "replacement" dwellings.

For over a year, while the Queensland government stone-walled to alter the specification of reconstruction funds, Mornington Islanders were condemned to survive in rotting army tents. BOEMAR was afraid to go public, fearing that the state would use destitution as an excuse to take control and forcibly disperse residents to the mainland.

At Burketown similar negligence occurred. Whereas most white housing was quickly replaced, more than twelve months later less than half the crisis grant of $950,000 for Aboriginal housing had been used. Here, in contravention of federal directives that homes be supplied on the basis of need, Killoran refused replacement shelter for ten families on the grounds that the people should be dealt with as itinerants who "should not be accommodated there" because no employment was available.

Bjelke-Petersen was furious to discover that nearly $2 million earmarked to replace Aboriginal housing had been charged against state grants rather than the national disaster fund. He bitterly accused Fraser of double-crossing the state: "… the concept of 'co-operation' appears to be interchangeable with 'capitulation', which is at all times a Commonwealth requirement". In a confidential letter to Fraser he slammed what he termed the " 'shadow' Public Service" comprised mainly of federally funded "so called 'voluntary' organisations" which were "developing and extending" into Queensland. This tier of intrusive operators usurped normal lines of power to such an extent that state ministers and senior bureaucrats "are not consulted on anything other than a rapidly dwindling sum of money".[38] Elsewhere he referred to DAA personnel as "traitors".

Killoran shared Bjelke-Petersen's rancour, irate because the political nous of agencies such as Legal Aid and the

Aboriginal and Islander Legal Service actively defied the state's supervisory licence. Successful challenges to wrongful detentions, arrests and fines undermined community compliance with departmental disciplinary regimes. Queensland officials saw these anti-conservative options as being fuelled by the 1975 *Racial Discrimination Act*, which Killoran described as the source of "continual ammunition for the Aboriginal Legal Aid Service to undermine the State Government". Summing up the position for Bjelke-Petersen's meeting with Fraser, Killoran declared: "This Act should be withdrawn forthwith".[39]

The paranoia intensified. By late 1977 Bjelke-Petersen was demanding that the DAA terminate funds to the Aboriginal and Torres Strait Islander Community Health Service which provided emergency care and family support in Townsville, because it "pursues a radical racist and militant philosophy". Queensland's own Aboriginal Health Program was seen as tainted by its direct funding and thereby a federal ploy to bypass state health services.[40] Killoran thwarted proposals for a centralised body to manage Aboriginal health issues arguing that "empire building" was antagonistic to state policy; moves to initiate community medical programs were described as unacceptable because they dealt with Aborigines "as guinea pigs".[41]

Prior to the 1977 state election Bjelke-Petersen even engineered the withdrawal of Fred Hollow's trachoma survey team, claiming that two "well-known radicals" travelling with him were associated with the federally funded "Land Rights Council" in Cairns, and, as Labor supporters, had contrived an upsurge in voter registrations. The team was recalled, although federal Health minister Ralph Hunt later admitted that there was "no substantial evidence of politicking by the two men", a statement corroborated by the state electoral officer who reported no swell of voter numbers in the north.

Even the media was perceived as actively working to destabilise government policy. Many analysts decry Queensland's "compliant" press, but the George Street hierarchy felt themselves besieged by what Porter later described as a "rabidly partisan" media, "prepared at all times to wage highly emotive war against the government". Aboriginal Affairs in particular suffered from "concealment and misrepresentation" by critics keen "to sell an anti-government 'line' … using the aboriginal and islander people themselves as just so much ideological cannon-fodder for the fray".[42]

For Queensland politicians and Aboriginal Affairs' bureaucrats, Canberra's refusal to withdraw the network of service providers advising Aboriginal individuals and communities only served to entrench suspicion and increase outrage. But it was the continuing pressure towards self-determination, through (largely unactivated) anti-discrimination options and the rhetoric of empowerment, that triggered the pitched battle over the Aurukun and Mornington Island communities which climaxed in 1978.

Brinkmanship

It could be argued that Aurukun and Mornington Island emerged as a test case for state sovereignty over Aboriginal affairs. While the state managed — apart from the odd eruption — to keep the lid on mounting activism and dissent on other Aboriginal communities, it was probably Killoran's deepening obsession with the church's "radical" influence at Aurukun and Mornington Island which convinced Bjelke-Petersen that the situation was untenable.

Through his minister, Killoran warned Cabinet in 1978 that they might already be losing control on these particular portions of Queensland: "Over the years BOEMAR deviated from accepted State policies in regard to management of the Reserves, and since the intrusion by the Commonwealth into Aboriginal Affairs administration in this State, have attempted to 'play off' one government against the other". He warned also of the enemy within: "These philosophies are being either promulgated, sponsored or encouraged ... by the Church as a body but also as a result of the recruitment of young, generally immature certainly inexperienced, and often, emotionally unstable staff".

Evidence of the covert land rights strategy of "decentralisation" was apparent in the positioning of Aboriginal family groups around the reserves, and Killoran reminded Cabinet that such " 'social experimentation', particularly at Aurukun, [is] contrary to State policy." [43] In vain did Rev Brown protest that outstations had always existed to farm fertile sites and as cattle camps: "Is it illegal for people of Aurukun to live permanently or temporarily on other parts of the reserve besides the Aurukun township?" he queried. He was soundly reprimanded, and a commitment extracted that BOEMAR would "manage the Communities consistent with the policies and philosophies applying throughout the State on all other Reserves."

In fact the government had resolved to act. Immediately after the Privy Council decision which endorsed Killoran's trusteeship over the reserves, and bolstered by a confidential legal opinion that a "legal vacuum" in church authority had been created by the merger of the Presbyterian church into the Uniting church, the government struck. On 20 March 1978 BOEMAR was given three weeks' notice to vacate the missions on a walk out/walk in basis, after more than seventy years' service.

Immediately the government went into damage control. The church had tried its best, but "obviously" the task was now beyond them. We were forced to step in, explained Porter, to rescue the people from the moribund communities where both health and education had broken down. Internal documents give a different twist: a nurse from the federally funded AHP informed her superior that the Aurukun hospital had been kept empty, saving the state $1,000 a week in wages.[44] But this was not BOEMAR's doing. As Porter was soon forced to admit, both education and health had been government responsibilities for several years.

Public furore erupted over this pre-emptive strike against community wishes. The Queensland government brushed aside threats of a challenge under federal laws, insisting that the matter centred only on the question of management competence. The Aurukun council appealed for federal intervention but the federal coalition was determined to avoid confrontation with Queensland. Disregarding existing legal options, the Fraser government threatened to introduce draft legislation facilitating self-management for any Queensland reserve. When Bjelke-Petersen said he would terminate funding from the end of March to abort the dispute, Fraser offered to direct-fund the councils for continued operation while a compromise was secured. In a tactic aimed at distorting public support Killoran suggested setting the police fraud squad onto an immediate investigation of alleged Aboriginal misuse of state and federal subsidies.[45]

At this point Bjelke-Petersen called a truce, ostensibly so that all parties could consider the impending federal legislation. A change of heart? Hardly. With malice aforethought he was acting on opinion solicited from valued supporter Sir Arnold Bennett QC: call a truce, Bennett advised, but at all times remain "poised for action". After all, he continued, "The Aborigines, a people easily swayed, are hardly likely to have realized the implications of Commonwealth control … The same applies to the public". You have several options, he informed the premier. As a delaying tactic, the Aboriginal reserves could be regazetted as national parks, thereby invalidating the imminent federal reserve legislation. Or the reserves could merely be cancelled, "accompanied by appropriate explanation and justification, including a statement that it is with a view to reorganisation".[46]

In the interim Killoran notified all community managers to ignore press speculation of imminent change: "The Department will continue to provide management … in terms of broad policy guide lines clearly identified in previous annual reports". And after a thirteen-hour meeting in Canberra the two governments struck an agreement. Joint church/state control would continue pending consultation with Aurukun and Mornington Island and a report from the Aboriginal and Islander Commission (a revamp of the former AAC) advising new management procedures for the two communities.

BOEMAR immediately denounced the deal as a sellout to state interests. And Bjelke-Petersen could hardly wait to boast that it represented a victory for Queensland. In a belated effort to extract some credibility for itself, the Fraser government reactivated the self-management legislation, passing the Aboriginal and Torres Strait Islanders (Queensland Reserves and Communities Self Management) Bill through the lower house in five hours on 5 April, "guaranteeing the right" of Aboriginal communities to manage their own affairs. Perhaps they went to bed well satisfied. But the following day, while the Bill was being debated in the Senate, Queensland revoked the reserve status of the Aurukun and Mornington Island communities, creating instead two new local government shires. For these now defunct Aboriginal reserves, the new federal legislation had no relevance.

For several months Queensland strung federal minister Ian Viner along through a convoluted "negotiation" process to establish operational guidelines for the newly designated "local government" communities. A draft of the enabling state legislation was sent to Viner to verify "mutual objectives", but if Viner thought the Aboriginal residents should have input he was immediately disabused: "Co-operation is imperilled and the purposes of the agreement are put in jeopardy if you persist with ... suggestions of anything being dependent on 'approval' of any group", commanded Porter. Certainly Viner's assumption that the new land tenure "would guarantee to the Aboriginal communities their traditional rights and secure their right to the use and occupation of the land" would have caused amusement.

Within a few weeks Queensland's Cabinet decreed that any further discussions would have to take place in Brisbane. The farcical status of these "joint discussions" can be judged by senator Neville Bonner's assessment, made after a preview of the Bill, that 21 of the 35 clauses breached the state/federal agreement. When he confronted fellow Liberal Charles Porter on this point in an acrimonious television debate, Porter snapped that the Bill would be pushed through state parliament "without a single amendment".

And so it was. Two weeks later, with the federal government's legislation still sitting in the Senate, Queensland rushed the new law through parliament in a nineteen-hour sitting. In May 1978 the *Local Government (Aboriginal Lands) Act* set out the "self-management" strategies for the new local shires. The existing community councils were incorporated and nominated as trustees operating leases over most of the former reserve areas; but unlike other shire councils they were prevented from selling, mortgaging or subdividing the lands, nor could they acquire or hold direct title to any area. Although hunting and gathering rights were preserved, so was the Crown's access to mining and control of all mineral rights. Council management was supervised by an advisory committee comprising state and federal ministers. The Governor in Council, effectively the Cabinet, retained the right to intervene in council matters at any time, an intervention euphemistically disguised as "directing a minister to provide assistance".

Within weeks both councils had rejected this format and advertised for funds to fight the imposed legislation. They sacked the government-appointed shire clerks and spurned state funding. Queensland retaliated by dismissing community-appointed white advisers and refusing permission for Aurukun to select a town clerk of their own choice. When Bjelke-Petersen and local government minister Russ Hinze made their "triumphant" tour of the new shires in August, the media circus was repudiated by the non-cooperative residents. Bjelke-Petersen accused BOEMAR of trucking people from the township at Mornington Island to prevent communication with the government party.

Furious at the sullen reception, the premier announced that the communities had been brainwashed by political activists keen to "disrupt orderly administration", and declared that Aurukun was held under a "reign of terror". Hinze sacked both councils and installed government administrators. In his added role as police minister he alleged a "breakdown in law and order" and ordered in the state police to take control, vowing to "mop up" all land rights activists. Council elections for the "self-managed" communities were withheld for eighteen months. Aurukun promptly re-elected all their previous councillors.

The Queensland hierarchy must have been greatly relieved that the much-touted federal self-management legislation was never activated to secure the purposes for which it was created. It would, after all, have been a relatively simple exercise to resubmit the federal reserves and self-management Bill with a retrospective clause to include also *former* Aboriginal reserves.

In the event, and faced with earnest petitions from a range of Aboriginal communities in Queensland — Yarrabah, Cherbourg, Kowanyama (previously Mitchell River), Woorabinda and Mossman Gorge — the Fraser government declined to exercise the provisions it had so publicly constructed. There is evidence on file that federal minister Fred Chaney may have been sidelined on the Yarrabah petition by Porter and Bjelke-Petersen to ensure non-intervention. On the other hand, Chaney elsewhere confided to Porter and Killoran that he had ignored the petitions "for the sake of avoiding competition between the Governments".[47]

* * *

It is clear from official records that federal governments were loathe to directly overrule state rights. The Whitlam Labor government declined to activate powers under the 1967 referendum to back Palm Island during the gastroenteritis epidemic of 1973, and the coalition government under Malcolm Fraser showed similar distaste for confrontation during the Aurukun/Mornington Island crisis five years later.

Nevertheless, through a mixture of moderate pressures and financial coercion, federal governments of both persuasions increased their operational involvement in Queensland's Aboriginal affairs. Each move and countermove in the state/federal clash over jurisdiction reformulated the contested areas of wage rates, health delivery, community affairs, housing availability, and reserve and land management.

Bjelke-Petersen crowed over his "defeat" of Canberra in 1978 and subsequent analysis rarely challenges this assessment. Within the public and political domain it would certainly appear that it was the federal government whose nerve "broke first".[48] But had the state won the war, or merely one of the battles in the long struggle to control Aboriginal affairs in Queensland?

10

The politics of deception

It is hardly surprising that Queensland's 1978 *Local Government (Aboriginal Lands) Act*, which ostensibly bestowed local government status on the former Aboriginal reserves of Aurukun and Mornington Island, has been criticised for providing neither land security nor self-management. Given the evidence from internal records, summarised in the previous chapter, it could be said that such "failure" is entirely consistent with Queensland's objective of frustrating federal interventions into what it saw as a state prerogative — namely, the continuation of full control of both Aboriginal communities and reserve lands.

During the 1980s all remaining Aboriginal communities in Queensland were granted deeds of grant in trust (DOGITs), and enabling legislation passed self-governance to the various councils. What were the circumstances giving rise to these apparently radical changes? And what exactly did the communities inherit from the state government?

Law and order?

The government's favoured cover story for the peremptory takeover of the Aurukun and Mornington Island communities was that "law and order" had broken down, that the communities were hostage to drunken, rioting individuals who scorned authority, that "for their own good" it was necessary for state administrators and state police to move in and restore order. Were these two communities out of control? What was the interlinking of alcohol, social breakdown and policing?

There is little doubt that the post-1971 availability of alcohol on the previously dry communities caused turmoil. Initially canteens operated for only two hours per night, selling opened cans in sheds lacking seating, food or any social amenities. Income soaked up through alcohol consumption was lost to the communities because for many years profits from liquor sales streamed into departmental coffers via the Welfare Fund.

Social order and cohesion were doubly jeopardised by sly grog running — excessive, illegal and exorbitantly priced supplies of alcohol, often including fortified wines and spirits, which fuelled binge drinking, aggression and family poverty. In any rural town such social upheaval would be quickly policed. For more than a decade, however, Aboriginal communities paid a high price in disturbances, injury and assault, while the basic social requirement of law enforcement was bandied about between the Police and the Aboriginal departments — because neither was prepared to foot the bill on these state institutions.

Officially a cost to the Aboriginal department, the police presence on most communities was restricted to the occasional one-day visit, unless, *after* violence had erupted, they were called in as an emergency measure. Although there was a token permanent police attendance at the government settlements of Woorabinda, Cherbourg and Palm Island, this was woefully inadequate. The manager on the latter community, complaining in 1977 that order could not be maintained with just two officers, pointed out that Charters Towers, with a comparable crime rate, was serviced by ten men. No change was made.

Given sporadic attendance and chronic undermanning, the quality of police performance was crucial. But here, once again, there was no surety of standard service on Aboriginal communities — because of the unreliable commitment and integrity of state police. Records reveal an *increase* in sly grog running and violence on more than one government settlement during the tenure of particular police. "It can be said without any hesitation that it was common gossip on Palm Island that the Police Station was totally ineffective", wrote Killoran in 1980, because the two officers "spent the period from 8 am to 4 pm generally playing chess in public view and were not seen after that time". Meanwhile the community paid the price for their neglect: "sly grog running reached an all time high, the Community was in a state of turmoil and it was only during a period of leave of the Sergeant and his subsequent transfer that relieving officers took firm control and brought a degree of stability to the Community".[1]

This was not an isolated incident. As late as 1983 safety at Woorabinda was compromised by state police whose apparent lack of interest in curbing the sly grog trade was startlingly exposed by the dramatic drop in canteen sales during their term of duty, and the correspondingly high levels of community turmoil. In the same year Cherbourg's welfare adviser wrote of the widespread "anger, depression, and frustration" that neither the police nor the council could control binge drinking, brawling and house breaking. According to Killoran himself, brawls, drunkenness and damage on many communities were "the result of lack of interest displayed over the years by the appointed conventional Queensland police".[2]

Additional difficulties arose because officers from the south often had no idea of conditions on Aboriginal reserves nor any awareness of Aboriginal customs. Such cultural dysfunction is understandable: evasion of duty is not. In the mid-1980s the Doomadgee council lodged complaints against the Burketown police practice of visiting only on quiet days, despite frequent requests to attend on pay and pension days when the need for patrols was most urgent. From Hopevale came protests that police refused to work after hours when trouble was most likely to occur. Here Killoran refused to pay penalty rates, directing that police roster their 40-hour period to cover the times when need was greatest.

Research of documents reveals that it was not uncommon for police to be *ordered* to serve on Aboriginal communities, compensated by advance promotion and other perks. Such enticement, as Killoran noted with considerable understatement, "does not always produce the most suitable type of person for duty within an Aboriginal Community environment".

This wealth of information of defective policing remained on closed file. The public position, that communities were adequately and more appropriately serviced by Aboriginal police operating under departmental direction, was a cruel deceit. Certainly, with proper instruction and status, internal policing may have succeeded. In practice, however, a stream of able-bodied "reliable" men were drafted into policing positions — often motivated by the expectation of better pay.

Once appointed, Aboriginal police were given no formal training whatever for their work, many were unaware of the regulations that they were supposed to enforce, and all were deeply compromised by family loyalties. Inevitable dissension with relatives generated, in the words of observers at Wujal Wujal (previously Bloomfield River), "tremendous tensions and crossed loyalties". Typically law enforcement was degraded: "The job turnover rate for Bloomfield policemen is very high. Most would never stay on for more than a month".[3]

Conflicts of interest arose because police were ultimately answerable to department managers rather than community councils. In one fight at Aurukun in the mid-1970s, community police threw their uniforms at the manager and sided with their relatives. In vain did BOEMAR and the council plead for a normal police presence, remarking of the community officers: "They say there are times when family authority patterns take precedence over training".

During the bitter stand-off with the Presbyterians in the 1970s it appears such tensions and disruptions were callously exploited by the department, demeaning BOEMAR's management to validate the planned government takeover. For years Killoran ignored desperate calls from both BOEMAR and the Mornington Island council that a permanent officer was essential to enforce law and to train Aboriginal police. Even the Burketown police called for a permanent station, citing rampant sly-grogging by trawler crews and regular raids on canteen supplies by residents. Even so, this community of almost 700 people was serviced, on Killoran's instruction, on only a three-monthly basis. Such crisis visits were described by BOEMAR as useless. In 1976, when the police department agreed to a permanent presence, the

Aboriginal department declined to supply the premises. Nothing was done.

Such was the turmoil on Aurukun that families were forced to camp in the bush for safety. Again sly-grogging, brawls and injuries prevailed, and again Killoran disdained to commission a permanent police presence. So bad was the violence that the teachers' and nurses' unions threatened to withdraw their members. The Police department argued the problem was not theirs to resolve. The Aboriginal department made no change.

Against this background, BOEMAR was incensed that the government callously played politics to claim that "law and order" problems on the two communities resulted from "inappropriate philosophies" of the church. In vain they protested that it was the duty of the government to protect lives and property. Killoran persisted in depicting social breakdown as a management problem, informing minister Claude Wharton that there was no need for any change in procedures. The local position, declared Killoran, "was the culmination of the policies adopted by BOEMAR of 'self determination and Aboriginality' which they had espoused from the Commonwealth". Somewhat illogically he continued: "The Queensland Police could not be expected and would not take on the role of a 'disciplinary force' ",[4] a statement entirely inconsistent with his previously noted lament that "lack of interest" by state police was responsible for much of the unrest on government communities.

Such callous manipulation of law enforcement for political expedience was strongly resented by Ray Whitrod, Queensland police commissioner between 1970 and 1976: "The government's view seems to be that the police are just another public service department, accountable to the premier and Cabinet through the police minister, and therefore rightly subject to directions, not only on matters of general policy, but also in specific cases".[5] For many decades collusion between police and Aboriginal departments produced a regular traffic in confidential police information and uncorroborated reports.

But police also profited from this unhealthy alliance. It is clear from the files that a regular corps of police "trackers" were retained as menial workers for rural officers, often at less than half the basic wage. Documents in 1966 reveal that Aboriginal administrators were aware that some men *lost up to $1,500* during their term of employment with police. In 1972, with great reluctance, the police department condescended to pay trackers $22 per week when the guaranteed minimum wage was $51.50. Two years later, opposing a public service board recommendation that the wage be set at $62.90 plus district allowances, the police protested that trackers were better off on $29.50 plus rations, because of high rural prices![6]

When free Legal Aid became available in the late 1970s to low income earners, and an Aboriginal and Torres Strait Islanders Legal Service (ATSILS) was set up, Aboriginal–police relations were irrevocably changed. For the first time legal representation was a feasible option, particularly for Aborigines in remote areas and isolated communities. Previous arrest and penalty rates were thrown into question: many charges were dropped or discounted; bail often replaced short-term imprisonment. Also challenged was the common practice of removing offenders hundreds of kilometres for arraignment in rural towns, only to abandon them after bail without the means to return. At Burketown, for instance, people from Mornington Island and Doomadgee were commonly left destitute, often to be re-arrested as vagrants.

Protection was now available against police verballing of Aborigines, a practice said to be so common in Brisbane in the 1970s that senator Neville Bonner introduced a private member's Bill offering safeguards against coercive testimony. The police unions, the premier and the Justice minister, Bill Lickiss, promptly labelled the Admissibility of Confessions Bill an example of "one law for the blacks and one for the whites". The Bill lapsed when parliament was prorogued prior to the 1977 election.

Access to outside scrutiny also exposed the hypocrisy of the so-called community court system. At the same time as the department dismissed complaints from legal aid personnel as being motivated by anti-government sentiment, officially delegated visiting justices routinely criticised the irregular procedures of Aboriginal police and courts. In some cases, appointed court officers had no knowledge of the by-laws, no idea what a summons was, and held no processing documents. Anomalous, and all too frequently illegal, community court dealings were indicative not only of negligent training but also of community distaste for imposed sanctions. Frequently courts declined to enforce attendance or set default terms for fines; councillors refused to exercise powers to search for liquor; and community police failed to prefer charges for violence and property destruction.

This brief review gives some indication of the context of "law and order" problems which undermined cohesion and frequently threatened safety on Aboriginal communities into the 1980s. In vain did councils and mission authorities call for conventional levels of policing and formal training. While the government openly blamed assaults and upheaval at Aurukun and Mornington Island on BOEMAR's self-determination philosophy, other communities were, by official default, left exposed to the public presumption that alcohol and violence were somehow "Aboriginal" problems.

Big brother

It was not only on matters of law and order that councils were emasculated. Giving the lie to public rhetoric of relative autonomy, all council meetings were attended by government-appointed managers. Frequently it was these officers who typed up the minutes, copies of which were always forwarded to Killoran, often with caustic comments added. Councils, and indeed all individuals, were stigmatised by an almost total lack of privacy. All communications — telephone calls, mail and telegrams — were relayed through the manager's office where, as Commissioner for Community Relations Al Grassby noted in 1979, they were frequently intercepted or delayed.

Killoran was almost obsessed with minimising contacts between federal agencies and community councillors. It was "essential" and "most important", Killoran warned managers, that they watch out for visiting DAA officers "and their affiliates" who might "continue to use their influences on your Community and pursue a philosophy with Council and residents" at odds with state policy. Attend all discussions with community residents, he ordered, "or failing your ability to meet this commitment, obtain feed-back from a reliable source in regard to proposals and commitment agreed upon. Finally, I must insist that you give priority in keeping me constantly informed on the activities of the Commonwealth in your area".[7] As late as 1980 the siege mentality was still apparent as Killoran stressed the imperative for managers to remain loyal to the state, reject any blandishments and make sure neither they nor the councillors allowed themselves to be manipulated.

This paranoia jeopardised projects which councils sought to establish independently of the department. At Doomadgee, for example, a cultural program drawn up by the Ngooderi Culture Company was initially rejected by mission authorities because of the "outside advice" by the Mornington Island chairman regarding federal subsidies. When the school took over the project at the council's request, minister Charles Porter angrily denounced it as bypassing his authorisation, even though his federal counterpart Ian Viner assured him that the program was "enthusiastically regarded by Teachers, Councillors, mission staff and pupils alike".

It was to the DAA that Doomadgee councillors turned in their efforts to retrieve council trucks hired to the Burke Shire Council for road upgrading and not returned after five years, and in their battle with missionary authorities for control of the council-owned community bus. DAA reports also exposed the hollowness of Killoran's boast that two new homes were provided for the community in 1978: both were for white teachers. Records of this period show 13 homes and 2 units for 48 whites at Doomadgee, compared with 88 homes and 8 camps for 700 permanent and 203 seasonal residents.

Council decisions were cursorily overruled when it suited Killoran, particularly where this related to access on reserves. At Lockhart River the council exercised its right to

refuse entry to school health inspectors. Despite his acknowledgment that Aboriginal communities were sick of
being treated like "guinea pigs" during "numerous visita-
tions ... for various purposes of enquiry, investigation, assessment or research", Killoran ordered the inspection to
proceed.[8]

Not only did Killoran trample council decisions, in a
notorious incident at Hope Vale in 1979, he pressured
other departments to do his bidding. Here a teacher had
called a "meeting" without the manager's authority. Acutely
sensitive that the AWU were canvassing mission workers at
the nearby Cape Flattery silica mines over the matter of
non-award wages, the Lutheran mission board requested
that the "radical" teacher be transferred, and Killoran demanded that the Education Department act immediately.
Unwilling to provoke union retaliation on such a slim issue,
the Education Department demurred, only to be steam-
rolled by Killoran who insisted that the matter be put
directly to Cabinet.

Meanwhile, deputy director Tom Murphy quizzed residents at Hopevale for "incriminating" evidence against the
teacher and passed to Killoran the names of those who
spoke also to the delegate from the teachers' union who
was preparing a defence. From Hopevale the Aboriginal
police lodged a protest denying government publicity that
they had been threatened by the teacher. After considerable pressure, the council bowed to Killoran's demands that
the teacher's residence permit be cancelled, but they set no
execution date to activate the eviction. Ultimately the
teacher was transferred, in blatant contempt of a petition
seeking his continuation, lodged with parliament on the
signatures of 172 of the 210 residents and three of the four

councillors.[9] Human Rights commissioner Al Grassby's official protest that refusal of access to union delegates breached federal anti-discrimination legislation was ignored; Cabinet had decreed it would have no dealing with this body.

The belligerent rejection of federal facilities, while publicly extolled by the Queensland hierarchy as a triumphant safeguarding of state rights, unquestionably exacerbated the area of greatest vulnerability, namely entrenched poverty on Aboriginal communities. Housing on the communities had deteriorated markedly since McMahon had refused further funds in 1972 until Aboriginal co-operatives were set up to manage development. This hiatus was readily exploited by DAA personnel who eagerly informed councils of the availability of large housing subsidies — subsidies disallowed because the state would not sanction the prerequisite incorporation of councils. In theory, council chairmen "endorsed" all state policy through the emasculated Aboriginal and Islander Commission (discussed below). In fact, the reality of plentiful funds and derelict housing tested "loyalty". As the manager at Yarrabah warned Killoran, the acute lack of housing "is being used to maximum political advantage by all anti-Department of Aboriginal and Islanders Advancement factions."

When the Fraser government proclaimed the *Aboriginal Councils and Associations Act* in 1976, it provided a federal platform for incorporation of Aboriginal bodies on state communities. Quick to realise such instrumentalities would escape his control, Killoran scorned the new provision as "another step aimed at disjointing the management of Aboriginal Reserves in this State." Aware that ATSILS was energetically promoting community incorporation to access DAA housing funds, Killoran, keen to block "another local government body additional and quite separate in law", urged that similar provisions be set up through amendments to the state's Aboriginal legislation.

Aboriginal housing has always been the area of greatest destitution in Queensland. But so inflexible was the state in its exclusion of funds not directly under departmental control that a $6.1 million grant for Aboriginal housing in rural areas was rejected because the money was allocated through the state housing commission, not through the Aboriginal department. Porter's implausible explanation was that the commission would "disturb the anonymity" of Aboriginal families who were "not identified" except through the Aboriginal department.[10]

It was not until the passage of the 1979 *Aborigines and Islanders Amendment Act* that Queensland sanctioned the incorporation of councils under the umbrella of state supervision. This and other, largely cosmetic, changes followed a highly public charade of Aboriginal and Islander consultation through the state-appointed Aboriginal and Islander Commission (AIC). Set up in 1976, internal records show that this body of four was compromised even before its inception. Early suggestions that it be a statutory body answerable to parliament were hastily stifled by Bjelke-Petersen who admonished: "… if the proposed body were to make recommendations contrary to present expectations the Government would find itself committed in advance to giving effect to those recommendations".[11] The AIC found itself operating as a publicity exercise within the department.

Starved of funds, set abortively brief travel itineraries, and denied access to information or personnel other than departmental officers, the AIC report which signalled the legislative changes predictably "endorsed" state policy, denouncing the "unrealistic degree of idealism" and the "dangerous policy of separate development" espoused by federal agencies. According to analysts from the Foundation for Aboriginal and Islander Research Action (FAIRA) 32 of the 34 pages of the report were "apparently written" by a departmental official.[12] The impotence of the AIC can be judged by the fact that it learned of BOEMAR's eviction from Aurukun and Mornington Island in March 1978 from the newspapers, despite a consultation with the minister only a week previously.

Touted as a major policy response to the AIC's report, the 1979 *Amendment Act* perpetuated this body to make recommendations (but not public reports) to the government. The new legislation also strengthened community council powers to refuse or evict unwanted persons, and introduced a right of appeal for aggrieved persons against decisions of Aboriginal courts. And, in a move aimed at pre-empting provisions in federal law, Aboriginal councils could now incorporate for grants in aid for services and maintenance, but under state superintendence.

No doubt well pleased with this intergovernmental accord, federal Aboriginal Affairs minister Fred Chaney toured the northern communities of Aurukun, Mornington Island and Yarrabah lauding the freeing up of subsidies for essential council projects. Things turned sour, however, when Aurukun chairman Donald Peinkinna demanded to know why the federal government had not activated its own legislation to accord self-management despite earnest entreaties from many Aboriginal communities. Killoran would have approved Chaney's assessment of this query as indicative of "outside agitation of simple blacks". With breathtaking hypocrisy Chaney elsewhere reflected: "Perhaps at times our rhetoric and thoughts led them to believe that [self-management] is available".[13]

There is no doubt that Queensland's Aboriginal communities were short-changed by a federal coalition government which lacked the stomach for public confrontation on matters of doctrine. Even so, the state had been forced to match the federal flanking strategy on community incorporation. But as the flow of federal funds accelerated the building of desperately needed homes and amenities from the late 1970s, pressure mounted on the Achilles' heel of state policy — namely wages.

Default

Queensland's triumphant "win" on Aurukun and Mornington Island had come at an extreme, although unstated, price. In degazetting the Aboriginal reserves of Aurukun and Mornington Island, Queensland had undercut its primary defence against charges of exploitation. Now that these two new local government areas were no longer subject to regulations crafted for Aboriginal reserves, s.68, which excluded Aboriginal wages from the province of industrial law, no longer applied.

Since the introduction of cash economies on the Aboriginal institutions in 1968, the department had consistently sacrificed income-earning positions rather than allocate the funds necessary to cover even the "training wage" of those wanting employment. Ignoring community stress and deprivation, the official line was that the available wage pool was sufficient to cover needs and was commensurate with the skills of employees. One among many who pleaded for jobs so families could feed their children, Hopevale's council secretary petitioned the minister directly, reporting that half the workforce was kept idle despite urgent projects. Killoran drafted the minister's rejection of increased funding citing "Australia's current economic situation".

Well aware of the wage exposure which degazettal would invite, Bjelke-Petersen took the opportunity of the false "truce" to throw down the gauntlet to Fraser. If full wages were a federal objective then their funding was a federal responsibility, he wrote. Compliance with demands to pay all Aboriginal workers the state's minimum wage would require an extra $3.6 million per year, and payment of award wages where due would raise the bill to $6.85 million.

The premier outlined his options. If the Commonwealth failed to provide the funds he would recoup the shortfall by reducing state services and increasing rents and charges on the communities, or by retrenching 850 workers to cover payment within current budget levels. Not only would this latter course cause "massive social problems" from unemployment and "other factors", he informed Fraser brutally, but it would leave the Commonwealth exposed to an additional $9.5 million in social security benefits.[14]

A deal was struck whereby bulk social security payments were paid directly to the Aurukun and Mornington Island councils to bankroll workers' wages. Euphemistically tagged the community development employment projects scheme (CDEP), this effectively transferred the running costs of the new local government communities from state to Commonwealth, at base using private pensions to bankroll the two rural towns. But this cosy arrangement did not resolve the wage position on other Aboriginal communities where the state anticipated a flow-on demand for normalised wages. Within months Bjelke-Petersen was once again bitterly denouncing "mounting pressures flowing from Commonwealth enactments".[15]

When Killoran was served with a complaint and summons on behalf of Yarrabah labourer Arnold Murgha, charging that non-payment of award wages on Aboriginal reserves breached state industrial law, Queensland detected the hidden hand of the Commonwealth: "The Department has been confidentially informed that the Aboriginal and Islander Legal Aid Service has been, in the background, actively promoting Murgha's cause and it is further understood that Federal Labour [sic] Parliamentarians have been involved with the Australian Workers' Union in promoting the action".[16]

File evidence suggests that the department assumed an arrogant — and misguided — stance. It appears Killoran ignored the compulsory conference convened by the arbitration commissioner, his attendance after three days secured by subpoena. The department argued that, as "special areas" (like prisons), Aboriginal reserves were not subject to industrial regulation, that the work was community aid and not employment, and that s.68 specifically placed reserves outside the industrial framework. They did not bother to dispute the status or standard of Murgha's work. This oversight brought stinging criticism from the industrial magistrate who declared that he had been left in "a legal vacuum" on the matter of Murgha's so-called "trainee" capacity.

The magistrate held, nonetheless, that s.68 invalidated his jurisdiction. The AWU appealed. It was then that Killoran received an unwelcome opinion from the government's Senior Counsel: "...[that] the *Industrial Conciliation and Arbitration Act* does apply and [that] the award is relevant and binding ... the claim must succeed". Settle as quickly and quietly as possible, was his eminent advice. Considering the threat that parallel civil action could be brought under the 1975 *Aboriginal and Torres Strait Islander (Queensland Discriminatory Laws) Act*, the Crown Solicitor confirmed: "In the net result there is a liability to pay the award rate of wages irrespective of how or where that liability is enforced".[17]

The government plotted its next move. Minister Charles Porter told his colleagues that his federal counterparts "seemed quite jubilant", over the successful appeal and "admitted Commonwealth legal officers had worked diligently for it". "The repercussions of this wage situation, sought and secured by the Commonwealth, are enormous", said Porter, outlining treasury estimates of $7.3 million annually for the 1600 eligible workers. If this amount was "unavailable", although a possible $1.5 million could be garnered through increased rents and charges, community workforces would have to be slashed by 50 per cent to keep within budget.

Either way, Porter argued, Queensland should blame the Commonwealth: "I am determined to make it quite clear to the peoples of reserves just who has caused the massive unemployment and the inevitable social trauma growing out of it", wrote Porter to Bjelke-Petersen. "Equally the electorate must be informed so that with the elections next year, the State's voters will know who to blame."[18]

The AWU's appeal against the industrial magistrate's decision was heard, and upheld, by the president of Queensland's industrial court. In his judgment of May 1979, he argued that without a clearly stated intention "to abridge the liberty of the subject" in paying less than award rates to Aboriginal workers on reserve, then s.68 of the Aboriginal Acts could not take precedence over the state's industrial laws. Effectively, the government had no legal right to refuse award wages to these employees. It quietly settled out of court. But it was the communities which paid the cost. Insisting that "a political solution" had to be secured between state and Commonwealth on the award wage question, Cabinet decreed that not one cent would be made available to cover the implementation of legal wages on the state-run communities.[19]

Stung by his loss in the courts, Killoran retaliated. Hearing that a Yarrabah councillor was canvassing union membership, he threatened to sack anyone who applied for award wages. If there were a strike, he warned, he would withhold state grants for essential services and force the council to extract from householders the revenue necessary to run the communities "including payment of wages at the rates demanded".[20] Eleven newly-signed union members were "stood down" for seeking award rates.

Again Killoran was forced to an industrial court hearing. Here he had no option but to agree that wages be almost doubled to reach the state minimum of $131. Lamely he sought to link this rise to a commitment that the AWU desist from any further action on award wages: the AWU ignored him. On this matter, however, Killoran bought time from the commissioner: award wages would be held in abeyance pending a full employment survey on all communities — a survey which dragged out for more than a year and was confidentially defined as a procedural guide to accommodate award wages at no cost to the government.

Forced to reinstate the eleven workers at Yarrabah, the

government fed the media an imaginative version of events: the men were not sacked, they had "rejected their previous positions". Killoran maintained the department's innocence, and patronisingly suggested that the men "might not have realised the significance of their action". They could be re-employed as trainees, he said, provided they adopted "a more meaningful and responsible attitude."[21]

In public, the government condemned "the abrupt change-over [to award wages] required by Union and Commonwealth interests". Behind-the-scenes efforts to pin the financial burden on the federal government were torpedoed when the latter agency rejected any obligation to subsidise a decision by a state industrial court. Caught between the federal veto and the state's hard line, the department turned its hand to some creative accounting: it was calculated that 101 store and stock workers whose wages totalled $900,000 could be costed from the Welfare Fund, and for the remaining 794 workers due award wages there would only be a shortfall of $1.5 million after factoring in the existing $5.5 million wage allocation. Raising the rents $20 would bring in an extra $1 million, "drastic cuts" could subtract a further $400,000 from the bill, and if treasury agreed to hand over the annual interest of $100,000 generated on the Welfare Fund, the books could be balanced.[22]

Killoran launched the 1980 year with confidential instructions to managers that workforces be cut by 25 per cent, despite his own assessment that such reductions "would seriously impair the operations of essential services on communities". Internal reports reveal the wretchedness of this scheme given existing low work numbers: at Barambah there were already 22 people to each wage earner, at Yarrabah 46, Lockhart River 26, Cherbourg 43,

Woorabinda 41, Edward River 50, Doomadgee 50, Weipa 61, Kowanyama 70 and Palm Island 99.[23]

A government proposal that a special industrial agreement be set for reserve workers was aborted in April 1980 when the AWU set a benchmark at current award rates. The following month Porter reluctantly reported that the Commonwealth had sunk any chance of a "political solution" by rejecting Queensland's bid to have the CDEP scheme extended to all communities. Already, however, Killoran had stockpiled $600,000 by underspending, and anticipated a further $300,000 through increased charges.

Despite mounting pressure of further industrial action, this time by two Cherbourg nurses, the government resolved to tough it out. At a private meeting between Killoran, Porter and federal minister Fred Chaney, Porter declared that "the matter would not be pursued further unless the union reactivated it". For his part, Chaney declared that payment of award wages, now costed at around $5 million above minimum wage levels, was inevitable.[24]

The Queensland government held fast to its June 1979 decision not to finance award wages. During 1980 the hoarding of funds intensified as the department withheld a promised increase of $3.50 per week, terminated subsidised electricity and retail store prices, planned "significant increases" in rentals, and, disregarding the previous years' commitment to bring wages to the $131 minimum grade, held rates at only $95. This achieved a stockpile of more than $595,000 for the year, a saving the government was anxious to conceal, given grossly substandard community conditions. New minister Ken Tomkins had the gall to state that Queensland's legislation was only retained on the insistence of the indigenous population in order to protect "social, economic, and political structures" on their "fragile communities". The same man elsewhere declared Aborigines needed at least "fifty years more evolution" before they could handle their own domestic affairs.

At the same time, the department was fighting a rear-guard action against the nurses union, with Killoran holding to the doctrine that maximum employment from a limited wages pool worked to the benefit of "those persons who, through lack of qualifications, have been unable to acquire suitable employment as one would expect to find in the general Australian Community".[25] This cut no ice with the Crown Solicitor, who advised that the policy of employing more persons than needed did not relieve the department from obligations under federal anti-discrimination laws. Further, although engaged through the department, the nurses at Cherbourg were actually employed by the Health department through the South Burnet Hospital Board and were thereby, in his opinion, due full wages. Killoran's calls for the Health department to back his stance were given short shrift.

Throughout 1981 the process of attrition continued with more than 500 jobs stripped from the communities, reducing employment levels to only $7^1/_2$ per cent. Already reeling under massive delays in maintenance, building and essential service programs, several managers baulked, risking professional retribution — the Yarrabah manager lamented "the recognized career dangers associated with appearing to question established policy". Community conditions further deteriorated as the department resorted to "internal manipulation", poaching funds from housing and enterprise projects to recoup wage deficits. Records reveal builders' wages were extracted from Commonwealth grants for housing, and nearly one hundred "marginal type employees" were charged against the Welfare Fund.

In three years reserve workforces were slashed 26 per cent, dropping from 1463 in 1979 to 1082. Ignoring its own commitment of August 1982 to "pursue the award wages objective", Cabinet retained a freeze on the necessary funding. There is no question that Cabinet was aware of its untenable legal stance: records show that new minister Val Bird reminded his colleagues in August 1983 that the department had moved towards award rates "in the knowledge, as previously conveyed to Cabinet, that payment for labour below Award rates is in breach of State industrial law and infringes certain laws of the Commonwealth".[26]

Bird appealed to Cabinet's political judgment, arguing that the "social and political consequences" of any further contractions "should be avoided". He appealed to their economic judgment: the reserve areas, he informed them with gross understatement, were "relatively depressed in economic terms" and lacked the capacity "to self-fund any reasonable contribution to higher wage costs". Treasury had agreed to find $500,000 to raise wages to $205.40, $35 above the minimum wage, so bringing some workers "close to the lower scales" of awards for unskilled labour. But it was imperative, Bird declared, that Cabinet authorise the $1.2 million necessary to cover this increase for the 1983–84 year. Failure to do so would necessitate a further 100 sackings.

Cabinet was unmoved. The impact on the cash-starved communities was horrendous. At Woorabinda, for instance, 81 per cent of the homes were already listed as overcrowded, and 42 per cent grossly so, with four or more persons per bedroom. Dwellings of three-bedrooms held up to 21 people, and two-bedrooms up to 10, and the manager reported "no alternatives are available for those they are sheltering". Many of the weatherboard homes were nearly forty years old, described as "in dire need of repair, requiring re-lining, laundries, toilets and bathrooms", and serviced by wood stoves and cold water.[27]

And Woorabinda, with its average house occupancy of 7.4 persons, was not the worst placed. A survey preceding increases in rents and charges revealed 7.3 people per house at Cherbourg, 11.8 at Palm Island, 10.7 at Yarrabah, 6.6 at Bamaga, 7.4 at Edward River, 7.3 at Kowanyama, 7.7 at Lockhart River, 13.7 at Weipa, 18.2 at Hopevale and 10.6 at Doomadgee. To bring occupancy to under eight persons, it was calculated a further 664 homes were needed at a cost of $32.5 million. Meanwhile, housing and maintenance funds were being secretly bled for wages.

When the Human Rights Commission contacted communities late in 1983 to offer support in wage challenges under federal laws, minister Val Bird disparaged the approach as "merely an attempt to discredit the Queensland Government". In his advice to Bjelke-Petersen, bearing all the hallmark's of Killoran's drafting, Bird endorsed Queensland's hard line: "I would suggest that we await any move against Queensland ... and consider the issue further should this occur". Once more, and against all the evidence of decimated workforces, the old refrain of maximum jobs in meaningful work was trotted out, along with an assertion, also oft-repeated, that the Murgha case "was not, in fact, determined by the Court but was settled between the Department and Mr Murgha";[28] hence, by inference, the department was under no legal obligation to pay award wages.

This charade fooled no one. In April 1984 the Human Rights commissioner again deplored the continuing "unlawful" practice of under-award payments on Queensland reserves. But he took heart in the knowledge that new minister Bob Katter was drafting legislation to grant self-management to community councils. This provided, noted the commissioner trenchantly, "an appropriate occasion to eliminate any discrimination against Aboriginal workers" on reserve communities.[29] He received an assurance from Katter that under the proposed law, "Employees presently engaged on the Departmental payroll will [thus] become Council employees at Award rates appropriate to the Awards adopted by Councils ... Long-standing concerns such as the one you have raised will be satisfied".

In a later section we will examine how — or indeed, whether — satisfaction was achieved on this matter. In the meantime it was the much more public battle — over land rights — which captured the attention of contemporary media and of subsequent historical and political commentators. How did the state deal with the push for land rights? What was the background to the self-management legislation of the mid-1980s?

Controlling the country

By a Cabinet decision in 1976, the Queensland government had set its face against any federally backed transferral of land, whether by lease or purchase, to Aboriginal people. Land areas under Aboriginal control were equated with "apartheid". Bjelke-Petersen depicted his state as the sole defender of national unity, declaring: "Queensland is the only state that hasn't fallen for their soft soap about land rights and mining rights", and accusing the prime minister,

Malcolm Fraser, of supporting "an independent nation, within a nation".[30] Warming to his theme in state parliament, the premier declared such "nations" would be "outside the laws of Australia", and since they were "capable of contracting with overseas nations hostile to Australia in the future" they would be bases for terrorist activities.

Resourced by the Aboriginal Land Fund Commission (ALFC) and backed by legal aid expertise, continued attempts were made by Aboriginal groups to acquire rural properties. From the late 1970s Queensland found itself skirmishing on several fronts to deny Aboriginal access. When John Koowarta of Aurukun purchased leases on properties at Archer River Bend in 1976, Queensland refused outright to transfer title. Seeking to reverse ALFC support, Lands minister Ken Tomkins (who served as Minister for Aboriginal Affairs between 1980 and 1982) told Aboriginal Affairs Minister Ian Viner the property was earmarked as a national park, that the ALFC had paid far too much, and that the land was not economically viable. According to ALFC evidence, however, no national park had been proposed at the time of sale, and claims of unprofitability were discredited by Tomkin's approaches to Comalco regarding possible purchase.

Information from within the ALFC suggests that Viner was keen to defer to Queensland's objections in the interests of state/federal relations during the Aurukun/Mornington Island crisis. When the ALFC purchased the station of Glenore near Normanton in March 1977, and Tomkins again refused to transfer title, this time on the pretext that the ALFC were not "fit" vendors, Viner assured his Queensland colleagues that neither the Glenore nor the Archer

River Bend deals would be proceeded with, publicly declaring both had lapsed for "technical" reasons.

ALFC personnel were furious at this politicisation of the commission's autonomy, privately vowing to concentrate on freehold properties and so avoid the requirement of ministerial consent for title transfers. When the Commissioner for Community Relations, Al Grassby, contacted the ALFC to say that Queensland's refusal to transfer leases to Aboriginal vendors apparently breached federal anti-discrimination legislation, he found willing listeners: the ALFC sought legal advice and briefed QCs for the challenge. Aghast at this unilateral undertaking at a time when Aurukun/Mornington Island "negotiations" were reaching a critical point, the federal government intimated it might not make funds available to pursue the case.[31]

In the meantime the ALFC briefed a solicitor as front man, amid rumours he stood for a group of Brisbane doctors, to stand for them when Glenore again came up for auction. He gained the property for $200,000 less than the original purchase price. Queensland again refused to transfer title, and the contract lapsed in February 1978. For the Aboriginal Affairs minister, Charles Porter, ALFC operations were evidence that they were out to acquire land in Queensland "by fair means or foul". The Lands minister, Ken Tomkins was moved to declare that "the northern half of Australia" was under threat.

Despite this blustering, 1980 saw Joh Bjelke-Petersen, the new Lands minister, Bill Glasson, and the new Aboriginal Affairs minister, Ken Tomkins, served with a Supreme Court writ by John Koowarta, charging that refusal to transfer title breached 1975 federal racial discrimination legislation. Queensland responded that Koowarta had no status to bring such an action, and that the federal legislation had no validity over state land transfers. They failed on both points. On referral to the High Court, the state now maintained that the transfer was not blocked in order to prevent Aboriginal control but because the area was earmarked as a national park. Did this convince the court? No. But neither did Koowarta gain control of the land. Correctly anticipating judgment against them, Queensland regazetted the area as national park shortly before Koowarta won the case in May 1982.

In an inventive twist to double-dealing, the newly renamed Aboriginal Development Commission (ADC), successor to the AFLC, acquired covert control of the Delta pastoral company by gaining a majority shareholding. This manoeuvre saw management of the property transferred to Aboriginal hands without any requirement of a ministerial-approved transfer. Poor losers, the government canvassed several spoiling tactics. Plans to block the renewal of leases due to expire in 1997 were dropped when legal advice suggested that such refusal would "provoke another Koowarta situation" and risk the property falling to Commonwealth control. The safer option, it was decided, was to let the lease run, thus retaining power and authority in the hands of Queensland's Lands minister. By the end of 1983, despite the state's best efforts, the ADC had secured eight properties in Queensland.

In the same month that Koowarta won his case, although not his land at Archer River Bend, Eddie Mabo launched a statement of claim on behalf of the people of Murray Island in the Torres Strait. By the time the matter reached the Supreme Court in 1986, Queensland had passed a law pre-empting native title on any coast island. It was not until

June 1992 — after ten years of legal battle — that judgment was handed down in a split High Court decision. The Murray Islanders had won recognition of their title.

Documents of the 1970s and 1980s indicate that the Queensland hierarchy were as much suspicious of federal control as they were antagonistic to Aboriginal occupation. In fact Killoran was convinced that Aboriginal enterprise was merely a cover, warning in 1983 that title to land acquired by the ADC "remains with the commission ... occupational rights instead are only given" to Aboriginal clients. "Because of this", he continued, "the whole cosmetic overlay dissolves".[32] Even land procured under the 1976 *Aboriginal Councils and Associations Act* was deemed vulnerable — legal advice confirmed it would revert to federal, rather than state, control if the Aboriginal corporation was wound up.

For some time Bjelke-Petersen had equivocated on the possibility of a more "appropriate" form of Aboriginal land tenure, prompting several communities, and the Aboriginal Advancement League, to pursue the possibility of perpetual leases. But it was not until April 1982 that Queensland passed the *Land Act (Aboriginal and Islander Land Grants) Amendment Act*. Aimed at defusing federal strategies and political criticism, the new law extended longstanding provisions available for public purposes use, namely the granting of trust deeds rather than open title.

The promise of deeds of grant in trust (DOGITs) for Aboriginal communities was a tactic with several appealing features: by advancing the promise of land tenure, it confounded embarrassing condemnation in time for Brisbane's brief passage of international glory during the Commonwealth Games; it suggested an appeasement of community demands for self-management; and it provided a breathing space by tacking the thorny award wage question to the mast of community administration, thus deferring the matter for several years. Katter's later assurance to the Human Rights Commissioner that councils would resolve this matter can be judged in the light of his contemporary commitment to colleagues: "State Government funds advanced to an Aboriginal Council cannot be spent except on approval of a senior officer of the Department of Community Services for a period of three years ... It should be noted", he stressed, "that funding will be at the rate of the current allowance paid each of the workers".[33]

The much-touted land security which DOGITs would afford Aboriginal communities vanished on closer scrutiny: the Governor-in-Council (i.e. Cabinet) could rescind DOGITs at the stroke of a pen; ministerial approval was required before councils could lease or rent land to residents; and the government was to retain control of service delivery and maintenance of facilities. Most importantly, of course, was the fact that the 1982 legislation actually *established* no DOGITs — it merely altered the statutory framework to allow for their possible creation.

In their first official meeting after the Act was proclaimed, the Aboriginal response was unambiguous. In a resounding rebuttal of state policy and propaganda, the Aboriginal Advisory Council voted overwhelmingly to reject the DOGIT format, nor would they consider any projected services legislation until amendments were introduced to protect security of tenure. The AAC was the government-sanctioned "liaison" body: it could not be dismissed as a bunch of unrepresentative radicals. But it was never convened again.

Fierce lobbying by Aboriginal and church groups forced federal minister Peter Baume to issue a "guarantee" of federal intervention if Queensland double-crossed the communities, a commitment in stark contrast to the Fraser government's initial acclaim. And by mid-1983 the Queensland Cabinet had agreed to transfer to parliament the power to revoke trust deeds. What would prompt this concession on the major point of contention? Although some commentators argue the Bjelke-Petersen government was finally "moving ground" on land rights, a cynic might suggest it had more to do with the imminent state election.

There is no doubt that the government had seriously misjudged Aboriginal response to the DOGIT legislation. Repudiation of the new "land title" by the AAC was a critical comment on Killoran's standing in the communities. Perhaps the government really believed that the concession on security of tenure would be sufficient to quell dissent and buy support. In a surprising confirmation of just how far out of touch he was with passions in the northern communities, Killoran stood for the North Queensland seat of Cook in the state election of October 1983. On temporary stand-down from his high-profile public service post, and rumoured to have utilised departmental facilities to mount his campaign, he ran on the National Party ticket. In what had only six years' previously been a safe seat under Aboriginal member Eric Deeral, Killoran was unceremoniously dumped, winning only 17 per cent of the vote.

It was this election which brought Bob Katter into the Aboriginal Affairs portfolio as member for the vast northwest Queensland seat of Flinders. He immediately began work on amendments to the *Land Act* to formalise Cabinet's promise to place DOGIT tenure in parliamentary hands.

Perhaps it was this determination which sparked his early clash with Killoran. Perhaps Killoran was still licking his wounds. Within two weeks of Katter's accession to the portfolio, according to Katter himself, Killoran approached Bjelke-Petersen to have him sacked.

For the first time, Killoran did not have a malleable minister. After the rapid succession of largely token ministers whose ready endorsement of Killoran's drafted letters, reports and Cabinet submissions is evident from the files, Katter must have presented an unwelcome aberration in Killoran's relatively seamless association with Bjelke-Petersen. For the first time also, the phrase "Aboriginal land rights" was heard at ministerial level. In February 1984 Katter's amendments passed through state parliament. The next step was to finalise the procedural framework under which the communities, when eventually they were declared DOGITs, could manage their own affairs.

Loathe to forgo a good media opportunity, Katter took a National Party committee on a brief tour of the communities to "consult" with councils. To Killoran's dismay, he proved adept at losing his departmental "minders" to talk directly to a range of people long ostracised as "radicals". The National Aboriginal Council chairman, Steve Mam, and the North Queensland Land Council chairman, Mick Miller, were just two of the Aboriginal and Islander leaders whose views Katter sought. Killoran would have been mortified to learn that his own "future and role" formed one of the topics for discussion with Aboriginal leaders.

Although Katter's acknowledgement of Aboriginal spokesmen was a conspicuous procedural deviation, his apparent contempt for democratic process ran true to form. He refused outright to discuss any details of the impending legislation with any of the communities who were to be subjected to the new "self-management" system, despite a press release claiming it was "in line with the needs and wishes of the people". Killoran also found himself on the outer, losing a bitter clash over the wisdom of extending such a degree of autonomy. Katter won the day, boasting that he had convinced Bjelke-Petersen "that it was better to make the Aborigines earn their own keep". In high dudgeon, according to media reports, Killoran tendered his resignation. The premier persuaded him to remain.

Community services

When the Community Services (Aborigines) Bill was introduced to parliament along with its counterpart for Torres Strait communities, 17 Torres Strait council chairmen and 25 of the 27 Aboriginal council chairmen had already informed Bjelke-Petersen they did not want Killoran appointed as undersecretary of the new Community Services department which would control Aboriginal Affairs. They were ignored. And despite Katter's boast that "the consultation process has worked admirably" and that community leaders had "expressed enthusiasm for the provisions", he was soon forced to concede that no community had been shown drafts of the legislation. They were not alone. Opposition members were given less than one hour to examine the provisions of the new laws which were rammed through parliament in a marathon 21-hour sitting. Aboriginal comunity chairmen told Katter they had been deceived.

Under the new law, all Aboriginal and Islander councils would gain qualified local government powers. Now, boasted Killoran, local government decisions would be made "by the people themselves", rather than by the Department of Community Services (DCS). There would, however, be a three-year transitional period while the new council staffs received the necessary training.

Under the community services legislation, councils could make executive decisions, hold elections, levy rates, borrow or invest funds and hire consultants. They were also made responsible for public works and collection of rents. But there were major differences in the running of "local government" for these Aboriginal and Islander communities, and procedures in place for ordinary authorities under the *Local Government Act*, including the shires of Aurukun and Mornington Island. The newest councils had to obtain ministerial approval for their budgets; all accounts had to be vetted and audited by the DCS; Killoran could initiate inspections of the communities, receive reports from visiting justices, administer deceased estates and control beer supplies for council-operated canteens.

With the passing of the services legislation, the department handed to the communities the ticking time bomb of award wages. Immediately councils declared that they would no longer be part of the charade of "community wage" rates. Killoran was furious, drafting letters for Katter in which he berated councils for their "reluctance to recognise the realities of Local Authority administration and decision making" by jettisoning what he described as the existing "guaranteed incomes policy, not necessarily equated to real term job positions". He threatened to cut Yarrabah's funding and their operational independence unless they toed the line on wages. Katter did not sign the letters.

Protesting that the state government would not make sufficient funds available to cover legal wage rates for their employees, the Woorabinda council approached the Human Rights Commission for assistance. Called to account for his department, Katter committed himself to full wages "one way or another". He wrote that it was his decision that all Aboriginal and Islander workers would move to award wages. Perhaps, he added, if Cabinet will not make provision as requested in the 1984–85 budget, council chairmen could solicit a 10 per cent subsidy from the DAA.[34]

The department's pretence that workers were somehow not doing "real" jobs was vehemently rejected by Cherbourg council, who informed Katter: "Council does not accept the argument that your Department has in the past funded positions on reserves that were not 'full-time', and thus, that payment of Award Wages for these positions as opposed to 'Community award' wages was and is not justified". It also warned that any further sackings "would result in serious reduction of services to the public".[35]

Again Killoran came under attack. Yarrabah council had approached the DAA declaring that state subsidies did not allow for legal wage rates. Called to question, Killoran alleged that "no Council has been forced into an untenable position by the Department" and mocked council concerns as "a fixation requiring an amount equivalent to an award rate for each person". "Notwithstanding inadequate funds to pay award rates", Killoran said that councils should "examine their options", and include a "strong social welfare component" so that "as many jobs as possible are available".[36]

By 1985 Katter was distancing himself from Killoran's position on the "social welfare" aspect of "community wages". This position was, after all, the same one Killoran had held since the introduction of cash economies on reserves nearly twenty years previously. Although Killoran continued his authoritarian domination of the Aboriginal communities, Katter was having serious doubts over the wisdom of calling the bluff of the many unions now lining up to take his department to court for breach of state industrial law.

It was only in April 1985, a month after the Queensland Nurses Union (QNU) approached the Human Rights commission on the matter, that Cabinet finally acted on the underpayment of community nurses. Cabinet commissioned the release of funds to pay award wages to staff at seven hospitals run by local hospital boards under the province of the Health department. This did not satisfy the QNU representatives. On six Aboriginal and twenty Torres Strait Island communities where hospitals were under DCS control, nurses continued to be underpaid by, as the QNU pointed out in disgust, the very authorities responsible for their "advancement".

On this matter Killoran made his stand. Although the increase was costed at only $73,000 per annum, Killoran was emphatic: to concede award wages for these nurses was to invite a flow-on to other health workers and indeed all employees, he informed Katter. Again official documents reveal that government personnel were deliberately flouting legal requirements. Acknowledging that "payment of below award rates is arguable as in breach of state industrial law and perhaps infringes certain laws of the Commonwealth", Killoran suggested making only a small increase "to forestall union action". And Katter's response? An internal DCS memo relates that when he read this advice at a meeting with QNU delegates, he screwed it up in disgust and dispatched it dramatically to the wastepaper basket. He informed them that he would ask Cabinet that award wages be paid to all health care workers.[37]

Killoran, it seemed, had fatally misjudged both his minister and the political climate. He apparently overrode Katter's directive that several grazing properties attached to Woorabinda, and the community's main income source, were to be handed over to council control as part of the DOGIT area. "I am terribly, terribly angry that my instructions have not been carried out", Katter reportedly told the Woorabinda people, as DCS officers mustered cattle without council consent. Cherbourg council also was said to be excluded from revenue-producing enterprises such as the store, the sawmill and the joinery.[38] Again Katter went public, condemning DCS personnel "who feel their jobs are threatened and are trying to stop self-management and to make fools of black people. I wish I could get clear enough evidence to act". He said that these people "seem to be devoting their entire waking hours to destroying the concept of self-management". The writing was on the wall for Killoran.

By 1986 the government was exposed to court challenges by the Transport Workers' Union (TWU), FEDFA and the QNU, each challenge involving the expensive probability of retrospective wage remuneration. Killoran was still advising Katter to hold course pending a federal/state solution, while at the same time conceding that the federal government denied any responsibility for meeting award rates of pay. Katter had in fact extracted a commitment from the federal Aboriginal Affairs minister, Clyde Holding, that funding might be directed to cover some positions when DOGITs were conferred, although Holding was at pains to stress that there would be no subsidies for "Mickey Mouse jobs".[39]

Killoran started the 1986 year with an attempt to marshall support from fellow bureaucrats. In a letter to the Public Service Board regarding ongoing challenges by several unions he argued that payment of award wages "may cause the reduction of the Community workforce below a viable level to support services", and urged "whatever action is necessary in the circumstances be taken to protect the department's interests". In a conspiratorial jibe, he drew attention to Katter's published statements regarding payment of nurses wages, and added mischievously: "Enquiry to the Cabinet Secretariat indicates no Cabinet Submission or Decision on the issue of wages for Aboriginal nursing aides".[40]

In a briefing statement for Katter's March Cabinet meeting, Killoran once again tried to bring Katter to heel: the move to award rates was tied to "the funds available and the workforce employed to absorb them". The average community wage was now around $240, compared with $355 for males and $300 for females in the general community. This had been achieved by stripping workforces from 2,500 in 1976 to 901 a decade later. In fact, continued Killoran, slipping easily into 1960s assimilationist mode, the current policy of underpayment was proving an incentive for workers to leave the communities. They were moving into "conventional urban situations" and becoming "integrated in the total community life of Queensland"; nearly two-thirds of the Aboriginal population currently "enjoys this standard of living", he enthused.

In contrast to this convenient transition, Killoran argued that insistence on immediate award wages would cost the government a further $21 million, which he had in fact requested for the 1985–86 year, yet treasury had allocated only $9 million, just enough to cover inflation on current rates. Without greater funding, said Killoran, award wages could only be met by slashing workforces a further 25 per cent–30 per cent. But administrative officers had reported there would be problems maintaining services if more workers were lost: sackings would mean worsening community hygiene, health and sanitation.[41] The inference was unmistakable: hold to the policy of gradualism.

But Katter had resolved to act. Discarding Killoran's ministerial brief, he told his colleagues that bulk employment on substandard wages was a "relic of past policy". Private enquiries, he said, had disproved the advice from his undersecretary [Killoran]: awards could be introduced without jeopardising community health and at a cost far less than $10 million; and the old furphy that the Murgha case was a win for the government was also wrong — it was settled out of court to avoid the inevitable unfavourable finding in the state industrial court. Contradicting his department's public doctrine, Katter now also confirmed that Queensland stood in breach of 1975 racial discrimination legislation.

The policy of calling the union's bluff was fraught with danger, continued Katter. Advice from the Solicitor General and from the ministers of Justice and Industrial Affairs confirmed that any of the present union challenges against the DCS was likely to succeed. Katter now insisted that award wages be introduced immediately. The cost, he said, would only be $3.8 million. The government took his message to heart. Far better to concede award rates than lose highly punitive court actions.[42]

The clash between minister and bureaucrat was settled decisively in Katter's favour. After nearly 25 years Killoran lost control of Aboriginal Affairs; the deputy chairman of the Public Service Board was appointed to replace him. A substitute role was organised for Killoran as "special adviser" to Bjelke-Petersen, but his authority was fatally compromised. Within three months he walked out of the department for the last time — with more than half a million dollars in superannuation.

Did Cabinet capitulation signal a major policy change? Hardly. Despite Katter's estimate that a further 32 per cent, or 245 persons, would have to be sacked to meet awards within current funding, Cabinet held to its decision of June 1979: not one cent would be made available. If Aborigines wanted award wages then Aborigines would pay. Faced with a barrage of objections from councils, Katter attempted to salvage some credibility by announcing in parliament that the federal government had promised to meet the costs. Clyde Holding promptly denied this "distortion of facts" — the DAA would only support community resource development.

Katter was now well and truly in damage-control mode, his credibility hinging on his ability to sell to the public mass retrenchments on these already traumatised communities. Conveniently ignoring internal reports of critically compromised service delivery, he now alleged that most communities had "highly inflated" employment programs. Parrotting Holding's remark, Katter stated that the DCS would not be funding "mickey mouse" jobs; and no, he would not be taking action against a "senior public servant" for providing misleading information.

The government now held writs against it from the

ACTU, FEDFA and the AWU, and knew it risked parting with several million dollars in back pay alone. After Yarrabah shed further jobs, award rates were scheduled from 1 June, with all other communities to be phased in over a six-month period. A survey team was dispatched to "assess" staff functions in order to "assist compliance" with government policy. In a confidential memo DCS officers were informed that there would be no funding increases: award rates depended on job shedding. Perhaps, suggested head office, some hospital staff could be graded as domestics, and Aboriginal police forces could be restructured. In December 1986 the Industrial Court found in favour of FEDFA and the DCS settled out of court rather than risk setting a precedent. Four months later another settlement was made, this time to the AWU.

These, then, were the conditions which Aboriginal councils inherited from the government as the deeds of grant in trust were ceremoniously bestowed on each community throughout 1987. Now, it was said, councils had "total responsibility for local government and the delivery of local government services", including housing and rentals. But hospital, police and administrative buildings remained the province of the various departments, as did nearly all revenue-producing enterprises. At Cherbourg, for instance, the store, pottery, artefacts, sawmill, dairy and piggery continued to pour profits into the DCS-controlled Welfare Fund, to the greater detriment of the community. Aboriginal communities were left dependent on rentals, alcohol profits, federal pensions and state handouts.

Old habits die hard. When the federal government passed the *Local Government (Financial Assistance) Act* in 1986 to better equip councils for executive and administrative functions, the DCS tried to block the funds, claiming such grants breached pre-existing Queensland legislation requiring all local government subsidies to be directed to the department. Not so, said the federal Local Government minister, Tom Uren. The state can not act as distributor for the funds unless it stipulated the exact targets for the allocations.[43]

Federal agencies were deeply suspicious of the state's propensity to distort community funding, and communities themselves immediately signalled an intent to deal direct. Although Katter boasted in mid-1988 that "Queensland leads Australia in the movement towards Aboriginal self management and self reliance", DCS officers positioned on every community were instructed to "continue to work closely with Councils and Council administrations".

In one of his last submissions for Cabinet preceding the deposing of Bjelke-Petersen as premier in November 1988, Katter showed how little attitudes had changed over the coalition's thirty-year term in power. The state's "positive" program was "increasingly hindered", wrote Katter, by arbitrary federal grants and the five hundred Commonwealth personnel "scattered throughout Queensland" plus the additional two hundred Aboriginal and Islander staff on the federal payroll. It was "through the agency of CDEP funding" that officers were gaining access to communities and at the same time "endeavouring to influence heavily Councils in their decisions on Council matters", according to Katter. The government should deny funds and refrain from handing control to councils "where these relationships with the Commonwealth exist", he declared.

It seems that the idea that councils should act autonomously in accessing information and expertise remained as much anathema to the guardian state as it had twenty years earlier. "It is important that State Government funding to Councils is not spent on the advice from any Commonwealth funded officer", because, as Katter assured his colleagues, such advice "would subvert the whole of the self management plan of the Queensland Government".[44]

* * *

Attention to Aboriginal affairs in Queensland during the 1970s and 1980s is generally focused on the struggle for land rights and self-determination. On the one hand, self-management legislation and the bestowal of DOGITs are seen to represent a "softening" of the government's entrenched belligerent stance. On the other hand, there is dismay and speculation as to why these "gains" have delivered far less in reality than was promised in rhetoric.

Analysis of internal documents suggests this is no surprise. Rather than any belated — and reluctant — program to liberalise controls and to recognise Aboriginal "rights", it would appear that policy changes are better understood as strategies to resolve specific crises — such as the regazetting of Aurukun and Mornington Island, the right of Aboriginal groups to incorporate, and the move to award wages. Over the last twenty years, in fact, there has been an intensification of surveillance and interventions in Aboriginal communities.

The real driving force for change in Aboriginal affairs has operated out of the public eye in the financial domain. Here federal pressures, coercions and legislative flanking strategies have impacted on state policy and practices, particularly in relation to accessibility to outside funding and expertise and to wage rates. Concerted union chal-

lenges set legal benchmarks which ultimately could not be
ignored. It was the misreading of the wages impasse which
brought the downfall of Patrick Killoran, only the third
department head in seventy-two years, and arguably himself
a "relic of past policy".

Records reveal the willingness of state bureaucrats and
politicians to manipulate the changing options of community management so as to sabotage "opponents" and entrench existing controls. They reveal the horrendous price
exacted on the communities as public officers charged as
guardians of Aboriginal interests deliberately decimated
workforces and infrastructure as wage rates lifted despite
them. Queensland's Aboriginal communities are today
struggling to overcome the legacy of nearly one hundred
years of such disgraceful management.

Conclusion

It is January 1997, the birth of the centenary of Aboriginal legislation, introduced in Queensland to "protect" those of Aboriginal heritage through land areas reserved "for their benefit" and officers delegated to act "in their interests". All too briefly this book has touched on some of the wide range of intertwined, overlapping and often conflicting programs and "expert knowledges" which have impacted on the lives of Aboriginal Queenslanders.

Many of these programs and much of the "expert" knowledge has not originated in race relations but has been translated from fields such as epidemiology, cultural anthropology, public health, census and statistics, and federal/state financing and welfare programs. Governments over time adopt, circulate, institutionalise and discard a range of these knowledges as they wrestle with circumstances and events which have become unacceptable. Too frequently such unacceptability relates to political sensitivity to unwelcome exposure rather than to the "best interests" of Aboriginal communities.

In attempts to defend the indefensible, bureaucrats and politicians readily invoke, and thus revalidate, the concept of an "Aboriginal problem". It has been all too easy to accumulate a raft of separate issues — territorial and cultural dispossession, erratic and unsafe food and water, under-supply and under-maintenance of housing, poverty arising from unpaid and underpaid labour, decades of defective teaching and medical attention — and file them under this convenient label. But these are problems of government. Chronic — bordering on criminal — under-funding has underwritten the defective, deadly and dispiriting conditions endured for most of this century by these reluctant wards of state.

The Aboriginal department in Queensland has operated since its inception as a closed, secretive and highly defensive agency of government. Remarkably, only three men held the position of chief administrator between 1914 and 1986, exercising almost total control over the lives of many thousands of Aboriginal Queenslanders, regulating freedom of movement, place of residence, employment, private savings and spending, marriage, adoptions and family cohesion.

Until the 1950s Aboriginal administration was largely run as a personal fiefdom. With the influx of federal funding and the accession of Killoran in the 1960s, however, Aboriginal affairs in Queensland was increasingly politicised as policies were articulated in the media and in parliament. By the late 1970s and 1980s Aboriginal affairs became a matter of state, rather than departmental, resolution. Killoran's close ideological affinity with premier Joh Bjelke-Petersen cemented a unified anti-federal stance as they rebuffed what they perceived were strategies to usurp state sovereignty and dictate state policies, particularly in issues such as land rights, self-management, and award wages.

Foucault's concept of *governmentality* has provided rich and unexpected rewards in the investigation and analysis of the complex field of Aboriginal affairs in Queensland. Adjusted legislation and new or refocused programs exemplify the striving for greater economy and competence in regulating this population group. During the first half of this century "eternal optimism" can be detected as much in the rhetoric of institutionalisation, training and assimilation (as an assumption of "progress"), as in the more sombre perceptions of husbanding a "dying race". Notwithstanding such rhetoric, however, the optimism of governmentality is generated by government expediency, which has no necessary coincidence with the best interests of the governed. This dichotomy is most apparent in the greatly politicised decades of the 1970s and 1980s where evidence reveals that the assertive focus of governmentality worked actively against the well-being of Aboriginal communities.

Whether in terms of administrative responsibilities of care or even in terms of achieving political agendas, the "congenital failure" of governments ever to secure fully their reformative intentions is disturbingly obvious. Diverse objectives, incompatible funding priorities and conflicting power strategies underwrite endemic ineffectuality and default. The extensive failures of government ambitions and of administrative practices have been masked by tight controls over the information repertoire, controls which operate to assist aggressive appropriation of the terms of debate. Poverty, derelict housing, low education and employment levels, alcoholism and domestic violence, individual despair and community upheaval are still — conveniently — interpreted as aspects of an Aboriginal, rather than a governmental, problem.

As I write, much of the land reserved for Aboriginal use

on Cape York has been ceded to multinationals for mineral extraction, dispossessing hundreds of Aboriginal people and bringing immense profits to the State. And the Coalition government of Rob Borbidge is at the forefront of a frenzied campaign to declare void a High Court decision that the rights of the Wik people of Cape York may never have been extinguished on pastoral leases which they have always frequented.

Seven elderly Palm Island workers are, once again, steeling themselves to bring the Queensland government to accountability over the non-payment of legal wages. These men and women have already proved "deliberate, knowing, and intentional" discrimination by the government before retired Supreme Court judge Bill Carter in an April 1996 hearing before the Human Rights and Equal Opportunities Commission. This finding followed desperate — but failed — attempts by government lawyers to prevent tabling of the evidence described in Chapter ten.

The Borbidge government has stated that it will ignore this adverse decision. And so the case is recommencing in the Federal Court. Once again the government will try to exclude evidence of official policies and practices; evidence which explodes official myths of workers in training, of maximising employment numbers, of welfare institutions, and of a legal right under s.68 to exempt Aboriginal community employees from state industrial law; evidence which exposes the critical gap between the rhetoric of government competence and the reality of government failure.

This knowledge of government operations cannot remain the property of governments, to be deployed only to government advantage. This knowledge is the rightful property of the Aboriginal people, whose lives are intricately and painfully etched on the documents of Aboriginal affairs. This knowledge is rightfully the property of all of us. Without it we cannot keep our governments honest in their dealings. Without it we cannot hope to understand fully the history of this state; nor can we hope to understand ourselves as Queenslanders and Australians, particularly, for most of us, as non-Aboriginal Australians.

Ignorant of our historical heritage, we remain vulnerable to manipulation by those who have the most to gain from a truncated and distorted debate. A wealth of previously untold experiences remains in archives controlled by governments. If we are to give real substance to the rhetoric of reconciliation on the eve of a new millenium, then we must retrieve, explore, understand and accommodate the whole spectrum of experiences of *all* Australians.

Notes

Preface

1. Most of the material that I researched at the Aboriginal department has now been transferred to Queensland State Archives. Wherever possible, references in this book carry the upgraded archival location number. The file content remains the same.

Introduction

1. Michel Foucault, "Governmentality", in Burchell, G., Gordon, C. and Miller, P. (eds), *The Foucault Effect: Studies in Governmentality*, University of Chicago Press, Chicago, 1991; and Miller, P. and Rose, N., "Governing Economic Life", *Economy and Society*, Vol. 19, No. 1, 1990.

1. Problems of law

1. Governor Brisbane, 1825. Quoted in R. Cilento and C. Lack, *Triumph in the Tropics*, Smith and Paterson Pty Ltd, Brisbane, 1959: 182.

2. A Castles *An Australian Legal History*, The Law Book Company, Sydney, 1982: 524.

3. For example, see M. Hartwig, "Aborigines and Racism; an Historical Perspective", in F. Stevens (ed.), *Racism: The Australian Experience*, vol. 2, ANZ Book Company, Sydney, 1973: 13.

4. Quoted in J. Little, "Legal Status of Aboriginal People: Slaves or Citizens" in F. Stevens (ed.) *Racism: The Australian Experience*, vol. 2, ANZ Book Company, 1973: 83.

5. See B. Bridges, "The Extension of English Law to the Aborigines for Offences Committed Inter Se, 1829–1842", in *Journal of the Royal Australian Historical Society*, vol. 59, Pt 4, 1973: 264–69; and J. Hookey, "Settlement and Sovereignty" in P. Hanks and B. Keon-Cohen, *Aborigines and the Law*, George Allen and Unwin, Sydney, 1984.

6. Quoted in L. Skinner, "Law and Justice for the Queensland Colony",

Royal Historical Society of Queensland Journal, vol. IX, no. 3, 1971–72: 100.

7. W. Coote, *A History of the Colony of Queensland,* vol. 1, Wm Thorne, Brisbane, 1882: 41.

8. C. Petrie, *Tom Petrie's Reminiscences of Early Queensland,* Angus & Robertson, Sydney, 1932: 216.

9. *The Simpson Letterbook,* undated transcription by G. Langevad, Cultural and Historical Records of Queensland, no. 1: 13.

10. *Triumph in the Tropics,* 1959: 185.

11. *A History of the Colony of Queensland,* 1882: 46.

12. J. Knight, *In the Early Days,* Sapsford & Co, Brisbane, 1898: 196.

13. Quoted in J. Bennett and A. Castles, *A Source Book of Australian Legal History,* The Law Book Company Ltd, Sydney, 1979: 189.

14. A. R. Radcliffe-Brown ("Former Numbers and Distribution of the Australian Aborigines" in *Official Year Book of Australia,* 1930: 687–96) suggests the figure of 100,000. But in a more recent work (*Our Original Aggression,* George Allen & Unwin, Sydney, 1983: 17), N. Butlin puts the pre-settlement population for Australia at over one million people. He alleges a "conspiracy of silence" masks massive deaths due to smallpox, the sterilisation effects of venereal disease, and starvation.

15. D. Cryle, *The Press in Colonial Queensland,* University of Queensland Press, St Lucia, 1989: 12.

16. R. W. Cilento, *Black War in Queensland,* undated typescript [University of Queensland, Fryer Library, mss 44/46].

17. Queensland State Archives (QSA) COL/A12, 15.1.1861, Commandant Morisset to colonial secretary.

18. R. Evans, "Don't you remember Black Alice, Sam Holt?", in *Hecate,* vol. VIII, no. 2, 1982: 98.

19. Quoted in D. Cryle, *The Press in Colonial Queensland,* 1989: 17.

20. W. Hill, *Forty-five Years Experiences in North Queensland* (1861 to 1905), H. Pole and Company, Brisbane, 1907: 31.

21. G. W. Rusden, *History of Australia,* vol. 3, Chapman and Hall, London, 1883: 231.

22. W. Ross Johnston, *The Long Blue Line,* Boolarong Publications, Brisbane, 1992: 91.

23. *The Press in Colonial Queensland,* 1989: 68.

24. QSA COL/A22, 22.22.1861, Clark & Co to colonial secretary.

25. *History of Australia,* 1883: 232.

26. B. Knox, *The Queensland Years of Robert Herbert, Premier,* University of Queensland Press, St Lucia, 1977: 236.

27. H. Golder, *High and Responsible Office: A History of the NSW Magistracy*, Sydney University Press, Sydney, 1991: 60.

28. *A History of the Colony of Queensland*, 1882: 233.

29. QSA COL/A18, 10.7.1861, Frederick Walker to Attorney General. Walker proposed that settlers who took retributive measures should be denied the "protection" of Native Police presence.

30. H. Reynolds, "Aboriginal–European Contact History: Problems and Issues", *Journal of Australian Studies*, no. 3, June 1978: 57.

31. QSA COL/A84, 10.1.1866, Rev Larkin to Sir George Bowen, and response.

32. QSA COL/A316 (81/2895), Rev D. McNab, "Notes on the condition of the Aborigines of Queensland".

33. *History of Australia*, 1883: 232.

34. J. Knight, *In the Early Days*, Sapsford & Co, Brisbane, 1898:370.

35. E. Kennedy, *The Black Police of Queensland*, Murray, London, 1902: 35.

36. QSA COL A/157, 29.5.1871, Police magistrate, Gilberton, to police commissioner.

37. R. Spencer Browne, *A Journalist's Memories (1877–1927)*, Read Press, Brisbane, 1927: 36.

2. Learning to labour

1. L. Radzinowicz, *Ideology and Crime*, Heinemann Educational Books, London, 1966: 31.

2. Introduction by Rev Tuckniss in H. Mayhew, *London Labour and the London Poor*, published 1861–62, reprinted by Frank Cass and Co Ltd, London, 1967.

3. Gillian Wagner describes several of these institutions in *Barnardo*, Weidenfeld and Nicholson, London.

4. *The Reformatory Schools Act, An Act for the better Care and Reformation of Youthful Offenders in Great Britain.*

5. By 1860 there were 4,000 children in 48 reformatories in Britain. By 1881 there were 17,000 in the institutions and by 1885 there were 20,000.

6. L. Radzinowicz and R. Hood, *A History of English Criminal Law and Its Administration from 1750*, Stevens and Sons, London, 1986: 180.

7. W. Ross Johnston, *Brisbane: The First Thirty Years*, Boolarong Publications, Brisbane, 1988: 111.

8. See J. Ramsland, *Children of the Back Lanes*, New South Wales Press, New South Wales, for colonial policies of removal and reform.

9. Police Department, *Annual Report*, 1879.

10. L. Goldman, "Child Welfare in 19th Century Queensland: 1865–1911", unpublished MA thesis, Queensland University, 1972: 41, 122.

11. QSA COL/A18, 13.8.1861, Chas Carvosso to colonial secretary.

12. QSA COL/A22, 22.11.1861, T. L. Zillman to colonial secretary.

13. QSA COL/A84, 10.1.1866, Rev Larkin to governor Sir George Bowen.

14. See *Ideology and Crime*, 1966: 157 for these debates.

15. Captain E. P. Brenton, quoted in *A History of English Criminal Law*, 1986: 137. Children as young as eight were sent abroad in indentured apprenticeships after only a few months' training.

16. *London Labour and the London Poor*, vol. IV, Introduction.

17. Quoted in G. Pearson, *The Deviant Imagination*, The Macmillan Press Ltd, London, 1975: 153.

18. Quoted in M. Bennett, *Christison of Lammermoor*, Alston Rivers Ltd, London, 1928: 95. Christison used Aboriginal workers almost exclusively and encouraged local tribes to remain on the property. D. May (*From Bush to Station*, History Department, James Cook University, Townsville, 1983) provides a wider analysis of Aboriginal pastoral labour in Queensland during this period.

19. *History of Australia*, 1883: 242.

20. Anglican Archives, *Bishop Hale's Correspondence*, 4.5.1876, Bridgman to Queensland treasurer W. Drew.

21. Report in *Port Denison Times*, 28.7.1877.

22. *Queensland Votes and Proceedings*, 1874: 439–42.

23. McNab, "Notes on the condition of the Aborigines of Queensland". The Home government referred to the British government, to whom colonial governments were accountable until 1901.

24. Police Department, *Annual Report*, 1877.

25. Police Department, *Annual Report*, 1875. Seymour refers to this commission as a Royal Commission, but this is surely an error since it is unlikely that the government would submit to two inquiries simultaneously.

26. McNab, "Notes on the Condition ..."

27. Quoted in Bennett, 1928: 88.

28. Anglican Archives, *Bishop Hale's Correspondence*, 25.5.1876, colonial secretary to Bishop Hale.

29. Anglican Archives, *Bishop Hale's Correspondence*, 31.5.1876, Drew to Bishop Hale.

30. J. W. Bleakley, *The Aborigines of Australia*, Jacaranda Press, Brisbane, 1961: 98–99. My thesis deals more fully with these reserves.

31. McNab, "Notes on the Condition ..."

32. *Port Denison Times*, 28.7.1877.

33. C. Petrie, *Tom Petrie's Reminiscences of Early Queensland*, Angus and Robertson Ltd, Sydney, 1932: 215.

34. Despite acknowledging that identification of suspects was impossible, journalist R. Spencer Browne wrote approvingly of the slaughter of "31 bucks bathing on a small beach ... all but three were accounted for". "Where murders of whites are committed", he continued, "there can be no arrests and no trial by jury" (*A Journalist's Memories, 1877–1927*, Read Press, Brisbane, 1927: 27–28). Described by Spencer Browne as "a spendid bushman, and well experienced with the Native Police", O'Connor was a relative of governor Sir Arthur Kennedy.

35. Police Department, *Annual Report*, 1878.

36. McNab, "Notes on the Condition ..."

37. *The Queenslander*, 19.5.1880.

38. *The Queenslander*, 15.5.1880.

39. Quoted in *Christison of Lammermoor*, 1928: 90.

40. McNab, "Notes on the Condition ..."

41. Quote in R. Fitzgerald, *From the Dreaming to 1915: A History of Queensland*, University of Queensland Press, St Lucia, 1986: 215.

42. Quoted in R. Evans, K. Saunders and K. Cronin, *Race Relations in Colonial Queensland*, 1988: 386–88.

43. *History of Australia*, 1883: 244.

44. Quoted in ibid, 1883: 244.

45. *Government Gazette*, 1881: 146.

46. B. Molesworth, "Kanaka Labour in Queensland (1863–1871), *Historical Society of Queensland Journal*, vol. 1, no. 3, 1917: 142.

47. C. Bernays, *Queensland Politics During Sixty Years (1859–1919)*, Government Printer, Brisbane, 1919: 66. By the 1880s nearly 11,500 Melanesians were employed in the cotton, cane and fishing industries.

48. H. Reynolds, *Invasion and Resistance*, 1982: 126.

49. N. Loos, *The Other Side of the Frontier*, 1982: 176.

50. *The Native Labourers' Protection Act*.

51. QSA COL/A409, 6.12.1884, H. E. Aldridge, Maryborough, to colonial secretary.

52. ibid., notation on letter.

53. Customs duties from the importation of opium for private use were a major revenue source for governments until 1905.

54. G. Bolton, *A Thousand Miles Away*, Australian National University Press, Canberra, 1972: 252.

55. R. Joyce, *Samuel Walker Griffith*, University of Queensland Press, St Lucia, 1984: 92.

3. Competing interests

1. J. and L. Haviland, "Lutherans and Aborigines Around Cooktown to 1900", *Aboriginal History*, 4:2, 1980: 140. Cooktown council passed a by-law in 1885 barring Aborigines from the town at night.

2. C. Anderson, "A Case Study in Failure", in T. Swain and D. Rose (eds), *Aboriginal Australians and Christian Missions*, The Australian Association for the Study of Religions, South Australia, 1988: 323.

3. Presbyterian Archives, 4.4.1903, *The Austral Star*, "Quarterly letter from Mapoon".

4. See J. Gribble, *Dark Deeds in a Sunny Land*, 1905, reprinted by University of Western Australia Press, Western Australia, 1987, for his own account of official persecution.

5. Rev. G. White, *Round About the Torres Straits*, Society for the Promotion of Christian Knowledge, London, 1925: 11. White was Bishop of Carpentaria from 1900 to 1915.

6. QSA A/70007, 3.10.1898, information contained in telegram from Lands Commission to commissioner of police.

7. QSA A/69417, 30.11.1894, committee secretary, Deebing Creek Aboriginal Mission to secretary for Public Instruction.

8. Published by the Government Printer in 1895.

9. Archibald Meston, *Report on the Aboriginals of Queensland*, Queensland Votes and Proceedings, vol. IV, 1896: 723–38.

10. W. E. Parry-Okeden, 19.2.1897, *Report of the Police Commissioner to Home Secretary*.

11. Queensland Votes and Proceedings 1897: 43–45, *Measures Recently Adopted for the Amelioration of the Aborigines*.

12. For these debates see *Queensland Parliamentary Debates* 1897: 1539–1633.

13. *Queensland Parliamentary Debates*, 1897: 1629, 1540.

14. *Queensland Parliamentary Debates*, 1901: 1139, 1142.

15. See for instance J. Allen, *Sex and Secrets*, Oxford University Press, Melbourne, 1990: 79.

16. QSA A/45209, 27.6.1900, Roth to home secretary.

17. *Annual Report of the Northern Protector of Aboriginals for 1900*: 1, 8.

18. *The Aboriginals Protection and Restriction of the Sale of Opium Act, 1901*.

19. QSA A/69490, 3.10.1901, petition to home secretary.

20. *Report of the Northern Protector of Aboriginals for 1899:* 2.
21. *Queensland Parliamentary Debates,* 1901: 210–13.
22. *Queensland Parliamentary Debates,* 1901: 217.
23. *Queensland Parliamentary Debates,* 1901: 1142.
24. See QSA COL/483a for Fraser Island documentation.
25. QSA HOM/J19, 24.2.06, Roth to home secretary.
26. QSA PRE/A163, 4.12.1903.
27. DAIA RK:107, 13.12.1901.
28. QSA A/58927, 18.4.1906, Roth to undersecretary.
29. *Annual Report,* 1905: 14.
30. *Croydon Mining News,* December 1906.
31. *Annual Report,* 1906.
32. *North Queensland Herald,* 29.10.06.
33. *The Austral Star,* 1.10.1897.
34. Presbyterian Archives, *Minutes of the General Assembly,* Heathen Mission Committee Report, 1898.
35. QSA A/44680, 1.1.04, Normanton protector to Roth.
36. *Annual Report,* 1905: 22, Rev Richter of Mapoon.
37. *Torres Straits Pearler,* 3.6.06.
38. QSA A/70007, 29.8.05, Gribble to Roth.
39. DAIA RK:165, 14.7.10, Mr Pointon to Howard, his emphases.
40. QSA A/58855, 15.2.09, Howard to undersecretary.
41. Presbyterian Archives, *Minutes of the General Assembly,* May 1914.
42. Anglican Archives, *Yarrabah Mission Correspondence,* 1909.
43. DAIA RK:87, 25.8.10, Howard to home secretary.
44. QSA A/58858, 5.4.11, Archbishop of Brisbane to home secretary.
45. See Anglican Archives, *Yarrabah Mission Correspondence* 1910/1911 for this sequence.
46. Anglican Archives, *Archbishop's Correspondence,* F15/A2, February 1915, note by Needham.
47. *Annual Report,* 1913: 16.
48. *Annual Report,* 1911: 11.
49. QSA A/4291, 19.1.14, Meston to undersecretary, and comment.
50. J. W. Bleakley, *The Aborigines of Australia,* Jacaranda Press, Brisbane, 1961: 124.
51. Presbyterian Archives, *Minutes of the General Assembly,* 1914: 50.
52. *The Aborigines of Australia,* 1961: 124.
53. See QSA A/69429 for this sequence.
54. *Annual Report,* 1914: 16.
55. Of these volunteers, 154 were enlisted, 18 were killed in action, 22 wounded and 5 gassed.

56. *The Aborigines of Australia*, 1961: 172.
57. *Annual Report*, 1919: 3.
58. *Queensland Parliamentary Papers*, 1919–20: 460.
59. *Annual Report*, 1916: 7.
60. QSA A/69434, 7.3.19, deputy chief protector to Mr Firth JP, of Townsville, who had written on behalf of a local man requesting a wife.
61. *Annual Report*, 1916: 8.
62. QSA TR1227:128, 22.9.19, Bleakley to home secretary.

4. The health dimension

1. R. Evans, "Aborigines", in D. Murphy, R. Joyce and C. Hughes (eds), *Labor in Power*, University of Queensland Press, St Lucia, 1980: 330.
2. F. S. Stevens (ed.), *Racism: The Australian Experience*, ANZ Book Co Pty Ltd, NSW, 1973: 128.
3. QSA A/69778, November 1918, Barambah Inquiry.
4. DAIA RK:165, 19.3.20, Bleakley to home secretary.
5. " 'Talking with Aunty Ettie' ", J. Bell, *Social Alternatives*, vol. 7, no. 1, 1988.
6. *Annual Report*, 1919: 5.
7. Anglican Archives, *Diocesan Year Book*, 1920: 184.
8. QSA A/69455, January 1919, *General Remarks in connection with The Inquiry into the Conduct of Officials of the Palm Island Aboriginal Settlement*.
9. QSA A/58792, 30.11.19, protector to Bleakley.
10. Anglican Archives, *Archbishop's Correspondence, F40/A7, Yarrabah Mission Report, 1921–22*.
11. *Annual Reports*, 1921 and 1922.
12. QSA A/69452, 15.3.23, *Report on the Office of The Chief Protector of Aboriginals*.
13. QSA A/69449, 23.10.24, memorandum for undersecretary William Gall.
14. ibid., 7.3.24, Bleakley to Lyon.
15. QSA A/58860, 1.10.23, Governor to home secretary.
16. QSA A/58858, 9.6.13, board of mission secretary to home secretary.
17. Anglican Archives, *Diocesan Year Book*, 1922. Board of missions report on Yarrabah.
18. R. Patrick, *A History of Health and Medicine in Queensland 1824–1960*, University of Queensland Press, St Lucia, 1987:251.
19. QSA A/69449, Yarrabah annual report for 1920.
20. QSA TR1227:92, 9.11.23, Bleakley to public health commissioner.

21. Presbyterian Archives, *Minutes of the General Assembly*, Heathen Mission Committee reports, 1921, 1922.
22. QSA A/58696, 19.1.25, Love to Bleakley.
23. Presbyterian Archives, *Correspondence Heathen Missions*, 14.12.25, Love to convener Heathen Missions.
24. Anglican Archives, *A.B.M. Review*, 12.5.1927.
25. QSA A/69483, 12.5.27, Colledge to Bleakley.
26. ibid., 20.2.28, Colledge to Bleakley.
27. Anglican Archives, *Archbishop's Correspondence*, F74/A13/J4, 15.1.30, Archbishop of Brisbane to Bishop of North Queensland.
28. Anglican Archives, *Archbishop's Correspondence*, F81/A15/J4, 1.1.31, Rev. Kernke to Archbishop Sharpe.
29. DAIA RK:168, 23.9.20, Report GMO to Bleakley; and 3.3.22, Public Health Department to Bleakley.
30. *Annual Report*, 1926: 5.
31. For a detailed treatise on Cilento's life and work, see F. Fisher, "Raphael West Cilento. Medical administrator, Legislator, and Visionary", M.A. thesis, University of Queensland, 1984.
32. R. W. Cilento, *New Guinea Letterbook*, 30.9.31, letter to Dr Phyllis Cilento (University of Queensland, Fryer Library, mss 44/10).
33. QSA A/8724, 17.5.30, Mr Rodie to manager *Smiths Newspapers Ltd*.
34. *New Guinea Letterbook*, 30.9.31, Cilento to Dr Phyllis Cilento.
35. DAIA RK:91, 23.1.32, *Fantome Island: Annual Report for 1931*.
36. G. D. Bradbury, *Report on the Aboriginal Settlements at Palm Island, Cherbourg and Woorabinda and the Aboriginal Missions at Yarrabah and Monamona, 1932*, University of Queensland, Fryer Library, mss 44/144.
37. R. W. Cilento, *Letterbook October 1932*, 28.10.32, letter to Dr Phyllis Cilento.
38. *New Guinea Letterbook*, 31.10.32, letter to Dr Phyllis Cilento.
39. R. W. Cilento, *Cilento Diaries*, (mss 44/23), 29.7.33.
40. ibid.
41. QSA: (R254 19A/11), 15.11.33, Bleakley to undersecretary.
42. QSA A/58774, 20.6.22, Curry to Bleakley.
43. ibid., 10.7.22, Bleakley to Curry.
44. QSA A/69436, 5.1.28, Bleakley to Thursday Island protector.
45. DAIA RK:90, Palm Island *Annual Report*, 1933.
46. DAIA (uncatalogued), 8.8.35, deputy chief protector Cornelius O'Leary to Bleakley.
47. DAIA RK:87, 14.3.34, Fantome Island *Annual Report*.
48. DAIA RK:115, 11.5.35, Dr Julian, Fantome Island to Bleakley.

49. Anglican Archives, *Archbishop's Correspondence*, 8.10.34, Bishop of North Queensland to Archbishop of Brisbane.

50. DAIA RK:12, 10.4.33, Bleakley to undersecretary.

51. QSA A/58856, 23.8.34, Bleakley to undersecretary.

52. *The Aborigines of Australia*, 1961: 178.

53. R. Evans, "Aborigines", 1980: 339.

54. QSA A/8724, 11.11.35, Bleakley to public service commissioner.

55. QSA A/69458, 24.8.36, Bleakley to Mrs E. Jones.

56. QSA A.69455, 10.4.33, Bleakley to home secretary.

57. DAIA RK:17, 28.3.34, Pastor Thiele to home secretary.

58. QSA A/38092, 18.7.34, *Circulars to Herberton Protector.*

59. QSA A/58784, 2.3.37, Report by director-general of Health and Medical Services.

60. QSA TR254 3A/18, 5.5.36, *Palm Island Report* for April 1936.

61. DAIA RK:168, 13.3.33, Bleakley to superintendent, Palm Island.

62. QSA TR254 6J/9, 11.9.40, Bleakley to Dr Julian, Fantome Island.

63. ibid., 31.8.38, Cilento to Bleakley.

64. ibid., 12.8.38, Cilento to minister for Health and Home Affairs.

65. ibid., 10.10.38, Cilento to Minister for Health and Home Affairs.

5. The new "experts"

1. "A. R. Radcliffe-Brown, 1880–1955", obituary by A.P. Elkin, *Oceania*, vol. XXVI, no. 4, June 1956.

2. A. P. Elkin, *Citizenship for the Aborigines*, Macmillan, Sydney, 1944: 10–21.

3. Quoted in C. D. Rowley, *The Destruction of Aboriginal Society*, Penguin, Harmondsworth, 1972: 328.

4. DAIA RK:44, 26.4.34, Thursday Island protector to Bleakley.

5. QSA A/69458, 11.1.37, Bleakley to Agent-General, Queensland Government Offices, London.

6. QSA A/69461, 10.6.31, "From all Aurukun people to the Chief Protector of Aboriginals".

7. For MacKenzie's detailed explanations *see* Presbyterian Archives, *Mission Correspondence*, 1931, 3.11.31, MacKenzie to Rev. Kirke.

8. DAIA RK:88 *Report to the Aboriginal Mission Committee of the Visit of the Convenor to the Mission Stations situated in the Gulf of Carpentaria, August–October 1934.*

9. D. Thomson, *Donald Thomson in Arnhem Land*, Currey O'Neil Ross Pty Ltd, South Yarra, 1983: 5, 6.

10. QSA A/69470, 6.4.33, O'Leary to Bleakley.

11. *The Sun*, 8 & 13.1.47.

12. *The Sun*, 8.1.47.

13. *Telegraph*, Brisbane, 23.3.50.

14. *Report to the Aboriginal Mission Committee* ..., op. cit.: 9.

15. QSA A/69984, 11.9.37, Bleakley to secretary, Aborigines Protection Board, Sydney.

16. Presbyterian Archives, *Mission Committee Correspondence*, 1935, 10.5.35, MacKenzie to mission committee secretary.

17. ibid., 10.5.35.

18. QSA A/69455, 3.10.34, Elkin to Hanlon.

19. Presbyterian Archives, *Aboriginal Mission Correspondence*, 1935, 25.11.34, Rev. Hey to mission committee secretary.

20. QSA A/69455, 20.6.35, O'Leary to Hanlon.

21. QSA A/69458, 24.8.36, Bleakley to Mrs Edith Jones.

22. QSA A/58856, 21.8.36, Bleakley memorandum.

23. DAIA RK:44, 26.4.34, Thursday Island protector to Bleakley.

24. *Raphael West Cilento* ..., 1984: 231.

25. *The Aborigines of Australia*, 1960: 321.

26. QSA A/69984, 11.9.37, Bleakley to secretary, Aborigines Protection Board, Sydney.

27. ibid., 14.3.34, Professor Elkin to Bleakley.

28. QSA A/69584, 6.6.34, Governor Leslie Wilson to acting premier Percy Pease.

29. ibid., 27.8.34, Semple to Bleakley.

30. ibid., 30.11.34, Bleakley to undersecretary.

31. QSA A/69455, 24.1.35, Semple to Bleakley.

32. QSA A/69584, 27.8.34, Semple to Bleakley.

33. QSA A/69984, 25.1.35, Semple to Bleakley.

34. *Courier-Mail*, 23.1.35.

35. *A.B.M. Review.* 1.2.37.

36. QSA A/69455, 14.2.35, Morley to premier W. Forgan Smith.

37. ibid., 12.8.36, Needham to Bleakley.

38. *A.B.M. Review.* 1.2.37.

39. QSA POL 9H/1 Winton Police Station, 15.9.32, *Circulars from chief protector*.

40. QSA A/38092, *Circulars to Herberton protector*, 19.11.35.

41. *Queensland Parliamentary Debates*, 1927: 308.

42. *Queensland Parliamentary Debates*, 1927: 308.

43. QSA A/58854, 6.6.27, Townsville Inspector to police commissioner. Thumbprints were reintroduced in April 1921 "as a further safeguard" for Aboriginal workers.

44. QSA A/58856, 9.11.32, *Report on the Inspector of the Office of the Chief Protector of Aboriginals.*
45. ibid., 24.8.32, Bleakley to Gall.
46. ibid., 15.3.33, note by Gall.
47. QSA TR254 1A/188, 30.6.29, extract from *Audit Report.*
48. QSA A/58856 undated memorandum by Bleakley, appendix B, attached to *Report on the Inspection of the Office of the Chief Protector of Aboriginals,* 9.11.32.
49. ibid., 15.3.33, undersecretary to premier and treasurer.
50. ibid., 19.9.31, memo from undersecretary.
51. *Queensland Parliamentary Debates,* 1935: 1101.
52. QSA A/70627, 6.11.35, Bleakley to undersecretary, replies for minister.
53. ibid.
54. QSA A/69455, 24.1.35, McConnel to deputy chief protector C. O'Leary.
55. ibid., 6.2.35, McConnel to O'Leary.
56. *Courier-Mail,* 23.1.35.
57. QSA A/69984, 11.9.37, Bleakley to secretary, Aborigines Protection Board.
58. DAIA RK:91, Press Release, February 1931.
59. DAIA (uncatalogued) 21.4.37, Press Release, Commonwealth Bureau of Census And Statistics.
60. QSA A/69458, 11.1.37, Bleakley to Agent-General, London.
61. QSA A/8724, 13.8.34, Gall to Governor Leslie Wilson.
62. DAIA RK:20, 13.2.34, Lyons to deputy premier.
63. QSA A/69452, 6.7.35.
64. ibid., 8.7.35.
65. ibid., 18.7.35.
66. QSA A/58856, 6.10.38, Bleakley to undersecretary.
67. QSA A/69470 undated, *Motion by Queensland Representative that a Uniform Policy and Legislation should be adopted for Aboriginal Protection.*
68. *Courier-Mail,* 23.1.35.
69. *Motion by Queensland Representative* ...
70. ibid.
71. For a detailed analysis of this conference see *The Destruction of Aboriginal Society,* 1972: 319–28.
72. See also remarks in his *Annual Report* for 1937.
73. QSA A/69980, Bleakley's summary of conference.
74. *The Aborigines of Australia,* 1960: 303.
75. *Citizenship for the Aborigines,* 1944: 20.

76. Anglican Archives, *Archbishop's Correspondence*, F132/A25/K1, 22.2.40, Bishop of Carpentaria to Archbishop of Brisbane.
77. *Queensland Parliamentary Debates*, 1939, vol. CLXXIV: 485, 486.
78. QSA TR254 18A/10, 26.11.56, O'Leary to undersecretary.
79. QSA A/69470, 25.5.38, *Survey of Aboriginal Protection Operations, Queensland.*
80. DAIA RK:11, 20.1.38, Bleakley to undersecretary.
81. *Queensland Parliamentary Debates*, 1937: 863.
82. *The Aborigines of Australia*, 1961: 183.
83. *Annual Report*, 1938: 11.
84. *Queensland Parliamentary Debates*, 1939: 452.
85. DAIA RK:35, 20.12.34, O'Leary to Laura protector.
86. DAIA RK:165, 30.11.34, Bleakley to undersecretary.
87. QSA POL 9H/1, 24.8.36, memorandum to all protectors.
88. QSA A/4291, 17.4.37, Bleakley to undersecretary.
89. QSA A/4291, 9.11.39, Bleakley to undersecretary.
90. *Annual Report 1938:* reports for the war years lack detail.
91. QSA A/4291 29.7.41, Public service commissioner's minute re *Investigation into the Sub-department of Native Affairs.*
92. ibid., 31.7.41, Bleakley to Public Service commissioner.
93. ibid., 12.8.41, Public service minute.
94. DAIA 1B/12, *Audit Report 1940.*
95. QSA A/69634, 29.7.43, memorandum for the minister.
96. ibid., 20.10.43, undersecretary Treasury to undersecretary Health and Home Affairs.

6. National priorities

1. QSA TR254 1A/21, 30.5.41 and 15.2.46.
2. D. Ball (ed.), *Aborigines in Defence of Australia*, Australian University Press, Sydney, 1991: 38, 39.
3. *The Aborigines of Australia*, 1961: 170.
4. QSA TR254 4A/88, 31.12.44, O'Leary to College.
5. Presbyterian Archives, *Aboriginal Mission Correspondence*, 9.7.42, committee secretary Dan Brown note of phone call.
6. QSA TR254 1A/119, 11.6.42, O'Leary to undersecretary.
7. QSA TR254 1A/135, 9.1.43, Colledge to O'Leary.
8. QSA TR254 1A/216, 5.4.44, police memo to department of Native Affairs.
9. QSA TR254 1A/120, 26.11.47, Woolloongabba police to O'Leary.
10. *Courier-Mail*, 19.4.45.

11. QSA TR254 1E/18, 23.3.43, secretary, department of the Army to moderator Presbyterian church of Queensland.

12. ibid., 20.1.43.

13. *Aborigines in Defence of Australia*, 1991: 41, 42.

14. ibid., 1991: 58.

15. Presbyterian Archives, *Mission Correspondence*, 29.6.42, Rev. Dan Brown to Mrs Balfour, president, Aboriginal Mission Auxiliary.

16. ibid., 6.1.42, MacKenzie to Brown.

17. QSA TR254 6K4, 31.3.42, *Quarterly Report*, Mornington Island.

18. QSA TR254 6K/14, correspondence 1943, 1944.

19. Presbyterian Archives, *Mission Correspondence*, 29.6.42, Brown to Mrs Balfour.

20. Anglican Archives, *Archbishop's Correspondence*, F147/A28/K2 4.7.41, superintendent MacLeod to Rev. A. Flint.

21. QSA TR254 1A/354, 15.1.41, Bleakley to O'Leary.

22. QSA TR254 3A/25, 21.1.42, Foote to O'Leary.

23. ibid., 23.4.42, O'Leary to undersecretary.

24. Quoted in *Aborigines in Defence of Australia*, 1991: 57. This statement is also on file QSA TR254 6B/8 18.5.42, letter from A. Stanfield Sampson to daughter of Pastor Schwartz.

25. QSA TR254 6B/8, 10.5.42, minutes of conference re evacuation.

26. QSA A/69716 (also on A/58916), 18.3.43, Dr D. Johnson, *Report on Inspection of The Aboriginal Settlement, Woorabinda*.

27. ibid., 22.3.43, response by Colledge to Dr Johnson's report.

28. ibid., O'Leary, *Review and Comments on the Report by Dr Johnson on Woorabinda Settlement*.

29. QSA TR254 1A/129:1, 19.8.43, O'Leary to undersecretary.

30. Presbyterian Archives, *Mission Correspondence*, 27.1.42, Rev. Brown to all missionaries in charge.

31. ibid., 29.6.42, Brown to Mrs Balfour, and 27.10.42, Brown to MacKenzie.

32. Presbyterian Archives, *Minutes of the General Assembly*, 1941.

33. Presbyterian Archives, *Mission Correspondence*, 28.7.42, MacKenzie to Brown, and 1.7.42, Braunholz to Brown.

34. QSA TR254 15A/9, 24.12.43, J. Beirne to minister E. Hanlon.

35. Presbyterian Archives, *Mission Correspondence*, 18.11.42, Cane to Brown.

36. Presbyterian Archives, *Minutes of the General Assembly*, 1944.

37. Presbyterian Archives, *Mission Correspondence*, 18.11.42.

38. Anglican Archives, *Archbishop's Correspondence*, F153/A29/K2, 19.1.42.

39. QSA TR254 1D/133, 19.9.49, Inspector Davies to deputy director.
40. QSA TR254 3D/12, quarterly reports by Dr Power, 1943, 1944.
41. QSA TR254 3D/8, 10.3.44, Matron Rynne to O'Leary.
42. QSA TR254 3D/16, 13.7.45, Dr Fryberg to deputy-general, Public Health.
43. QSA TR254 4A/22, 27.2.40 and 28.11.41, visiting justice to O'Leary.
44. QSA TR254 3D/23, 30.3.50, Dr Macken to Dr Fryberg.
45. QSA TR254 4D/20, 10.11.47, quarterly inspection report.
46. QSA TR254 3D/8, 28.10.47, Dr Short to O'Leary, and 20.6.47, baby welfare yearly report.
47. QSA TR254 3D/23, 30.3.50, Dr Macken to director-general Health and Medical Services.
48. QSA TR254 4D/20, 14.3.47, Dr Monz to Semple.
49. QSA TR254 1D/106, 19.7.43, Coen protector to O'Leary.
50. QSA TR254 1B/69, *Audit Report 1964/1965*.
51. QSA POL 9H/1, these are extracted from the file of the Winton protector.
52. QSA TR254 1D/12, 25.7.41, Croydon protector to O'Leary.
53. ibid., 11.5.52, letter to O'Leary.
54. QSA A/58762, 2.6.41, Coen protector to Bleakley.
55. QSA: (R254 7C/14), 9.3.53, E. Weston to O'Leary.
56. QSA TR254 1D/111, Cooktown community.
57. QSA TR254 1D/66, Talwood and Texas communities.
58. QSA 1D/131, Gympie community.
59. DAIA 01-017-001, Beaudesert community.
60. P. Memmott, "Queensland Aboriginal Cultures and the Deaths in Custody Victims", *Regional Report of Inquiry*, Royal Commission into Aboriginal Deaths in Custody, 1991: 250.
61. QSA TR254 7C/16, 8.10.48, acting deputy director Native Affairs to undersecretary.
62. QSA A/69470, 3.2.37, Bleakley to home secretary.
63. D. Murphy and R. Joyce, *Queensland Political Portraits, 1859–1952*, University of Queensland Press, 1978: 445.
64. QSA TR254 1A/267, 23.4.46, memorandum to minister.
65. P. Hasluck, *Shades of Darkness*, Melbourne University Press, 1988: 77.
66. QSA TR254 1A/267, 22.6.54, O'Leary to undersecretary.
67. QSA TR254 1A/129:1, 18.3.53, prime minister's department to Wakefield.
68. QSA TR254 3A/207, 12.10.49, O'Leary to superintendent Palm Island.

69. DAIA 01-057-007, 5&6.1.48, *Minutes of Settlement Superintendents' Conference*.
70. Presbyterian Archives, *Mission Correspondence* 1947, Report on Conference with director of Native Affairs.
71. QSA TR254 1A/267, 13.4.59, Thomas Hiley to Nicklin.
72. QSA TR254 1A/467, 10.7.59, press statement by minister for social services.
73. ibid., 14.7.59, press statement for *Telegraph*.

7. Besieged

1. QSA TR254 6G/20, 15.3.53, O'Leary to undersecretary.
2. Presbyterian Archives, *Mission Correspondence*, 31.12.51, *Annual Report*, Mapoon.
3. QSA TR254 6G/20, 14.7.52, McCarthy to O'Leary.
4. See QSA TR254 6G/20 for this crisis.
5. Presbyterian Archives, *Mission Correspondence*, 27.9.52, Holmes to committee manager.
6. Presbyterian Archives, *Minutes of the General Assembly*, 1953.
7. QSA TR254 1E/45, 7.7.53, O'Leary to undersecretary.
8. *Sunday Mail*, 9.8.53; and Presbyterian Archives, *Minutes of the General Assembly*, 1954.
9. QSA A/69497, 16.10.53, O'Leary memorandum.
10. QSA TR254 6G/20, 29.3.54, O'Leary to undersecretary.
11. ibid., 19.5.54, minutes of conference between department, board of missions, and undersecretary.
12. ibid., 26.7.54, conference minutes. S. Wylie was the Board of Finance chairman, Rev. James Sweet was secretary of the Aboriginal and Foreign Missions Committee, Rev. Victor Coombes was general secretary of the Sydney-based Australian Board of Missions until 1958, Rev. James Stuckey held this position between 1960 and 1972.
13. ibid., 28.4.54, O'Leary to undersecretary.
14. ibid., 19.5.54, conference minutes.
15. ibid., 6.8.54, Rev. Sweet to minister.
16. QSA A/69497, 7.9.54, Rev. Sweet to minister.
17. ibid., 30.8.54, O'Leary to undersecretary.
18. QSA TR254 6G/20, 26.9.54, Sweet to O'Leary.
19. ibid., 26.9.55, O'Leary to undersecretary.
20. *Courier-Mail*, 4.6.75.
21. Presbyterian Archives, *Minutes of the General Assembly, 1957*. For an analysis of church and mining company correspondence see Geoffrey Wharton, "The Day They Burned Mapoon: A Study of the

Closure of a Queensland Presbyterian Mission", BA Hons thesis, University of Queensland, 1996.

22. QSA TR254 6G/20, 25.9.56, O'Leary to Killoran.
23. Presbyterian Archives, *Minutes of the General Assembly*, 1957.
24. ibid.
25. QSA TR254 6G/20, 21.8.57, Mawby to Sweet.
26. ibid., 6.11.57, O'Leary to undersecretary.
27. Presbyterian Archives, *Minutes of the General Assembly*, 1958.
28. ibid.
29. QSA TR254 6G/20, 28.5.62, Rev. James Stuckey to editor *Nation*.
30. QSA A/69497, 31.1.58, Sweet to Noble.
31. QSA TR254 6G/20, 1.10.58, Sweet to Comalco.
32. ibid., 4.12.57, quoted in Noble to Sweet.
33. ibid., 12.11.57, Comalco to Noble.
34. QSA TR254 1E/57, 18.12.58, conference between department, government and Anglican and Presbyterian church officials.
35. DAIA 01-059-002, 30.6.58, O'Leary to undersecretary.
36. QSA TR254 1E/57, 18.12.58, conference between department, government and Presbyterian and Anglican church officials.
37. ibid.
38. QSA TR254 19A/25, 16.10.61, O'Leary to bishop of Brisbane.
39. ibid., 28.3.63, O'Leary to director-general of education.
40. QSA TR254 15D/1, 29.2.56, health inspector's report.
41. QSA: (R254 1D/183), 1.9.59, Wordworth to Noble.
42. QSA TR254 15A/34, 17.7.59, Bartlam to O'Leary.
43. ibid., 30.9.59, O'Leary to undersecretary.
44. QSA TR254 1E/57, 18.12.58, conference with representatives of Anglican and Presbyterian committees and government.
45. QSA TR254 6J/8, 11.5.61, summary of meeting between church and department.
46. DAIA RK:61, 3.11.65, Killoran to director-general of education.
47. QSA A/70008, 15.4.59, Comalco to Sweet.
48. QSA TR254 6G/20, 21.8.59, Byrne to Noble.
49. ibid., 9.5.62, Stuckey to Killoran.
50. QSA A/69497, 20.1.58, O'Leary to undersecretary.
51. QSA TR254 1E/58, 11.4.58, Sweet to O'Leary.
52. QSA A/69497, 1.5.58, Killoran to O'Leary.
53. QSA TR254 1E/58, 16.6.59, Sweet to O'Leary.
54. QSA TR254 6G/20, 20.8.59, O'Leary to undersecretary.
55. ibid., 9.9.59.

56. ibid., joint observations following visit and discussions at Mapoon 7 and 9 September 1960.
57. QSA 1A/578, 3.1.62, Filmer to O'Leary.
58. QSA TR254 6G/20, 5.7.61, Killoran to Sweet.
59. ibid., Sweet's rebuttal of pamphlet "They Made Our Rights Wrong".
60. QSA A/69497, 3.5.63, O'Leary to director-general of education.
61. QSA TR254 6G/20, 11.1.63, Stuckey to Killoran.
62. ibid., Stuckey to O'Leary.
63. ibid., 8.5.62, Stuckey to Killoran.
64. QSA A/69497, 1.7.63, Stuckey memo of Killoran conversation.
65. *Weekend Australian*, 20–21.8.1994.
66. *Cairns Post*, 27.11.63, letter to the editor.
67. QSA TR254 6G/20, 19.10.62, Stuckey to O'Leary.
68. QSA TR254 16A/11, 16.2.65, Stuckey to Killoran.
69. ibid., 14.7.65, Killoran to board of missions.
70. ibid., 21.9.65, Killoran to director-general of education.
71. *Cairns Post*, 18.11.65.
72. QSA TR254 16A/15, 23.6.66, co-ordinator general of public works to premier Nicklin.
73. *Australian*, 7.6.67.
74. DAIA RK:148, 8.10.69, Killoran to minister Neville Hewitt.

8. Double standards

1. QSA TR254 3A/241, 7.7.57, report of visiting justice.
2. A. Burger, *Neville Bonner: A Biography*, Macmillan, South Melbourne, 1979: 30.
3. QSA TR254 1E/57, 15.12.59, minutes of meeting between mission committee and department.
4. DAIA 01-007-006, 13.9.57, BWIU to Noble.
5. QSA TR254 3A/241, 23.8.57, O'Leary to undersecretary.
6. DAIA 01-057-007, 11 & 12.10.60, settlement superintendents' conference.
7. DAIA 01-007-006, 29.11.63, TLC to Noble.
8. QSA: (R254 1A/29), 7.12.50 and 21.2.52, Killoran to undersecretary.
9. QSA TR254 1A/29, 22.10.56, Richards to O'Leary.
10. DAIA RK:38 (probably QSA TR1227:258), 23.1.57, UGA deputation with minister, undersecretary and O'Leary.
11. QSA TR254 1E/25, 26.11.59, superintendent Green, Edward River, to O'Leary.
12. See DAIA 01-017-010 for stations in the Normanton area; and DAIA 01-017-006 for stations round Cloncurry.

13. Joe McGuiness, Aborigines and Torres Strait Island Advancement League, transcript of ABC new item, 25.11.61 on QSA TR254 1A.29. Men working an 8 hour day dropped from £2 2s to £2, but 6 hours on the hourly rate dropped from £2 8s to £1 11s 6d; women working 8 hours dropped from £2 to £1, but 6 hours on the hourly rate dropped from £2 8s to 15s.

14. QSA TR254 1A/29, 9.11.64, Killoran to Ruby Langford.

15. ibid., 27.11.64, UGA to minister Jack Pizzey.

16. ibid., 23.12.64, Killoran to director-general of education.

17. ibid., 28.5.65, Menzies to Nicklin.

18. QSA TR254 1A/467, 10.7.59, press statement.

19. ibid., April 1959, memo from O'Leary.

20. QSA: (R254 4A/192), 9.3.60, Jack Arnold to premier.

21. QSA TR254 1A/345, 19.5.59, *Citizenship Rights for Aborigines*.

22. DAIA RK:87, 23.12.57, Noble to Queensland TLC.

23. QSA TR254 1A/519, 2.12.60, O'Leary memo.

24. DAIA 01-057-007, 11.10.60, O'Leary, superintendent's conference.

25. QSA TR254 1A/345:1, 24.1.62, Confidential Savingram to all posts.

26. DAIA RK:145, 10.12.62, bishop of Carpentaria to Freedom from Hunger Campaign.

27. *Commonwealth House of Representatives Debates*, vol. 35, 1962: 1709, 1706.

28. *Cairns Post*, 4.8.62.

29. QSA TR254 1A/519, 19.9.61, special committee meeting.

30. QSA: (R254 1A/455), 17&18.9.60, assimilation conference, Cairns.

31. QSA TR254 1A/580, undated draft summary of changes.

32. DAIA 01-057-007, 12.10.60, superintendents' conference.

33. QSA TR254 1A/580, 19.5.64, Killoran to director-general of education.

34. ibid., 9.10.64, premier Frank Nicklin to minister.

35. DAIA 01-095-004, 17.1.66, ministerial proposal.

36. QSA TR254 1A/580, extract from undated report by FCAATSI (the Federal Council of Aborigines and Torres Strait Islanders).

37. quoted in B. Rosser, *Dreamtime Nightmares*, AIAS, Canberra, 1985: 136.

38. QSA TR254 15A/101, 13.1.65, Killoran to superintendents seeking submissions.

39. ibid., 10.1.66, Murphy to Killoran; and QSA TR254 3A/276, 5.2.66, Bartlam to Killoran.

40. QSA TR254 15A/101, 27.1.66, Killoran to Murphy.

41. QSA TR254 3A/276, 28.8.68, Bartlam to Killoran.

42. DAIA 01-007-006, 15.3.66, TLC to Pizzey.

43. QSA TR254 3A/276, 28.8.68, Bartlam to Killoran.

44. QSA TR254 15A/101, 5.6.68, Killoran to Yarrow.

45. ibid., 19.5.69 and 24.9.69, Yarrow to Killoran.

46. H. C. Coombs, *Trial Balance*, Macmillan, South Melbourne, 1981: 268.

47. QSA TR254 1A/267, 2.3.66, Killoran to director-general of education.

48. DAIA 01-042-003, 21.8.68, telegram, Wentworth to Sullivan.

49. QSA TR254 1D/185, 10.10.60, O'Leary to undersecretary.

50. QSA TR254 1A/267, 16.6.60, Killoran to undersecretary.

51. DAIA RK:32, Nicklin to Menzies.

52. ibid., 24.10.61, Menzies to Nicklin.

53. QSA 1D/138, 15.11.60, O'Leary to undersecretary.

54. QSA TR254 1A/580, 7.12.62, prepared answer to question in state parliament.

55. *Neville Bonner: A Biography*, 1979: 45, 46.

56. QSA TR254 1D/185, 27.11.62, commissioner H. Galvin to O'Leary.

57. ibid., 11.9.62, memo for file.

58. For an analysis of exploitation of wages and trust funds see R. Kidd, "You can trust me, I'm from the government", *Queensland Review*, vol. 1, 1994.

59. DAIA 01-042-003, 23.10.68, quoted by Stan Edenborough, treasurer of the Presbyterian board of missions, to Killoran.

60. ibid., 9.12.68, Killoran to Edenborough.

61. ibid., 18.9.70, Wentworth to minister Neville Hewitt.

62. ibid., 3.9.68, Killoran to Reardon.

63. ibid., 11.6.70, Dexter to Killoran.

64. DAIA RK:9, 12.2.60, Rockhampton health inspector to director-general of health department.

65. QSA TR254 3D/35, 4.12.62, Bartlam to O'Leary.

66. ibid., 3D/35, 2.11.62.

67. Dr D. Jose, Dr J. Welch, "Report on Health of Aboriginal Children on Queensland Settlements and Missions, 1967–1969", summarised in Queensland Institute of Medical Research *Annual Report*, 1970.

68. QSA TR254 1A/653, February 1969, revised transcript of article for *Sunday Mail*.

69. DAIA 01-039-004, 3.9.68, memorandum for director-general of health.

70. QSA TR254 1A.653, 28.7.69, extract from report.

71. QSA TR254 3A/298, September 1972, *Quarterly Report of Supplementary Feeding Scheme.*

72. ibid., September 1972, *Quarterly Report on Supplementary Feeding Scheme.*

73. DAIA 1A/819, 3.9.68, memorandum for director-general of health.

74. QSA TR254 1A.653, 6.8.69, Killoran to director-general of health.

75. ibid.

76. ibid., 11.10.67, note for DAIA Inspector John Burless.

77. DAIA 01-094-078, 10.11.67, notes for training course.

78. ibid., 10.11.67, *Duties and Responsibilities of Liaison Officers.*

79. QSA TR254 12L, 1.6.73, *Duties of the Domestic Adviser.*

80. DAIA 01-042-003, 29.4.71, Killoran to Dexter.

81. DAIA RK:74, 26.11.73, acting manager to Killoran.

9. A state of paranoia

1. QSA TR254 1A/345 Batch 2 (ii) undated (probably late April 1970), draft cabinet submission.

2. Killoran, quoted in L. Ryan, "Policy Making for Aborigines and Islanders: Recent Queensland Experience", Research Lecture Series, Griffith University, 1984: 5.

3. DAIA 01-057-007, 14.2.73, Dexter's comments to managers' conference.

4. QSA TR254 1A/804, 25.7.72, Howson to Hewitt.

5. ibid., 24.10.73, Cavanagh to Hewitt.

6. QSA TR254 6C/8, 21.11.69, Hewitt to ministers.

7. ibid., 21.11.69, Hewitt to ministers.

8. DAIA 01-039-004, 14.4.72, Dr Musgrave to Dr Patrick.

9. QSA TR254 3D/35, 10.10.73.

10. DAIA 1A/1174, 25.2.74, Killoran to undersecretary, department of Health.

11. ibid., 8.5.75, Burless to Killoran.

12. QSA TR1855 1A/846, 25.11.74, Hewitt to ministers.

13. QSA TR254 6A/52, 1.10.1973, Killoran to BOEMAR.

14. I. Palmer, *Buying Back the Land,* Aboriginal Studies Press, Canberra, 1988:20. Palmer also argues McMahon was opposed by pastoral interests in Cabinet who demanded the *status quo* be maintained.

15. DAIA RK:130, 31.8.72, Hewitt advice to ministers.

16. ibid., 10.2.71, Hewitt to ministers.

17. H. Lunn, *Joh,* University of Queensland Press, St Lucia, 1987: 150.

18. DAIA RK:127, 29.11.73, Hewitt to Bjelke-Petersen.

19. QSA TR254 1A/804, 15.1.74, memo to acting Director.

20. DAIA RK:70 (Oct 1974), Bennett opinion.

21. DAIA RK:19, 4.12.74, Cavanagh to Mr Wallis-Smith.

22. DAIA 01-007-006, 11.10.74, Palm Island manager to Killoran.

23. B. Rosser, *This is Palm Island*, AIAS, Canberra, 1978: 85.

24. QSA TR254 6A/52, 26.3.74, Killoran to undersecretary.

25. DAIA 01-041-002, 23.10.74, Cavanagh to Hewitt.

26. ibid, 25.11.74, Hewitt to ministers.

27. QSA TR254 9M/27, September 1975, Claude Wharton to ministers.

28. C. Porter, *The "Gut" Feeling*, Boolarong Publications, Brisbane, 1981: 66.

29. DAIA RK:138 (probably mid-1977), *Notes for Discussion with Prime Minister regarding Commonwealth Department of Aboriginal Affairs in Queensland.*

30. *Joh*, 1987: 327.

31. QSA TR254 6K/46, 21.12.73, Killoran to BOEMAR.

32. QSA: (R254 6A/35), November 1969, draft submission for Hewitt for Cabinet, presented 5.11.69.

33. DAIA RK:70, 12.9.75, Brown to Killoran.

34. QSA A/70006, 27.1.76, *Chronological brief of mining negotiations since 1968 at Aurukun, Queensland.*

35. R. Howitt, *Beyond the Geological Imperative*, Research Paper No. 23, School of Geography, University of New South Wales, Newcastle, 1969: 23.

36. DAIA RK:96, 16.12.75, minutes of meeting between Wharton, Killoran and BOEMAR.

37. QSA TR254 1E/94 (ii), 24.2.77, Killoran to Wharton.

38. QSA A/69991, 19.9.77, Bjelke-Petersen to Fraser.

39. DAIA RK:138, mid-1977, *Notes for Discussion with Prime Minister regarding Commonwealth Department of Aboriginal Affairs in Queensland.*

40. DAIA 01-056-007, 1979, deputy director Tom Murphy to minister Charles Porter.

41. QSA TR1855 1A/1472, 18.8.78, Killoran to Porter.

42. *The "Gut" Feeling*, 1981: 121, 122.

43. DAIA RK:70, February 1978, undated historical precis "Management of Aurukun and Mornington Island Communities", for Cabinet consideration 24.2.78.

44. ibid., 14.2.78, confidential letter to Dr Musgrave.

45. QSA TR254 1E/94 (ii), 3.4.78, Killoran to Porter.

46. DAIA RK:70, 3.4.78, opinion by Sir Arnold Bennett.

47. QSA TR254 1E/94 (i), 5.4.78, enclosure from Yarrabah manager to

Killoran; and DAIA 01-069-007, 20.6.80, minutes of meeting between Porter, Chaney and Killoran.
48. C. Hughes, *The Government of Queensland*, University of Queensland Press, St Lucia, 1980: 296.

10. The politics of deception

1. DAIA RK:168, 18.6.80, Killoran to Porter.
2. ibid.
3. E. Young and E. Fisk (eds), *The Aboriginal Component in the Australian Economy. Town Populations*, ANU, Canberra, 1982: 102.
4. DAIA RK:46, 28.6.77, Killoran to Wharton.
5. quoted in *Joh*, 1987: 246, 247.
6. See DAIA RK:98, and DAIA 1A/172, for correspondence relating to trackers' exploitation.
7. QSA TR254 19A/114, 19.7.77, Killoran to managers.
8. DAIA 19-017-001, 21.7.78, Killoran to director of school health services.
9. See QSA TR254 6B/24 for this incident.
10. QSA TR1855 1A/975, 5.9.79 and 15.10.79.
11. QSA TR254 1A/1252, 1.9.76, Bjelke-Petersen to Wharton.
12. FAIRA Ltd, *Beyond the Act*, Brisbane, 1979.
13. *The Age*, 17.4.79; and a quote from S. Bennett, *Aborigines and Political Power*, Allen and Unwin, Sydney, 1989: 79.
14. DAIA 01-007-006, 2.5.78, Bjelke-Petersen to Fraser.
15. ibid., 2.5.78.
16. ibid., 5.2.79, Porter to ministers.
17. ibid., 2.2.79, crown solicitor to Killoran.
18. ibid., 5.6.79, Porter to Bjelke-Petersen.
19. ibid., 12.6.79, decision.
20. ibid., 30.7.79, Killoran to Porter.
21. ibid., 30.7.79, *Prospects of Readmission of Those for Whom Alternative Employment was Sought*.
22. QSA TR254 1C/190, 24.9.79, DAIA accountant to Killoran.
23. ibid., undated, DAIA accountant to Killoran.
24. DAIA 01-069-007, 20.6.80.
25. DAIA 01-007-006, 10.7.80, Killoran to Crown Solicitor.
26. ibid., 25.3.83.
27. DAIA 01-042-010, June 1983, manager's report.
28. DAIA 01-007-006, 24.10.83, Bird to Bjelke-Petersen.
29. ibid., 27.4.84.
30. *Courier-Mail*, 12.9.81.

31. See Ian Palmer, *Buying Back the Land*, Aboriginal Studies Press, Canberra 1988, for ALFC dealings.
32. DAIA 01-049-001, 10.11.83, Killoran to Katter.
33. DAIA 19-049-002, 24.8.84, Katter to ministers.
34. DAIA 001-007-006, 7.8.84, Katter to commissioner for Community Relations.
35. ibid., 30.4.85.
36. ibid., 4.6.85, Killoran to regional director, DAA.
37. ibid., 9.12.85, internal minute of meeting.
38. *Sunday Mail*, 22.12.85.
39. DAIA 001-007-006, 4.9.85, Holding to Katter.
40. ibid., 31.1.86, Killoran to assistant commissioner to the Public Service Board.
41. ibid., 27.2.86, Killoran to Katter.
42. ibid., 6.4.86, Katter to ministers.
43. DAIA 01-038-012, 10.4.87, Uren to Bjelke-Petersen.
44. ibid., undated (June 1988), draft submission to Cabinet.

Index